KT-197-715

Driving
Standards
Agency

The OFFICIAL DSA
THEORY TEST
for Car Drivers

London: TSO

Written and compiled by the Learning Materials section of the Driving Standards Agency (DSA).

Questions and answers are compiled by the Item Development Team of DSA.

Published with the permission of the Driving Standards Agency on behalf of the Controller of Her Majesty's Stationery Office.

First published 1996
Sixteenth edition 2012
Fourth impression 2013

ISBN 978 0 11 553231 3

A CIP catalogue record for this book is available from the British Library.

Other titles in the Driving Skills series

The Official DSA Guide to Driving – the essential skills
The Official DSA Theory Test for Car Drivers (DVD-ROM)
The Official DSA Guide to Learning to Drive
Prepare for your Practical Driving Test (DVD)
DSA Driving Theory Quiz (DVD)
The Official Highway Code Interactive CD-ROM

The Official DSA Theory Test iPhone App
The Official DSA Theory Test Kit iPhone App
The Official Highway Code iPhone App

The Official DSA Guide to Riding – the essential skills
The Official DSA Theory Test for Motorcyclists
The Official DSA Theory Test for Motorcyclists (DVD-ROM)
The Official DSA Guide to Learning to Ride
Better Biking – official DSA training aid (DVD)

The Official DSA Guide to Driving Buses and Coaches
The Official DSA Guide to Driving Goods Vehicles
The Official DSA Theory Test for Drivers of Large Vehicles
The Official DSA Theory Test for Drivers of Large Vehicles (CD-ROM)
Driver CPC – the official DSA guide for professional bus and coach drivers
Driver CPC – the official DSA guide for professional goods vehicle drivers

The Official DSA Guide to Tractor and Specialist Vehicle Driving Tests

The Official DSA Guide to Hazard Perception (DVD)

We're turning over a new leaf.

RECYCLED
Paper made from
recycled material
FSC® C002151

Find us online

> GOV.UK – Simpler, clearer, faster

GOV.UK is the best place to find government services and information for

- car drivers
- motorcyclists
- driving licences
- driving and riding tests
- towing a caravan or trailer
- medical rules
- driving and riding for a living
- online services.

Visit **www.gov.uk and try it out!**

You can also find contact details for DSA and other motoring agencies like DVLA at **www.gov.uk**

You'll notice that links to **GOV.UK**, the UK's new central government site, don't always take you to a specific page. This is because this new kind of site constantly adapts to what people really search for and so such static links would quickly go out of date. Try it out. Simply search what you need from your preferred search site or from **www.gov.uk** and you should find what you're looking for. You can give feedback to the Government Digital Service from the website.

> Message from Lesley Young, the Chief Driving Examiner

Learning to drive is an exciting experience. As with getting to grips with any new skill, you may be nervous and it may be challenging at first. But before long, you'll be ready to take the step towards getting your full licence and enjoying the freedom that comes with it.

A sound understanding of driving theory will help you reach that stage and to carry on improving right through your driving life. Understanding and practice come together in a safe and responsible driver, so my advice is to get at least some practical lessons with a qualified instructor under your belt while you're studying for your theory test. It helps to make the theory meaningful, and that helps it to stick.

And you'll be glad of that on the day of your theory test!

I wish you safe driving for life.

Lesley Young
Chief Driving Examiner

Contents

About the theory test

In this section, you'll learn about

- how to use this book
- getting started
- the theory test
- after the theory test
- Pass Plus
- using the questions and answers sections
- using this book to learn and revise.

How to use this book

To prove that you have the right knowledge, understanding and attitude to be a safe and responsible driver, you'll need to pass the theory test.

It includes

- a multiple choice test, to assess your knowledge of driving theory
- a hazard perception test, to assess your hazard recognition skills.

This book contains hundreds of questions, which are very similar to the questions you'll be asked in the test and cover the same topics. It's easy to read, and explains why the answers are correct. References to the source material also appear with each question.

Everyone learns in different ways, so this book has features to help you understand driving theory whatever kind of learner you are, including

- bite-size chunks of information, which are easier to understand at your own pace
- lots of photographs and images to illustrate what you're learning
- fourteen topic-specific case studies and six mixed-topic ones, just like those you'll get in the test
- things to discuss and practise with your instructor, to put your learning about each topic into practice
- meeting the standards, to help you understand how each topic relates to the National Driving Standard.

This book is designed to help you learn about the theory of driving and to practise for the test. To prepare thoroughly, you should also study the source materials that the questions are taken from, which are

The Official Highway Code
Know Your Traffic Signs
The Official DSA Guide to Driving – the essential skills

There's always more you can learn, so keep your knowledge up to date throughout your driving career.

Getting started

> Applying for your licence

You must be at least 17 years old to drive a car. As an exception, if you receive Disability Living Allowance at the higher rate, you're allowed to start driving at 16. You must have a valid provisional driving licence before you can drive on the road.

Driving licences are issued by the Driver and Vehicle Licensing Agency (DVLA). You'll need to fill in application form D1, which you can request from **www.gov.uk** or collect from any post office. In Northern Ireland, the issuing authority is the Driver and Vehicle Agency (DVA; online at **dvani.gov.uk**) and the form is a DL1. For more information, see **nidirect.gov.uk/learner-and-new-drivers.htm**

Send your form to the appropriate office, as shown on the form. You must enclose the required passport-type photographs, as all provisional licences are now photocard licences.

When you receive your provisional licence, check that all details are correct before you drive on the road. If you need to contact DVLA, the telephone number is 0300 790 6801 (DVA is 0845 402 4000).

You'll need to show both the photocard and the paper counterpart of your provisional licence when you take your theory test.

> Residency requirements

You can't take a test or get a full licence unless you're normally resident in the United Kingdom. Normal residence means the place where you live because of personal or occupational (work) ties. However, if you moved to the United Kingdom having recently been permanently resident in another state of the EC/EEA (European Economic Area), you must have been normally resident in the UK for 185 days in the 12 months before you apply for a driving test or full driving licence.

Choosing an instructor

DSA in Great Britain and DVA in Northern Ireland approve instructors, who are then able to teach learner drivers in return for payment. These instructors have their standards checked regularly.

Approved driving instructors (ADIs) must

- pass a series of difficult examinations
- reach a high standard of instruction
- be registered with DSA or DVA
- display an ADI's certificate while giving professional driving instruction (except in Northern Ireland).

These professional driving instructors will give you guidance on

- your practical skills
- how to study and practise
- when you're ready for your tests
- further training after your practical test under the Pass Plus scheme (not applicable in Northern Ireland).

DSA and DVA regulate ADIs, and both organisations place great emphasis on professional standards and business ethics. A code of practice (not applicable in Northern Ireland) has been created, within which all instructors should operate. To find your nearest fully qualified ADI, please visit **www.gov.uk**

About the theory test

You'll take the theory test on-screen in two parts. It's designed to test your knowledge of driving theory – in particular, the rules of the road and best driving practice.

The first part is a series of multiple choice questions. Some multiple choice questions will be presented as a case study. More information about this part of the test is given on pages 17–19. The revision questions are given in the main part of the book, beginning on page 30.

Each question has references to the learning materials; for example

DES s4, HC r159, p131, KYTS p13

DES s indicates the section within *The Official DSA Guide to Driving – the essential skills.*

HC r/HC p indicates the rule or page in *The Official Highway Code.*

KYTS p indicates the page in *Know Your Traffic Signs.*

The second part of the theory test is the hazard perception part. More information about this is given on pages 19–20.

Can I take the practical test first?

No. You must pass your theory test before you can book a practical test.

Does everyone have to take the theory test?

Most people in the UK who are learning to drive will have to take the theory test. However, you won't have to if

- you're upgrading in the same category, eg B (car) to B+E (car with trailer)
- you already have a full B1 entitlement because you have a full motorcycle licence issued before 1 February 2001 (not applicable in Northern Ireland).

If you have any questions about whether you need to take a theory test, write to DSA theory test enquiries, PO Box 381, Manchester M50 3UW. Tel 0300 200 1122 or email **customercare@pearson.com**

For Northern Ireland, contact the Driver Licensing Division, County Hall, Castlerock Road, Coleraine BT51 3TB. Tel 0845 402 4000.

Foreign licence holders: if you hold a foreign licence issued outside the EC/EEA, first check with DVLA (Tel 0300 790 6801; for Northern Ireland call 0845 402 4000), to see whether you can exchange your driving licence. If you can't, you'll need to apply for a provisional licence and take a theory and a practical driving test.

⊙ Preparing for your theory test

Although you must pass your theory test before you can take your practical test, it's best to start studying for your theory test as soon as possible – but don't actually take it until you have some practical experience of driving.

To prepare for the multiple choice part of the theory test, DSA strongly recommends that you study the books from which the theory test questions are taken, as well as the questions you'll find in this book.

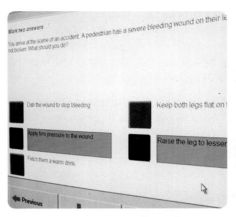

The Official Highway Code This is essential reading for all road users. It contains the very latest rules of the road, up-to-date legislation and provides advice on road safety and best practice.

Know Your Traffic Signs This contains most of the signs and road markings that you're likely to see.

It's important that you study, not just to pass the test but to become a safer driver.

The Official DSA Guide to Driving – the essential skills This is the official reference book, giving practical advice and best driving practice for all drivers.

These books will help you to answer the questions correctly and will also help you when studying for your practical test. The information in them will be relevant throughout your driving life, so make sure you always have an up-to-date copy.

Other study aids

The Official DSA Theory Test for Car Drivers (DVD-ROM) This is an alternative way of preparing for the multiple choice part of the theory test. It contains all the revision questions and answers, and also allows you to take mock tests.

The Official DSA Guide to Hazard Perception (DVD) We strongly recommend that you use this, preferably with your instructor, to prepare for the hazard perception part of the test. The DVD is packed with useful tips, quizzes and expert advice. It also includes interactive hazard perception clips, which you can use to test yourself and see if you're ready to take the real test.

The Official DSA Complete Theory Test Kit for Car Drivers This contains the above two products, giving you all the information you need to prepare for the complete theory test, at a reduced price.

DSA Driving Theory Quiz (DVD) A fun way to revise for your theory test – pit your wits against your family and friends to prove who has the best driving knowledge.

The Official DSA Theory Test iPhone Apps The ideal way to prepare for your test on the go. Choose either the Theory Test app, which covers the multiple choice part of the test, or the Theory Test Kit, which covers both the multiple choice and hazard perception parts of the test. There's also a free version to try before you buy.

The Official Highway Code iPhone App All the latest rules of the road and traffic signs at your fingertips.

You can buy official DSA learning materials online at **safedrivingforlife.info/shop** or by calling our expert publications team on **0870 600 5522**. The team can give you advice about learning materials and how to prepare for the tests and beyond. They can also help you select a suitable learning material if you have a special need; for example, if you have a learning disability or English isn't your first language.

DSA publications are also available from book shops and online retailers. DSA apps can be downloaded from the iPhone app store and eBooks are available from your device's eBook store.

Why do the questions in the theory test keep changing?

To make sure that all candidates are being tested fairly, questions and video clips are under continuous review. Some questions may be changed as a result of customer feedback. They may also be altered because of changes to legislation, and DSA publications are updated so that the revision questions reflect these changes.

Can I take a mock test?

You can take a mock test for the multiple choice part of the theory test online at **safedrivingforlife.info/practicetheorytest**

The theory test

Booking your theory test

Visit **www.gov.uk** to book your theory test online (for Northern Ireland, use **dvani.gov.uk**).

If you have any special needs for the theory test, call 0300 200 1122 (0845 600 6700 for Northern Ireland).

If you have hearing or speech difficulties and use a minicom machine, call 0300 200 1166. If you're a Welsh speaker, call 0300 200 1133.

You'll need your

- DVLA or DVA driving licence number
- credit or debit card details (the card holder must book the test). We accept Mastercard, Visa, Delta and Visa Electron.

You'll be given a booking number and you'll receive an appointment email on the same day if you book online.

If you book over the phone and don't provide an email address, you'll receive an appointment letter within 10 days.

Where can I take the test?

There are over 150 theory test centres throughout England, Scotland and Wales, and six in Northern Ireland. Most people have a test centre within 20 miles of their home, but this will depend on the density of population in your area. To find your nearest test centre, please visit **www.gov.uk**

What should I do if I don't receive an acknowledgement?

If you don't receive an acknowledgement within the time specified, please visit **www.gov.uk** or telephone the booking office to check that an appointment has been made. We can't take responsibility for postal delays. If you miss your test appointment, you'll lose your fee.

When are test centres open?

Test centres are usually open on weekdays, some evenings and some Saturdays.

How do I cancel or postpone my test?

You can cancel or postpone your test online by visiting **www.gov.uk** or by telephone. You should contact the booking office at least **three clear working days** before your test date, otherwise you'll lose your fee.

Booking by post If you prefer to book by post, you'll need to fill in an application form. The form can be downloaded from **www.gov.uk**, or your instructor may have one.

You should normally receive confirmation of your appointment within 10 days of posting your application form. This will be by email if you have provided an email address or by post if not.

If you need the theory test in a language other than English or if you need support for special needs, please turn to page 16.

Taking your theory test

Arriving at the test centre You must make sure that when you arrive at the test centre you have all the relevant documents with you. If you don't have them, you won't be able to take your test and you'll lose your fee.

You'll need

- your signed photocard licence **and** paper counterpart, or
- your signed old-style paper driving licence and valid passport (your passport doesn't have to be British).

No other form of identification is acceptable in England, Wales or Scotland.

Other forms of identification may be acceptable in Northern Ireland; please check **dvani.gov.uk** or your appointment letter.

All documents must be original. We can't accept photocopies.

The test centre staff will check your documents and make sure that you take the right category of test.

Remember, if you don't bring your documents your test will be cancelled and you'll lose your fee.

Make sure you arrive in plenty of time so that you aren't rushed. If you arrive after the session has started, you may not be allowed to take the test.

It's an on-screen test and is made up of a multiple choice part and a hazard perception part.

Watch the 'How to pass the theory test' video on DSA's YouTube channel, which explains how to prepare for the theory test, what to expect on the day and what you need to do to pass.

> **youtube.com/dsagov**

Languages other than English

In Wales, and at theory test centres on the Welsh borders, you can take your theory test with Welsh text on-screen. A voiceover can also be provided in Welsh.

You can listen through a headset to the test being read out in one of 20 other languages as well as English. These are Albanian, Arabic, Bengali, Cantonese, Dari, Farsi, Gujarati, Hindi, Kashmiri, Kurdish, Mirpuri, Polish, Portuguese, Punjabi, Pushto, Spanish, Tamil, Turkish, Urdu and Welsh.

At some theory test centres you may bring a translator with you so that you can take your test in any other language. The translator must be approved by DSA (DVA in Northern Ireland) and you must make arrangements for this when you book your test. You have to arrange and pay for the services of the translator yourself.

Tests with translators can be taken at the following test centres: Aldershot, Birmingham, Cardiff, Derby, Edinburgh, Glasgow, Ipswich, Leeds, Milton Keynes, Preston, Southgate and all test centres in Northern Ireland.

Provision for special needs

Every effort is made to ensure that the theory test can be taken by all candidates.

It's important that you state your needs when you book your test so that the necessary arrangements can be made.

Reading difficulties There's an English-language voiceover on a headset to help you if you have reading difficulties or dyslexia.

You can ask for up to twice the normal time to take the multiple choice part of the test.

You'll be asked to provide a letter from a suitable independent person who knows about your reading ability, such as a teacher or employer. Please check with the Special Needs section (call on the normal booking number; see page 13) if you're unsure who to ask.

We can't guarantee to return any original documents, so please send copies only.

Hearing difficulties If you're deaf or have other hearing difficulties, the multiple choice part and the introduction to the hazard perception part of the test can be delivered in British Sign Language (BSL) by an on-screen signer.

A BSL interpreter, signer or lip speaker can be provided if requested at the time of booking. If you have any other requirements, please call the Special Needs section on the normal booking number (see page 13).

Physical disabilities If you have a physical disability that would make it difficult for you to use a touch screen system or a mouse button in the theory test, we may be able to make special arrangements for you to use a different method if you let us know when you book your test.

Multiple choice questions

The first part of the theory test consists of 50 multiple choice questions. Some of these will be in the form of a case study. You select your answers for this part of the test by touching the screen or using a mouse.

Before you start, you'll be given the chance to work through a practice session for up to 15 minutes to get used to the system. Staff at the test centre will be available to help you if you have any difficulties.

The questions will cover a variety of topics relating to road safety, the environment and documents. Only one question will appear on the screen at a time.

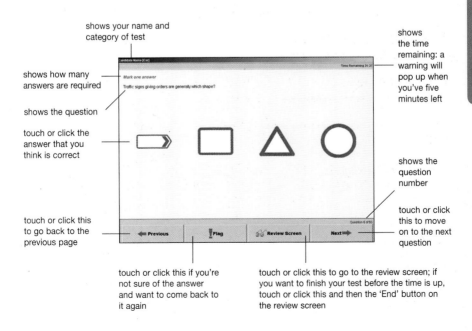

shows your name and category of test

shows the time remaining: a warning will pop up when you've five minutes left

shows how many answers are required

shows the question

touch or click the answer that you think is correct

shows the question number

touch or click this to move on to the next question

touch or click this to go back to the previous page

touch or click this if you're not sure of the answer and want to come back to it again

touch or click this to go to the review screen; if you want to finish your test before the time is up, touch or click this and then the 'End' button on the review screen

Most questions will ask you to mark one correct answer from four possible answers. Some questions may ask for two or more correct answers from a selection, but this will be shown clearly on the screen.

If you try to move on without marking the correct number of answers, you'll be reminded that more answers are needed.

To answer, you need to touch or click the box beside the answer or answers you think are correct. If you change your mind and don't want that answer to be selected, touch or click it again. You can then choose another answer.

Take your time and read the questions carefully. You're given 57 minutes for this part of the test, so relax and don't rush. Some questions will take longer to answer than others, but there are no trick questions. The time remaining is displayed on the screen.

You may be allowed extra time to complete the test if you have special needs and you let us know when you book your test.

You'll be able to move backwards and forwards through the questions and you can also 'flag' questions you'd like to look at again. It's easy to change your answer if you want to.

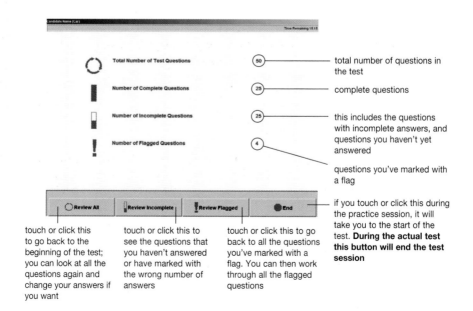

Try to answer all the questions. If you're well prepared, you shouldn't find them difficult.

Before you finish this part of the test, if you have time, you can use the 'review' feature to check your answers. If you want to finish your test before the full time, touch or click the 'review' button and then the 'end' button on the review screen. When you touch or click the review button, you'll see the screen on the previous page.

> Case studies

Some of the multiple choice questions will be presented as part of a case study. Case studies are designed to test

- knowledge (basic recall of facts)
- comprehension (basic understanding)
- application (practical use of knowledge and understanding).

This is done by creating a set of circumstances that you may encounter in a real-life situation. You'll then be asked some questions relating to the scenario, and you'll have to decide how you would react or behave in each case. For an example of a case study, see page 462.

The case studies at the end of each section in this book set out scenarios and then ask you relevant questions. This is to help you test your knowledge in a format similar to the case studies in the theory test. However, the layout isn't the same as the theory test screens.

> Hazard perception

After you've finished the multiple choice part, there's a break of up to three minutes before you start the hazard perception part of the test. You can't leave your seat during this break. This part of the test is a series of film clips, shown from a driver's point of view. You'll be using a mouse for this part of the theory test.

Before you start this part of the test, you'll be shown a short video that explains how the test works and gives you a chance to see a sample film clip. This will help you to understand what you need to do. You can play this video again if you wish.

During the hazard perception part of the test, you'll be shown 14 film clips. Each clip contains one or more developing hazards. You should press the mouse button **as soon as you see** a hazard developing that may need you, the driver, to take some action, such as changing speed or direction.

The earlier you notice a developing hazard and make a response, the higher your score. There are 15 hazards for which you can score points.

Your response won't change what happens in the scene in any way. However, a red flag will appear on the bottom of the screen to show that your response has been noted.

Before each clip starts, there'll be a 10-second pause to allow you to see the new road situation.

The hazard perception part of the test lasts about 20 minutes. For this part of the test no extra time is available, and you can't repeat any of the clips – you don't get a second chance to see a hazard when you're driving on the road.

> Trial questions

We're constantly checking the questions and clips to help us decide whether to use them in future tests. After the hazard perception part of the test, you may be asked to try a few trial questions and clips. You don't have to do these if you don't want to, and if you answer them they won't count towards your final score.

> Customer satisfaction survey

We want to make sure our customers are completely satisfied with the service they receive. At the end of your test you'll be shown some questions designed to give us information about you and how happy you are with the service you received from us.

Your answers will be treated in the strictest confidence. They aren't part of the test and they won't affect your final score or be used for marketing purposes. You'll be asked if you want to complete the survey, but you don't have to.

> The result

You should receive your result at the test centre within 10 minutes of completing the test.

You'll be given a score for each part of the test (the multiple choice part and the hazard perception part). You'll need to pass both parts to pass the theory test. If you fail one of the parts, you'll have to take the whole test again.

Why do I have to retake both parts of the test if I only fail one?

It's really only one test. The theory test has always included questions relating to hazard awareness – the second part simply tests the same skills in a more effective way. The two parts are only presented separately in the theory test because different scoring methods are used.

What's the pass mark?

To pass the multiple choice part of the theory test, you must answer at least 43 out of 50 questions correctly. For learner car drivers and motorcyclists, the pass mark for the hazard perception part is 44 out of 75.

If I don't pass, when can I take the test again?

If you fail your test, you've shown that you're not fully prepared. You'll have to wait at least three clear working days before you can take the theory test again.

Good preparation will save you both time and money.

After the theory test

When you pass your theory test, you'll be given a certificate. Keep this safe as you'll need it when you go for your practical test.

This certificate is valid for two years from the date of your test. This means that you have to take and pass the practical test within this two-year period. If you don't, you'll have to take and pass the theory test again before you can book your practical test.

> Your practical driving test

Your next step is to prepare for and take your practical driving test. To help you, DSA has produced a book called *The Official DSA Guide to Learning to Drive* and a DVD called *Prepare for your Practical Driving Test*.

Both products explain the standards required to pass the practical driving test. They include information about each of the 24 key skills examined within the test, with tips from the experts, and they explain what the examiner is looking for during the test. The DVD also shows a test in action so that you can see what happens.

Pass Plus

(not applicable in Northern Ireland)

After passing the practical driving test, you're at greater risk of being involved in a road traffic incident than older, more experienced drivers. That risk is reflected in car insurance premiums.

There are likely to be many driving situations that you haven't experienced during your lessons. The Pass Plus scheme can help by showing you how to deal with these situations so that you can drive with confidence.

Pass Plus is aimed at improving your driving skills and making you a safer driver. It can also lead to insurance discounts. Pass Plus will take you through driving

- in town
- on rural roads
- in all weathers
- on dual carriageways and motorways
- in the dark.

The structured syllabus gives you the extra experience you need at a time when you're most likely to be involved in a collision. It builds on your existing skills and there's no test to take at the end.

The amount of money you save on insurance could cover the cost of the course. Many car insurers recognise the benefits of the scheme and will give you substantial discounts when you insure your car. To find out more about the Pass Plus scheme, insurance discounts and Pass Plus instructors in your area,

- ask your driving instructor
- visit **www.gov.uk**
- call the Pass Plus hotline on **0115 936 6504**
- email **passplus@dsa.gsi.gov.uk**

You can take the Pass Plus course at any time in your driving career, but it's mainly aimed at new drivers in the first year after passing their test.

Saving money on your car insurance should bring a smile to your face.

Using the questions and answers sections

Sections 1 to 14 contain the revision questions for the multiple choice part of the theory test. These are very similar to the questions you'll be asked in the test and cover the same topics.

The questions are in the left-hand column with a choice of answers below.

For easy reference, the questions are divided into topics. Although this isn't how you'll find them in your test, it's helpful if you want to look at particular subjects.

At the start of each topic, before the questions, there are a few pages of useful information to help you learn more about each topic.

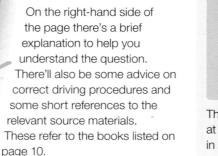

On the right-hand side of the page there's a brief explanation to help you understand the question. There'll also be some advice on correct driving procedures and some short references to the relevant source materials. These refer to the books listed on page 10.

The correct answers are at the back of the book, in section 16.

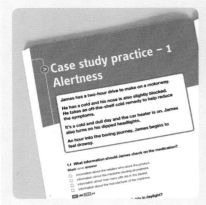

Don't just learn the answers; it's important that you know why they're correct. To help you do this, there's a short scenario at the end of each question section with five questions to answer. This will give you an idea of how the case study part of the theory test will assess your understanding of the subject covered. This knowledge will help you with your practical skills and prepare you to become a safe and confident driver.

Taking exams or tests is rarely a pleasant experience, but you can make your test less stressful by being confident that you have the knowledge to answer the questions correctly.

Make studying more enjoyable by involving friends and relations. Take part in a question-and-answer game. Test those 'experienced' drivers who've had their licence a while: they might learn something too!

Some of the questions in this book won't be relevant to Northern Ireland theory tests. These questions are marked as follows: **NI EXEMPT**

Best wishes for your theory test. Once you're on the road, remember what you've learnt and be prepared to keep learning.

Using this book to learn and revise

We're all different. We like different foods, listen to different music and learn in different ways.

This book is designed to help you learn the important information that you'll need for the theory test in a variety of different formats, so you can find a way of learning that works best for you.

Features

A summary, at the start of each section, of what you'll learn.

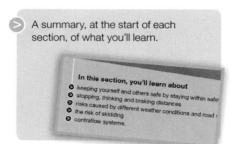

All the key information presented in bite-size chunks with clear headings.

Images to help you relate the information to the real world.

Diagrams and tables to help make information clear and summarise key points.

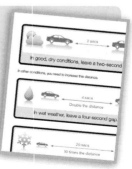

> Links and QR codes to online videos and interactive activities, to further increase your knowledge and skills. Scan the QR code on your smart phone (you'll need a QR code reader app) to access the online content.

> Links to other relevant publications, like *The Official Highway Code* and *The Official DSA Guide to Driving – the essential skills.*

Would you be able to stop, or safely avoid them, in time?

HC r205–206 DES s7, 10

> Tips containing useful extra information about driving safely.

At night, if a vehicle overtakes you, dip your headlights as soon as it passes you otherwise your lights could dazzle the other driver.

HC r115

> A summary, at the end of each section, of what you'll need to know and be able to do to meet the National Driving Standard.

Meeting the standards

> Pages for your own notes, with suggested things to think about.

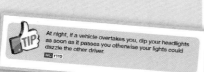

Notes

Think about

> Ideas to discuss with your driving instructor and practise when driving.

Things to discuss and pra your instructor

These are just a few examples of what you could

> Self-assessment – revision questions like the ones you'll get in the test.

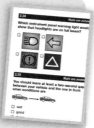

Which instrument panel warning light would show that headlights are on full beam?

You should leave at least a two-second gap between your vehicle and the one in front when conditions are

> Case studies showing how the information might work in practice, and related questions.

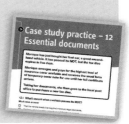

Case study practice – 12
Essential documents

The theory test is just one part of the process of learning to drive. You need to learn the facts, but it's important to understand how they relate to real driving.

The combination of knowing driver theory and having good practical driving skills won't only help you pass your test; it will also make you a safer driver for life.

> What kind of learner are YOU?

Ask yourself these questions

- Why are you doing this? What's motivating you?
- When have you learned best in the past? What helped you to remember what you needed to know?
- What are your strengths and weaknesses as a learner?

Think about the way that you learn best. You could try any combination of the following ideas.

I remember what I see or read

- Create flashcards with important facts or statistics
- Make diagrams and charts
- Use mind maps
- Use colour coding
- Watch the DSA short films
- Make your own notes
- Cross-reference information using a variety of books, eg *The Official Highway Code*
- Draw your own diagrams to show key information.

I remember best when I physically do something

- Short study sessions
- Do things – create models or diagrams; make lists
- Use props
- Try the interactive activities
- Watch and copy what your driving instructor does
- Mime or act out different driving moves.

I remember what I hear

- Repeat rules out loud
- Use a voice recorder to make recordings of key information
- Work with others and discuss things
- Watch and listen to the DSA video content.

Top tips

Remember your motivation

Think about the reason you're learning to drive. Is it for independence? For work? To drive a dream car? Remind yourself, from time to time, of your motivation for learning. Don't give up!

Relate to your personal experience

Information is more memorable when it's linked to what you already know. Try to picture yourself in the position of the driver. The case studies throughout the book can help you think about how the ideas would work in real life.

Use mnemonics

Mnemonics are little sayings, stories or techniques that help you remember something. A classic example is 'Richard Of York Gave Battle In Vain', which you can use to remember the colours of the rainbow (red, orange, yellow, green, blue, indigo, violet). You can use similar techniques to memorise statistics, facts or information for your driving career.

Question format

However you choose to learn the content, make certain you're familiar with the format of the test and how the questions will be presented. Go through the self-assessment questions in each chapter and see if you can answer them. Mark any you struggle with and try them again at a later date.

Plan your study

Set yourself timelines and targets. Try to set aside dedicated time for study, when you're feeling awake and are unlikely to be interrupted. The environment in which you study is important – try to find an area where you can concentrate.

Getting help

Think about the people you can speak with to ask questions, get advice or share experiences about driving – such as your driving instructor, parents, friends or colleagues at work.

Taking your test

Don't rush into the theory test before you're ready. You need to be confident with the information, and have enough practical experience to give you a deep understanding of the information too.

> Section one
Alertness

In this section, you'll learn about

- observing what's going on around you
- being seen by other road users
- being aware of other road users
- anticipating what other road users are going to do
- keeping your concentration on the road
- avoiding distractions.

Alertness

Being alert to what's going on around you is vital to driving safely and will help you to avoid dangerous situations.

> Observation and awareness

It's important to be aware of what's happening around you while you're driving, including

- other road users
- pedestrians
- signs and road markings
- weather conditions
- the area you're driving through.

Keep scanning the road ahead and to the sides, and assess the changing situations as you drive.

Before you move off, you should

use your mirrors to check how your actions will affect traffic behind you

look around for a final check, including checking the **blind spots** around your car

signal, if necessary.

HC r159–161 **DES** s4

31

blind spot
the area behind you that you're unable to see in mirrors

Getting a clear view

If you can't see behind you when reversing, ask someone to guide you to make sure that you reverse safely.

If your view is blocked by parked cars when you're coming out of a junction, move forward slowly and carefully until you have a clear view.

Watch the 'Test your awareness' TFL video.

> **youtube.com/ watch?v=Ahg6qcgoay4**

Overtaking

Observation is particularly important when you're overtaking another vehicle. Make sure you can see the road ahead clearly, looking out for

- vehicles coming towards you
- whether you're near a junction – vehicles could come out of the junction while you're overtaking
- whether the road gets narrower – there may not be enough space for you to overtake
- bends or dips in the road, which will make it difficult for you to see traffic coming towards you
- road signs that mean you **MUST NOT** overtake.

Before you overtake, check that

- it's safe, legal and necessary
- you have enough time to complete the overtaking manoeuvre.

HC r162–163, 165 **DES** s7 **KYTS** p64

Being seen by others

It's important for other road users to know you're there.

- Switch on your lights when it starts to get dark, even if the street lights aren't on.
- Where you can't be seen, such as at a hump bridge, you may need to use your horn.

HC r113–115

If you're following a large vehicle, stay well back. This will help the driver to see you in their mirrors. Staying back will also help you see the road ahead much more clearly. This is especially important if you're planning to overtake the vehicle.

HC r164

Remember: if you can't see a large vehicle's mirrors, the driver can't see you.

⊗ Anticipation

Anticipation can help you to avoid problems and incidents so that you can drive more safely. For example, a 'give way' sign warns you that a junction is ahead, so you can slow down in good time.

Look at the road signs and markings: these give you information about hazards. You should

- follow their advice
- slow down if necessary.

DES s6 **KYTS** p10, 62

Circles
give orders

Triangles
give warnings

Rectangles
give information

When turning right onto a **dual carriageway**, check that the **central reservation** is wide enough for your vehicle to stop in, especially if you're towing a trailer. Do this in case you have to wait before joining the traffic. If there's not enough space for your vehicle, only emerge when it's clear both to the right and left.

dual carriageway
a road that has a central reservation to separate the carriageways

central reservation
an area of land that separates opposing lanes of traffic

If you're approaching traffic lights that have been green for some time, be prepared to stop because they may change.

Road conditions will affect how easy it is to anticipate what might happen. It's more difficult when

- the weather is very wet or windy
- the light is poor
- the traffic volume is heavy
- the route you're driving is new to you.

In these conditions, you need to be particularly aware of what's happening around you.

DES s7

Anticipating what other road users might do

Watch other road users. Try to anticipate their actions so that you're ready if you need to slow down or change direction.

Be aware of more vulnerable road users. Watch out for

pedestrians approaching a crossing, especially young, older or disabled people who may need more time to cross the road

cyclists – always pass slowly and leave plenty of room, especially if the cyclist is young and may have little experience of dealing with traffic

motorcyclists, who may be difficult to see

horses, which may be startled by the noise of your vehicle – pass them slowly and leave plenty of room.

HC r204–218 **DES** s10

Always be ready to stop

However well prepared you are, you may still have to stop quickly in an emergency.

Keep both hands on the wheel as you brake to help you to keep control of your vehicle.

DES s5, 10

⊛ Staying focused

Driving safely takes a lot of concentration – as well as controlling the car, you need to be aware of what's happening on the road and what could happen next. Stay focused on driving and try not to get distracted.

Always plan your journey so that you

- know which route you need to take
- have regular rest stops.

Avoiding tiredness

You won't be able to concentrate properly if you're tired. It's particularly easy to feel sleepy when driving on a motorway, especially at night, so

- don't drive continuously for more than two hours
- keep fresh air circulating in the car
- if you start to feel drowsy, leave at the next exit. Find a safe and legal place to stop and take a break.

Stop in a safe place and have a cup of coffee or another caffeinated drink. Remember that this is only a short-term solution: it isn't a substitute for proper rest. If possible, take a short nap.

HC r91, 262 **DES** s1, 11

See the Think! road safety website for more information about driving and tiredness.

⊛ **http://think.direct.gov.uk/ fatigue.html**

Distraction

It's easy to be distracted by what's happening in your car. Devices such as phones, music players and navigation systems can divide your concentration between the road ahead and what you're hearing.

Losing your concentration, or just taking your eyes off the road for a second, could be disastrous. At 60 mph, your vehicle will travel 27 metres in one second.

HC r149–150 **DES** s1

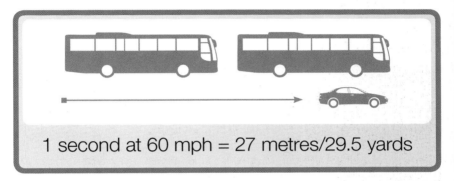

1 second at 60 mph = 27 metres/29.5 yards

Be careful that your passengers don't distract you. Joking about or having an argument can pull your attention away from the road for vital seconds.

DES s1

Watch DSA's 'Out of time' video to find out more about the risks of distraction.

➔ **youtube.com/dsagov**

Using a mobile phone while you're driving is illegal; it also drastically increases the chance of being involved in a collision. Even using a hands-free phone isn't safe because you can still be distracted from driving by making a call.

HC r149–150 **DES** s1

Be safe: switch your phone off or put it on voicemail. Wait until you're parked legally in a safe place before you use your mobile phone to

- retrieve any messages
- make any calls
- send or receive texts
- go online.

If you're driving on a motorway, you should leave the motorway and stop in a safe place before using your phone.

DES s11

See the Think! road safety website for more information about mobile phones and driving.

⊘ **http://think.direct.gov.uk/ mobile-phones.html**

If you have a navigation system, stop in a safe place before using the system.

You could also be distracted by something that has happened on the road, such as an incident on the other side of a motorway. Don't slow down or try to see what's happening; continue with your journey and keep your concentration on your driving.

Meeting the standards

The National Driving Standard sets out the skills, knowledge and understanding that DSA believes are required to be a safe and responsible driver. If you know, understand and are able to do the things described in the standard then you'll be not only in a great position to pass your test but well on your way to becoming a safe driver for life.

You can view the National Driving Standard at **www.gov.uk**

You must be able to

decide if you're fit to drive. You shouldn't be

- too tired
- too ill
- too emotional
- under the influence of drugs or alcohol

manage your passengers so that they don't stop you driving safely

be aware of what's around you (nearby and far away) at all times

drive at such a speed that you can always stop in the clear space ahead of you.

You must know and understand

how a poor seating position and bad posture can make you tired

how to deal with passengers if they make it hard for you to concentrate on the road

that some cars have large pillars that block your view, and how to deal with this

how to read the road ahead and be prepared for the unexpected.

Notes

You can use this page to make your own notes or diagrams about the key points you need to remember.

Think about

- Which clues can you use to help you anticipate what other road users might do? For example, a filling station at the side of the road could mean traffic slowing down to pull in, or vehicles pulling out.
- Why is it important to keep well back from large vehicles?
- What might you use to plan a long journey, and how would you make sure you took breaks at suitable points?
- Can you find a way to remind yourself to switch off your phone or put it to voicemail before you begin driving?

Your notes

Things to discuss and practise with your instructor

These are just a few examples of what you could discuss and practise with your instructor. Read more about alertness to come up with your own ideas.

Discuss with your instructor

- what you need to take into account before overtaking, eg road markings, bends, etc
- what could distract you while driving, eg friends, loud music, etc
- how to avoid getting bored while driving long distances.

Practise with your instructor

- your observation when making a turn in the road
- your alertness to other road users on narrow country lanes
- your ability to ignore your mobile phone. Arrange for someone to call you during your lesson so that you can practise your reaction. (Although *The Official Highway Code* advises you to turn your phone off while driving, sometimes you may forget.)

Before you make a U-turn in the road, you should

☐ give an arm signal as well as using your indicators

☐ signal so that other drivers can slow down for you

☐ look over your shoulder for a final check

☐ select a higher gear than normal

If you want to make a U-turn, slow down and ensure that the road is clear in both directions. Make sure that the road is wide enough to carry out the manoeuvre safely.

As you approach this bridge you should

☐ move into the middle of the road to get a better view

☐ slow down

☐ get over the bridge as quickly as possible

☐ consider using your horn

☐ find another route

☐ beware of pedestrians

This sign gives you a warning. The brow of the hill prevents you seeing oncoming traffic so you must be cautious. The bridge is narrow and there may not be enough room for you to pass an oncoming vehicle at this point. There is no footpath, so pedestrians may be walking in the road. Consider the hidden hazards and be ready to react if necessary.

In which of these situations should you avoid overtaking?

☐ Just after a bend

☐ In a one-way street

☐ On a 30 mph road

☐ Approaching a dip in the road

As you begin to think about overtaking, ask yourself if it's really necessary. If you can't see well ahead stay back and wait for a safer place to pull out.

This road marking warns

☐ drivers to use the hard shoulder

☐ overtaking drivers there is a bend to
the left

☐ overtaking drivers to move back to the left

☐ drivers that it is safe to overtake

You should plan your overtaking to take into account any hazards ahead. In this picture the marking indicates that you are approaching a junction. You will not have time to overtake and move back into the left safely.

**Your mobile phone rings while you are
travelling. You should**

☐ stop immediately

☐ answer it immediately

☐ pull up in a suitable place

☐ pull up at the nearest kerb

The safest option is to switch off your mobile phone before you set off, and use a message service. Even hands-free systems are likely to distract your attention. Don't endanger other road users. If you need to make a call, pull up in a safe place when you can, you may need to go some distance before you can find one. It's illegal to use a hand-held mobile or similar device when driving or riding, except in a genuine emergency.

Section one Questions

Why are these yellow lines painted across the road?

These lines are often found on the approach to a roundabout or a dangerous junction. They give you extra warning to adjust your speed. Look well ahead and do this in good time.

☐ To help you choose the correct lane

☐ To help you keep the correct separation distance

☐ To make you aware of your speed

☐ To tell you the distance to the roundabout

You are approaching traffic lights that have been on green for some time. You should

☐ accelerate hard

☐ maintain your speed

☐ be ready to stop

☐ brake hard

The longer traffic lights have been on green, the greater the chance of them changing. Always allow for this on approach and be prepared to stop.

Which of the following should you do before stopping?

☐ Sound the horn

☐ Use the mirrors

☐ Select a higher gear

☐ Flash your headlights

Before pulling up check the mirrors to see what is happening behind you. Also assess what is ahead and make sure you give the correct signal if it helps other road users.

1.9 | **Mark one answer** | **DES s6, HC r221**

When following a large vehicle you should keep well back because this

☐ allows you to corner more quickly

☐ helps the large vehicle to stop more easily

☐ allows the driver to see you in the mirrors

☐ helps you to keep out of the wind

If you're following a large vehicle but are so close to it that you can't see the exterior mirrors, the driver can't see you.

Keeping well back will also allow you to see the road ahead by looking past either side of the large vehicle.

1.10 | **Mark one answer** | **DES s4, 10, HC r161**

When you see a hazard ahead you should use the mirrors. Why is this?

☐ Because you will need to accelerate out of danger

☐ To assess how your actions will affect following traffic

☐ Because you will need to brake sharply to a stop

☐ To check what is happening on the road ahead

You should be constantly scanning the road for clues about what is going to happen next. Check your mirrors regularly, particularly as soon as you spot a hazard. What is happening behind may affect your response to hazards ahead.

1.11 | **Mark one answer** | **DES s10**

You are waiting to turn right at the end of a road. Your view is obstructed by parked vehicles. What should you do?

☐ Stop and then move forward slowly and carefully for a proper view

☐ Move quickly to where you can see so you only block traffic from one direction

☐ Wait for a pedestrian to let you know when it is safe for you to emerge

☐ Turn your vehicle around immediately and find another junction to use

At junctions your view is often restricted by buildings, trees or parked cars. You need to be able to see in order to judge a safe gap. Edge forward slowly and keep looking all the time. Don't cause other road users to change speed or direction as you emerge.

Mark two answers

Objects hanging from your interior mirror may

☐ restrict your view

☐ improve your driving

☐ distract your attention

☐ help your concentration

Ensure that you can see clearly through the windscreen of your vehicle. Stickers or hanging objects could affect your field of vision or draw your eyes away from the road.

Mark two answers

On a long motorway journey boredom can cause you to feel sleepy. You should

☐ leave the motorway and find a safe place to stop

☐ keep looking around at the surrounding landscape

☐ drive faster to complete your journey sooner

☐ ensure a supply of fresh air into your vehicle

☐ stop on the hard shoulder for a rest

Plan your journey to include suitable rest stops. You should take all possible precautions against feeling sleepy while driving. Any lapse of concentration could have serious consequences.

Mark two answers

You are driving at dusk. You should switch your lights on

☐ even when street lights are not lit

☐ so others can see you

☐ only when others have done so

☐ only when street lights are lit

Your headlights and tail lights help others on the road to see you. It may be necessary to turn on your lights during the day if visibility is reduced, for example due to heavy rain. In these conditions the light might fade before the street lights are timed to switch on. Be seen to be safe.

1.15 Mark four answers DES s1, HC r148–150

Which FOUR are most likely to cause you to lose concentration while you are driving?

☐ Using a mobile phone
☐ Talking into a microphone
☐ Tuning your car radio
☐ Looking at a map
☐ Checking the mirrors
☐ Using the demisters

It's easy to be distracted. Planning your journey before you set off is important. A few sensible precautions are to tune your radio to stations in your area of travel, take planned breaks, and plan your route. Except for emergencies it is illegal to use a hand-held mobile phone while driving. Even using a hands-free kit can distract your attention.

1.16 Mark one answer DES s1, HC r149

You should ONLY use a mobile phone when

☐ receiving a call
☐ suitably parked
☐ driving at less than 30 mph
☐ driving an automatic vehicle

It is illegal to use a hand-held mobile phone while driving, except in a genuine emergency. Even using a hands-free kit can distract your attention. Park in a safe and convenient place before receiving or making a call or using text messaging. Then you will also be free to take notes or refer to papers.

1.17 Mark one answer DES s5

You are driving on a wet road. You have to stop your vehicle in an emergency. You should

☐ apply the handbrake and footbrake together
☐ keep both hands on the wheel
☐ select reverse gear
☐ give an arm signal

As you drive, look well ahead and all around so that you're ready for any hazards that might occur. There may be occasions when you have to stop in an emergency. React as soon as you can whilst keeping control of the vehicle.

Mark three answers

DES s4, 5, HC r159–161

When you are moving off from behind a parked car you should

☐ look round before you move off

☐ use all the mirrors on the vehicle

☐ look round after moving off

☐ use the exterior mirrors only

☐ give a signal if necessary

☐ give a signal after moving off

Before moving off you should use all the mirrors to check if the road is clear. Look round to check the blind spots and give a signal if it is necessary to warn other road users of your intentions.

Mark one answer

DES s10, HC r212

You are travelling along this narrow country road. When passing the cyclist you should go

Look well ahead and only pull out if it is safe. You will need to use all of the road to pass the cyclist, so be extra-cautious. Look out for entrances to fields where tractors or other farm machinery could be waiting to pull out.

☐ slowly, sounding the horn as you pass

☐ quickly, leaving plenty of room

☐ slowly, leaving plenty of room

☐ quickly, sounding the horn as you pass

Mark one answer

DES s1, HC r149

Your vehicle is fitted with a hand-held telephone. To use the telephone you should

☐ reduce your speed

☐ find a safe place to stop

☐ steer the vehicle with one hand

☐ be particularly careful at junctions

Your attention should be on your driving at all times. Except in a genuine emergency never attempt to use a hand-held phone while on the move. It's illegal and very dangerous. Your eyes could wander from the road and at 60 mph your vehicle will travel about 27 metres (89 feet) every second.

1.21 Mark one answer DES s1, 18

You lose your way on a busy road. What is the best action to take?

☐ Stop at traffic lights and ask pedestrians

☐ Shout to other drivers to ask them the way

☐ Turn into a side road, stop and check a map

☐ Check a map, and keep going with the traffic flow

It's easy to lose your way in an unfamiliar area. If you need to check a map or ask for directions, first find a safe place to stop.

1.22 Mark one answer DES s5, 10

Windscreen pillars can obstruct your view. You should take particular care when

☐ driving on a motorway

☐ driving on a dual carriageway

☐ approaching a one-way street

☐ approaching bends and junctions

Windscreen pillars can obstruct your view, particularly at bends and junctions. Look out for other road users, particularly cyclists and pedestrians, as they can be hard to see.

1.23 Mark one answer DES s9, HC r202

You cannot see clearly behind when reversing. What should you do?

☐ Open your window to look behind

☐ Open the door and look behind

☐ Look in the nearside mirror

☐ Ask someone to guide you

If you want to turn your car around try to find a place where you have good all-round vision. If this isn't possible and you're unable to see clearly, then get someone to guide you.

1.24 Mark one answer DES s4, HC r159

What does the term 'blind spot' mean for a driver?

☐ An area covered by your right-hand mirror

☐ An area not covered by your headlights

☐ An area covered by your left-hand mirror

☐ An area not covered by your mirrors

Modern vehicles provide the driver with well-positioned mirrors which are essential to safe driving. However, they cannot see every angle of the scene behind and to the sides of the vehicle. This is why it is essential that you check over your shoulder, so that you are aware of any hazards not reflected in your mirrors.

Using a hands-free phone is likely to

☐ improve your safety

☐ increase your concentration

☐ reduce your view

☐ divert your attention

Unlike someone in the car with you, the person on the other end of the line is unable to see the traffic situations you are dealing with. They will not stop speaking to you even if you are approaching a hazardous situation. You need to be concentrating on your driving all of the time, but especially so when dealing with a hazard.

You are turning right onto a dual carriageway. What should you do before emerging?

☐ Stop, apply the handbrake and then select a low gear

☐ Position your vehicle well to the left of the side road

☐ Check that the central reservation is wide enough for your vehicle

☐ Make sure that you leave enough room for a vehicle behind

Before emerging right onto a dual carriageway make sure that the central reserve is deep enough to protect your vehicle. If it's not, you should treat it as one road and check that it's clear in both directions before pulling out. Neglecting to do this could place part or all of your vehicle in the path of approaching traffic and cause a collision.

You are waiting to emerge from a junction. The windscreen pillar is restricting your view. What should you be particularly aware of?

Windscreen pillars can completely block your view of pedestrians, motorcyclists and pedal cyclists. You should particularly watch out for these road users; don't just rely on a quick glance. Where possible make eye contact with them so you can be sure they have seen you too.

☐ Lorries

☐ Buses

☐ Motorcyclists

☐ Coaches

Your vehicle is fitted with a navigation system. How should you avoid letting this distract you while driving?

☐ Keep going and input your destination into the system

☐ Keep going as the system will adjust to your route

☐ Stop immediately to view and use the system

☐ Stop in a safe place before using the system

Vehicle navigation systems can be useful when driving on unfamiliar routes. However they can also distract you and cause you to lose control if you look at or adjust them while driving. Pull up in a convenient and safe place before adjusting them.

Case study practice – 1
Alertness

> James has a two-hour drive to make on a motorway.
>
> He has a cold and his nose is also slightly blocked. He takes an off-the-shelf cold remedy to help reduce the symptoms.
>
> It's a cold and dull day and the car heater is on. James also turns on his dipped headlights.
>
> An hour into the boring journey, James begins to feel drowsy.

1.1 What information should James check on the medication?
Mark one answer

- ☐ Information about the retailers who stock the product
- ☐ Information about the medicine causing drowsiness
- ☐ Information about how many pills are in the packet
- ☐ Information about the manufacturer of the medicine

HC r96 **DES** s1

1.2 Why would James be using lights in daylight?
Mark one answer

- ☐ To observe other vehicles more clearly
- ☐ To improve his view of the road
- ☐ To catch sight of road signs easily
- ☐ To maximise his visibility to others

HC r115

1.3 How's the boring journey physically affecting James?

Mark **one** answer

- ☐ He becomes happy
- ☐ He becomes drowsy
- ☐ He becomes angry
- ☐ He becomes attentive

HC **r262** **DES** **s11**

1.4 What should James do about his condition?

Mark **one** answer

- ☐ Keep driving, slow down a little while taking a caffeinated drink
- ☐ Drive more slowly, turn the vehicle around and go back home
- ☐ Stop in a service area, drink a caffeinated drink and then rest
- ☐ Stop on the hard shoulder, recline the seat fully back and rest

HC **r91** **DES** **s1**

1.5 How could James help himself stay alert in the short term?

Mark **one** answer

- ☐ Open the window
- ☐ Turn up the heater
- ☐ Turn on the radio
- ☐ Open a can of drink

DES **s1**

Section two
Attitude

In this section, you'll learn about

- showing consideration and courtesy to other road users
- how to follow other road users safely
- giving priority to emergency vehicles, buses and pedestrians.

Attitude

Safe driving is all about developing the correct attitude and approach to road safety, together with a sound knowledge of driving techniques.

However modern, fast or expensive your vehicle, it's you, the driver, who determines how safe it is.

❯ Good manners on the road

Be considerate to other road users. Other drivers, cyclists and horse riders have just as much right to use the road as you. If you drive in a competitive way, you'll make the road less safe for everyone using it.

DES s1

It's also important to be patient with other road users. Unfortunately, not everyone obeys the rules. Try to be calm and tolerant, however difficult it seems. For instance, if someone pulls out in front of you at a junction, slow down and don't get annoyed with them.

HC r147 **DES** s1

Helping other road users

You can help other road users know what you're planning to do by signalling correctly and moving to the correct position at junctions. For instance, if you want to turn right, get into the right-hand lane well before the junction. A badly positioned vehicle could obstruct traffic behind it.

HC r143 **DES** s7, 8

If you're driving a slow-moving vehicle, consider other drivers behind you. If there's a long queue, pull over as soon as you can do so safely and let the traffic pass. Think how you would feel if you were one of the drivers following behind you. They may not be as patient as you are.

HC r169 **DES** s10

 TIP If a large vehicle is trying to overtake you but is taking a long time, slow down and let it pass. It will need more time to pass you than a car would.

HC r168 **DES** s7

If you're travelling at the speed limit and a driver comes up behind flashing their headlights or trying to overtake, keep a steady course and allow them to overtake. Don't try to stop them – they could become more frustrated.

HC r168 **DES** s7, 11

Using your horn and lights

Only sound your horn if there's danger and you need to let others know you're there. Don't sound it through impatience.

HC r112 **DES** s5–8, 13

At night, don't dazzle other road users. Dip your lights when you're

following another vehicle

meeting another vehicle coming towards you.

HC r114 **DES** s13

If you're queuing in traffic at night, use your handbrake rather than keeping your foot on the brake, as your brake lights could dazzle drivers behind you.

You should only flash your headlights to show other road users you're there. It's not a signal to show priority, impatience or to greet others.

HC r110–111 DES s5, 10

Animals on the road

Horses can be frightened easily and a rider could lose control of their horse. When passing horses

- keep your speed right down
- give them plenty of room.

HC r214–215 DES s10

See the Think! road safety website for more information about horses on the road.

❯ **http://think.direct.gov.uk/ horses.html**

Take care if there are animals, such as sheep, on the road. If the road is blocked by animals, or if you're asked to, stop and switch off your engine until the road is clear.

HC r214

❯ Following safely

Driving too closely behind another vehicle – known as tailgating – is

- intimidating and distracting for the road user in front
- very dangerous, as it could cause an incident if the vehicle stops suddenly.

DES s10

Travelling too closely to another vehicle also means that you can see less of the road ahead, so keep well back, especially from large vehicles. You'll be able to see further down the road and spot any hazards ahead more easily.

DES s7, 10

Keep a safe distance from the vehicle in front.

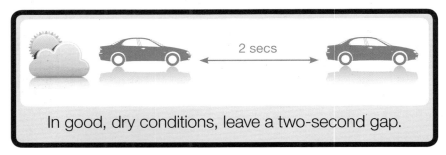

In good, dry conditions, leave a two-second gap.

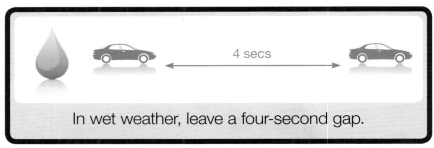

In wet weather, leave a four-second gap.

HC r126 **DES** s7, 10, 11

Use a fixed point, like a road sign, to help you measure the gap between you and the vehicle in front.

See section 4, Safety margins, for more information about the amount of space to leave between you and the vehicle in front.

When you're following large vehicles, you may see them move to the centre of the road before turning left – this is because they need more room to manoeuvre. Keep well back and don't try to pass on the left as the rear of the vehicle will cut in.

If the road user behind is following too closely, gradually increase the gap between you and the vehicle in front. This will give you a greater safety margin. If another road user cuts in front of you, drop back until you've restored your safety margin.

HC r168

> Giving priority to others

Who has priority on the road at any time can vary. Sometimes traffic going in one direction is given priority, and this is shown by a road sign. Having priority doesn't mean you can demand right of way. Be careful: the driver coming towards you may not have seen or understood the road sign.

Priority over oncoming vehicles

Emergency vehicles

Always give priority to emergency vehicles. It's important for them to move quickly through traffic because someone's life might depend on it. Pull over to let them through as soon as you can do so safely.

HC r219 **DES** s7

As well as fire, police and ambulance services, other emergency services also use a blue flashing light, including those shown here.

HM coastguard

Bomb disposal

Mountain rescue

Blood transfusion

Doctors' vehicles may use green flashing lights when answering an emergency call.

Watch the Blue Light Aware video to find out more about how to help emergency vehicles get through traffic.

> **motoringassist.com/bluelightaware**

Priority for buses

Give priority to buses pulling out from bus stops, as long as you can do so safely. In some areas, bus lanes allow buses to proceed quickly through traffic. Be aware of road signs and markings so that you don't use bus lanes while they're in operation.

HC r223 **DES** s6, 7, 10

Unmarked crossroads

At unmarked crossroads, no-one has priority. Slow down, look both ways and only emerge into the junction when you can do so safely.

Pedestrian crossings

Be particularly careful around pedestrian crossings so that you're ready to stop if necessary.

Type of crossing	What you need to be aware of
Zebra crossing 	Watch out for pedestrians at or approaching a zebra crossing. • Be ready to slow down and stop. • Be patient if they cross slowly. • Don't encourage them to cross by waving or flashing your headlights – there may be another vehicle coming. **HC** r195 **DES** s7
Pelican crossing 	If you're approaching a pelican crossing and the amber light is flashing • give way to pedestrians on the crossing • don't move off until the crossing is clear. **HC** r196–198 **DES** s7

Type of crossing	What you need to be aware of
Puffin crossing 	Puffin crossings are electronically controlled. Sensors ensure that the red light shows until the pedestrian has safely crossed the road. These crossings don't have a flashing amber light; they have a steady amber light, like normal traffic lights. **HC** r199 **DES** s7
Toucan crossing 	Toucan crossings, which work in a similar way to puffin crossings, allow cyclists to cross at the same time as pedestrians. **HC** r199 **DES** s7

Meeting the standards

You must be able to

help other road users to understand what you intend to do by signalling correctly

support the signals that you make with the position of your vehicle. For example, if you're turning right, position the car in good time and use the right-turn lane if there is one

control your reaction to other road users. Try not to get annoyed or frustrated

give other road users enough time and space.

You must know and understand

what can happen if you wrongly use the headlights or the horn as a signal

what lane discipline is and why it's important

that it's an offence to drive

- without due care and attention
- without reasonable consideration for other road users.

Notes

You can use this page to make your own notes or diagrams about the key points you need to remember.

Think about

- To which vehicles do you need to give priority?
- What would you do if someone was tailgating you?
- In what conditions should you keep a four-second distance between you and the vehicle in front?
- What problems might you cause if you're impatient and inconsiderate while driving?

Your notes

Things to discuss and practise with your instructor

These are just a few examples of what you could discuss and practise with your instructor. Read more about attitude to come up with your own ideas.

Discuss with your instructor

- the different crossings you may come across (puffin, toucan, etc) and who can use them
- which emergency vehicles you may see on the road (police, doctors, etc) and how to react to them
- what the 'two-second rule' means and how it may change in different weather conditions.

Practise with your instructor

- driving in an area with bus lanes, to practise how to react when they're in operation
- driving at night, to get used to using your dipped and main beam headlights
- driving in heavy traffic, to get used to other vehicles that may be following you too closely.

At a pelican crossing the flashing amber light means you MUST

☐ stop and wait for the green light

☐ stop and wait for the red light

☐ give way to pedestrians waiting to cross

☐ give way to pedestrians already on the crossing

Pelican crossings are signal-controlled crossings operated by pedestrians. Push-button controls change the signals. Pelican crossings have no red-and-amber stage before green. Instead, they have a flashing amber light, which means you MUST give way to pedestrians already on the crossing, but if it is clear, you may continue.

You should never wave people across at pedestrian crossings because

☐ there may be another vehicle coming

☐ they may not be looking

☐ it is safer for you to carry on

☐ they may not be ready to cross

If people are waiting to use a pedestrian crossing, slow down and be prepared to stop. Don't wave them across the road since another driver may not have seen them, may not have seen your signal and may not be able to stop safely.

'Tailgating' means

☐ using the rear door of a hatchback car

☐ reversing into a parking space

☐ following another vehicle too closely

☐ driving with rear fog lights on

'Tailgating' is used to describe this dangerous practice, often seen in fast-moving traffic and on motorways. Following the vehicle in front too closely is dangerous because it

- restricts your view of the road ahead

- leaves you no safety margin if the vehicle in front slows down or stops suddenly.

2.4   Mark one answer   DES s7, 10, HC r222

Following this vehicle too closely is unwise because

☐ your brakes will overheat

☐ your view ahead is increased

☐ your engine will overheat

☐ your view ahead is reduced

Staying back will increase your view of the road ahead. This will help you to see any hazards that might occur and allow you more time to react.

2.5   Mark one answer   DES s7, 10, 11, HC r126

You are following a vehicle on a wet road. You should leave a time gap of at least

☐ one second

☐ two seconds

☐ three seconds

☐ four seconds

Wet roads will reduce your tyres' grip on the road. The safe separation gap of at least two seconds in dry conditions should be doubled in wet weather.

2.6   Mark one answer   DES s7, HC r168

A long, heavily laden lorry is taking a long time to overtake you. What should you do?

☐ Speed up

☐ Slow down

☐ Hold your speed

☐ Change direction

A long lorry with a heavy load will need more time to pass you than a car, especially on an uphill stretch of road. Slow down and allow the lorry to pass.

2.7   Mark three answers   DES s7

Which of the following vehicles will use blue flashing beacons?

☐ Motorway maintenance

☐ Bomb disposal

☐ Blood transfusion

☐ Police patrol

☐ Breakdown recovery

When you see emergency vehicles with blue flashing beacons, move out of the way as soon as it is safe to do so.

65

When being followed by an ambulance showing a flashing blue beacon you should

☐ pull over as soon as safely possible to let it pass

☐ accelerate hard to get away from it

☐ maintain your speed and course

☐ brake harshly and immediately stop in the road

Pull over in a place where the ambulance can pass safely. Check that there are no bollards or obstructions in the road that will prevent it from doing so.

What type of emergency vehicle is fitted with a green flashing beacon?

☐ Fire engine

☐ Road gritter

☐ Ambulance

☐ Doctor's car

A green flashing beacon on a vehicle means the driver or passenger is a doctor on an emergency call. Give way to them if it's safe to do so. Be aware that the vehicle may be travelling quickly or may stop in a hurry.

Diamond-shaped signs give instructions to

These signs only apply to trams. They are directed at tram drivers but you should know their meaning so that you're aware of the priorities and are able to anticipate the actions of the driver.

☐ tram drivers

☐ bus drivers

☐ lorry drivers

☐ taxi drivers

On a road where trams operate, which of these vehicles will be most at risk from the tram rails?

☐ Cars

☐ Cycles

☐ Buses

☐ Lorries

The narrow wheels of a bicycle can become stuck in the tram rails, causing the cyclist to stop suddenly, wobble or even lose balance altogether. The tram lines are also slippery which could cause a cyclist to slide or fall off.

2.12 | Mark one answer | DES s3, 5, 10, HC r112

What should you use your horn for?

☐ To alert others to your presence

☐ To allow you right of way

☐ To greet other road users

☐ To signal your annoyance

Your horn must not be used between 11.30 pm and 7 am in a built-up area or when you are stationary, unless a moving vehicle poses a danger. Its function is to alert other road users to your presence.

2.13 | Mark one answer | DES s7, 8, HC r143

You are in a one-way street and want to turn right. You should position yourself

☐ in the right-hand lane

☐ in the left-hand lane

☐ in either lane, depending on the traffic

☐ just left of the centre line

If you're travelling in a one-way street and wish to turn right you should take up a position in the right-hand lane. This will enable other road users not wishing to turn to proceed on the left. Indicate your intention and take up your position in good time.

2.14 | Mark one answer | DES s7, 8, HC r179

You wish to turn right ahead. Why should you take up the correct position in good time?

☐ To allow other drivers to pull out in front of you

☐ To give a better view into the road that you're joining

☐ To help other road users know what you intend to do

☐ To allow drivers to pass you on the right

If you wish to turn right into a side road take up your position in good time. Move to the centre of the road when it's safe to do so. This will allow vehicles to pass you on the left. Early planning will show other traffic what you intend to do.

2.15 | Mark one answer | DES s7, HC r25, KYTS p124

At which type of crossing are cyclists allowed to ride across with pedestrians?

☐ Toucan

☐ Puffin

☐ Pelican

☐ Zebra

A toucan crossing is designed to allow pedestrians and cyclists to cross at the same time. Look out for cyclists approaching the crossing at speed.

Mark one answer

DES s1, 11, HC r168

You are travelling at the legal speed limit. A vehicle comes up quickly behind, flashing its headlights. You should

☐ accelerate to make a gap behind you

☐ touch the brakes sharply to show your brake lights

☐ maintain your speed to prevent the vehicle from overtaking

☐ allow the vehicle to overtake

Don't enforce the speed limit by blocking another vehicle's progress. This will only lead to the other driver becoming more frustrated. Allow the other vehicle to pass when you can do so safely.

2.17

Mark one answer

DES s5, 10, HC r110–111

You should ONLY flash your headlights to other road users

☐ to show that you are giving way

☐ to show that you are about to turn

☐ to tell them that you have right of way

☐ to let them know that you are there

You should only flash your headlights to warn others of your presence. Don't use them to greet others, show impatience or give priority to other road users. They could misunderstand your signal.

2.18

Mark one answer

DES s8, HC r146

You are approaching unmarked crossroads. How should you deal with this type of junction?

☐ Accelerate and keep to the middle

☐ Slow down and keep to the right

☐ Accelerate looking to the left

☐ Slow down and look both ways

Be extra-cautious, especially when your view is restricted by hedges, bushes, walls and large vehicles etc. In the summer months these junctions can become more difficult to deal with when growing foliage may obscure your view.

2.19

Mark one answer

DES s7, 10, 11, HC r126

The conditions are good and dry. You could use the 'two-second rule'

☐ before restarting the engine after it has stalled

☐ to keep a safe gap from the vehicle in front

☐ before using the 'Mirror-Signal-Manoeuvre' routine

☐ when emerging on wet roads

To measure this, choose a fixed reference point such as a bridge, sign or tree. When the vehicle ahead passes the object, say to yourself 'Only a fool breaks the two-second rule.' If you reach the object before you finish saying this, you're TOO CLOSE.

2.20   Mark one answer   DES s7, HC r199

At a puffin crossing, which colour follows the green signal?

☐ Steady red

☐ Flashing amber

☐ Steady amber

☐ Flashing green

Puffin crossings have infra-red sensors which detect when pedestrians are crossing and hold the red traffic signal until the crossing is clear. The use of a sensor means there is no flashing amber phase as there is with a pelican crossing.

2.21   Mark one answer   DES s7, 10, 11, HC r126

You are in a line of traffic. The driver behind you is following very closely. What action should you take?

☐ Ignore the following driver and continue to travel within the speed limit

☐ Slow down, gradually increasing the gap between you and the vehicle in front

☐ Signal left and wave the following driver past

☐ Move over to a position just left of the centre line of the road

It can be worrying to see that the car behind is following you too closely. Give yourself a greater safety margin by easing back from the vehicle in front.

2.22   Mark one answer   DES s7, 10, HC r223

A bus has stopped at a bus stop ahead of you. Its right-hand indicator is flashing. You should

Give way to buses whenever you can do so safely, especially when they signal to pull away from bus stops. Look out for people leaving the bus and crossing the road.

☐ flash your headlights and slow down

☐ slow down and give way if it is safe to do so

☐ sound your horn and keep going

☐ slow down and then sound your horn

You are driving on a clear night. There is a steady stream of oncoming traffic. The national speed limit applies. Which lights should you use?

Use the full beam headlights only when you can be sure that you won't dazzle other road users.

☐ Full beam headlights

☐ Sidelights

☐ Dipped headlights

☐ Fog lights

You are driving behind a large goods vehicle. It signals left but steers to the right. You should

Large, long vehicles need extra room when making turns at junctions. They may move out to the right in order to make a left turn. Keep well back and don't attempt to pass on the left.

☐ slow down and let the vehicle turn

☐ drive on, keeping to the left

☐ overtake on the right of it

☐ hold your speed and sound your horn

You are driving along this road. The red van cuts in close in front of you. What should you do?

There are times when other drivers make incorrect or ill-judged decisions. Be tolerant and try not to retaliate or react aggressively. Always consider the safety of other road users, your passengers and yourself.

☐ Accelerate to get closer to the red van

☐ Give a long blast on the horn

☐ Drop back to leave the correct separation distance

☐ Flash your headlights several times

You are waiting in a traffic queue at night. To avoid dazzling following drivers you should

☐ apply the handbrake only

☐ apply the footbrake only

☐ switch off your headlights

☐ use both the handbrake and footbrake

You should consider drivers behind as brake lights can dazzle. However, if you are driving in fog it's safer to keep your foot on the footbrake. In this case it will give the vehicle behind extra warning of your presence.

You are driving in traffic at the speed limit for the road. The driver behind is trying to overtake. You should

☐ move closer to the car ahead, so the driver behind has no room to overtake

☐ wave the driver behind to overtake when it is safe

☐ keep a steady course and allow the driver behind to overtake

☐ accelerate to get away from the driver behind

Keep a steady course to give the driver behind an opportunity to overtake safely. If necessary, slow down. Reacting incorrectly to another driver's impatience can lead to danger.

Section two Questions

A bus lane on your left shows no times of operation. This means it is

Don't drive or park in a bus lane when it's in operation. This can cause disruption to traffic and delays to public transport.

☐ not in operation at all

☐ only in operation at peak times

☐ in operation 24 hours a day

☐ only in operation in daylight hours

A person herding sheep asks you to stop. You should

Allow the sheep to clear the road before you proceed. Animals are unpredictable and startle easily; they could turn and run into your path or into the path of another moving vehicle.

☐ ignore them as they have no authority

☐ stop and switch off your engine

☐ continue on but drive slowly

☐ try and get past quickly

When overtaking a horse and rider you should

Horses can become startled by the sound of a car engine or the rush of air caused by passing too closely. Keep well back and only pass when it is safe; leave them plenty of room. You may have to use the other side of the road to go past: if you do, first make sure there is no oncoming traffic.

☐ sound your horn as a warning

☐ go past as quickly as possible

☐ flash your headlights as a warning

☐ go past slowly and carefully

2.31   Mark one answer   DES s7, HC r195

You are approaching a zebra crossing. Pedestrians are waiting to cross. You should

☐ give way to the elderly and infirm only

☐ slow down and prepare to stop

☐ use your headlights to indicate they can cross

☐ wave at them to cross the road

Look out on the approach especially for children and older pedestrians. They may walk across without looking. Zebra crossings have flashing amber beacons on both sides of the road, black and white stripes on the crossing and white zigzag markings on both sides of the crossing. Where you can see pedestrians waiting to cross, slow down and prepare to stop.

2.32   Mark one answer   DES s8, HC r147

A vehicle pulls out in front of you at a junction. What should you do?

☐ Swerve past it and sound your horn

☐ Flash your headlights and drive up close behind

☐ Slow down and be ready to stop

☐ Accelerate past it immediately

Try to be ready for the unexpected. Plan ahead and learn to anticipate hazards. You'll then give yourself more time to react to any problems that might occur.

Be tolerant of the behaviour of other road users who don't behave correctly.

2.33   Mark one answer   DES s7, HC r199, KYTS p123

You are approaching a red light at a puffin crossing. Pedestrians are on the crossing. The red light will stay on until

☐ you start to edge forward on to the crossing

☐ the pedestrians have reached a safe position

☐ the pedestrians are clear of the front of your vehicle

☐ a driver from the opposite direction reaches the crossing

The electronic device will automatically detect that the pedestrians have reached a safe position. Don't proceed until the green light shows it is safe for vehicles to do so.

Which instrument panel warning light would show that headlights are on full beam?

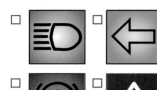

You should be aware of where all the warning lights and visual aids are on the vehicle you are driving. If you are driving a vehicle for the first time you should take time to check all the controls.

You should leave at least a two-second gap between your vehicle and the one in front when conditions are

- ☐ wet
- ☐ good
- ☐ damp
- ☐ foggy

In good, dry conditions an alert driver, who's driving a vehicle with tyres and brakes in good condition, needs to keep a distance of at least two seconds from the car in front.

You are driving at night on an unlit road behind another vehicle. You should

- ☐ flash your headlights
- ☐ use dipped beam headlights
- ☐ switch off your headlights
- ☐ use full beam headlights

If you follow another vehicle with your headlights on full beam they could dazzle the driver. Leave a safe distance and ensure that the light from your dipped beam falls short of the vehicle in front.

2.37 | Mark one answer | DES s10, HC r169

You are driving a slow-moving vehicle on a narrow winding road. You should

☐ keep well out to stop vehicles overtaking dangerously

☐ wave following vehicles past you if you think they can overtake quickly

☐ pull in safely when you can, to let following vehicles overtake

☐ give a left signal when it is safe for vehicles to overtake you

Try not to hold up a queue of traffic. Other road users may become impatient and this could lead to reckless actions. If you're driving a slow-moving vehicle and the road is narrow, look for a safe place to pull in. DON'T wave other traffic past since this could be dangerous if you or they haven't seen an oncoming vehicle.

2.38 | Mark two answers | DES s4, HC p130

You have a loose filler cap on your diesel fuel tank. This will

☐ waste fuel and money

☐ make roads slippery for other road users

☐ improve your vehicle's fuel consumption

☐ increase the level of exhaust emissions

Diesel fuel is especially slippery if spilled on a wet road. At the end of a dry spell of weather you should be aware that the road surfaces may have a high level of diesel spillage that hasn't been washed away by rain.

2.39 | Mark one answer | DES s14, HC p130

To avoid spillage after refuelling, you should make sure that

☐ your tank is only three quarters full

☐ you have used a locking filler cap

☐ you check your fuel gauge is working

☐ your filler cap is securely fastened

When learning to drive it is a good idea to practise filling your car with fuel. Ask your instructor if you can use a petrol station and fill the fuel tank yourself. You need to know where the filler cap is located on the car you are driving in order to park on the correct side of the pump. Take care not to overfill the tank or spill fuel. Make sure you secure the filler cap as soon as you have replaced the fuel nozzle.

2.40 | Mark one answer | DES s1

What style of driving causes increased risk to everyone?

☐ Considerate

☐ Defensive

☐ Competitive

☐ Responsible

Competitive driving increases the risks to everyone and is the opposite of responsible, considerate and defensive driving. Defensive driving is about questioning the actions of other road users and being prepared for the unexpected. Don't be taken by surprise.

> Case study practice – 2
Attitude

Sam is driving in heavy traffic.

It has rained, but now bright sun is causing glare on the wet road.

A car overtakes, then pulls back sharply into the traffic just in front of Sam.

Further on there's a roundabout with two lanes on approach. Sam needs to take the first exit, turning left. A large vehicle in front signals left but straddles both lanes.

The traffic is still heavy, and there's a zebra crossing up ahead. There are people waiting to cross.

2.1 If affected by the road condition, how should Sam react?
Mark **one** answer

- ☐ Slow down and, if necessary, stop
- ☐ Speed up to get out of the sunlight
- ☐ Turn around and go back home
- ☐ Turn on hazard lights and wipers

HC r237 **DES** s12

2.2 What should Sam do about the overtaking vehicle?
Mark **one** answer

- ☐ Become upset, slow down and use the horn
- ☐ Stay focused, speed up and lessen the gap
- ☐ Remain calm, slow down and increase the gap
- ☐ Feel annoyed, speed up and use the horn

HC r147, 168 **DES** s1

2.3 How should Sam be positioned on approach to the roundabout?

Mark **one** answer

☐   In the right-hand lane while signalling right
☐   In the left-hand lane without signalling
☐   In the left-hand lane while signalling left
☐   In the right-hand lane without signalling

HC r186 **DES** s8

2.4 Why might the large vehicle be taking this position?

Mark **one** answer

☐   The driver isn't sure which way to go
☐   The indicators aren't working properly
☐   The load being carried is extremely heavy
☐   The vehicle needs more room to turn

HC r187, 221 **DES** s8

2.5 What should Sam do at the zebra crossing?

Mark **one** answer

☐   Stop and then wave them across
☐   Rev the engine until they cross
☐   Stop and wait for them to cross
☐   Inch forward slowly as they cross

HC r195 **DES** s7

Section three
Safety and your vehicle

In this section, you'll learn about

- carrying out basic maintenance on your car
- what to do if your car has a fault
- using your car's safety equipment effectively
- making your car secure
- parking safely
- being aware of the environment
- avoiding congestion.

Safety and your vehicle

Look after your car and it will look after you, not only by being less likely to break down, but also by being more economical and lasting longer. Remember that an efficient engine is kinder to the environment.

> Looking after your car

Regular maintenance should ensure that your car is safe and fit to be on the road. It will also help to make sure that your car uses fuel as efficiently as possible and keep its exhaust emissions to a minimum.

Lights, brakes, steering, the exhaust system, seat belts, horn, speedometer, wipers and washers must all be working properly.

HC p128–130 **DES** s12, 14

Check the following items on a regular basis.

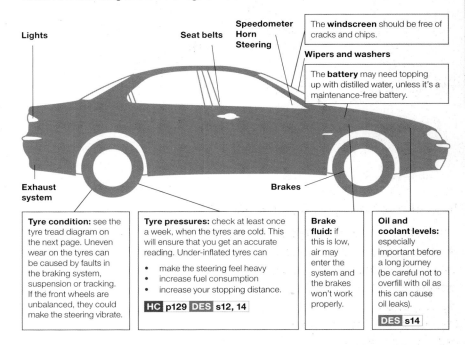

Lights

Seat belts

Speedometer
Horn
Steering

The **windscreen** should be free of cracks and chips.

Wipers and washers

The **battery** may need topping up with distilled water, unless it's a maintenance-free battery.

Exhaust system

Brakes

Tyre condition: see the tyre tread diagram on the next page. Uneven wear on the tyres can be caused by faults in the braking system, suspension or tracking. If the front wheels are unbalanced, they could make the steering vibrate.

Tyre pressures: check at least once a week, when the tyres are cold. This will ensure that you get an accurate reading. Under-inflated tyres can

- make the steering feel heavy
- increase fuel consumption
- increase your stopping distance.

HC p129 **DES** s12, 14

Brake fluid: if this is low, air may enter the system and the brakes won't work properly.

Oil and coolant levels: especially important before a long journey (be careful not to overfill with oil as this can cause oil leaks).

DES s14

The tread on car and trailer tyres must be at least 1.6 mm deep across the centre three-quarters of the breadth of the tyre and around the entire outer circumference. It's illegal to drive with tyres that have cuts or defects in the side walls.

HC p129 **DES** s14

Tread must be at least **1.6 mm** across the central three-quarters of the tyre …

… all the way around the tyre

Find out more about tyre safety in this video.

❯ **tyresafe.org/tyre-safety/ meet-the-mcintyres**

Dry steering is when you turn the steering wheel while the car isn't moving. It can cause unnecessary wear to the tyres and steering mechanism.

DES s3

To check the condition of the shock absorbers, 'bounce' the vehicle. Push down hard over each wheel: there should be no more than one rebound when released.

HC p130 **DES** s14

Watch the three 'Show me, tell me' videos on DSA's YouTube channel.

❯ **youtube.com/dsagov**

Here's another useful summary about the maintenance checks you'll need to be able to do for your driving test.

❯ **youtube.com/ watch?v=ixJERW-hN2I**

❯ Dealing with faults

A basic understanding of how your car works will help you recognise when there's a problem with it. It's important that your car is checked regularly by a qualified mechanic, especially the brakes and the steering.

Warning lights on the dashboard tell you about the performance of the engine and warn you of any faults.

- Check your vehicle handbook to make sure that you know what all the warning lights mean.
- Don't ignore a warning: it could affect your safety.

HC p128 **DES** s3, 14

The anti-lock braking system (ABS) warning light should go out when the car's travelling at 5–10 mph. If this doesn't happen, have the ABS checked by a qualified mechanic.

'Brake fade' is when the brakes become less effective because of overheating. It may happen if you use them continuously, such as on a long, steep downhill stretch of road. In this situation, use a lower gear to help you control the vehicle's speed.

DES s7

Visit a garage as soon as possible if

- the steering vibrates – the wheels may need **balancing**
- the vehicle pulls to one side when you brake – your brakes may need adjusting.

DES s14

Definition

balancing
making sure that the wheels and tyres are adjusted to minimise any vibrations in the vehicle

❯ Safety equipment

Modern cars are fitted with equipment designed to keep you as safe as possible, but you need to make sure that you use it correctly for it to be effective.

Seat belts and restraints

Always wear your seat belt and make sure your passengers wear theirs (unless exempt). The driver is responsible for making sure that children under 14 wear a suitable restraint.

HC r99, 100

Adults aged 14 and over, and children over 1.35 metres (approx 4ft 5 ins) in height or 12 or 13 years, **MUST** wear a seat belt unless exempt.

Children aged from 3 to 12 years, or up to 1.35 m in height, **MUST** use a suitable child restraint. If a suitable child restraint isn't available in the rear seat for children aged 3 to 12, an adult seat belt **MUST** be used.

Children under 3 years of age **MUST** use a suitable child seat. Never fit a rear-facing baby seat in a seat protected by an active airbag. The airbag **MUST** be deactivated first.

HC r99–102 **DES** s2

Safety before you start driving

Make sure that you're safe and comfortable before you begin your journey.

When you get into the car

 adjust the seat so that you can reach all the controls comfortably

 adjust the head restraint to help prevent neck injury in a collision

 wear suitable shoes so that you can keep control of the pedals

 adjust the mirrors so that you can see as clearly as possible all around. Convex mirrors give a wider view but can make vehicles look further away than they are. If you can't see behind you when you're reversing, get someone to guide you.

HC r97 **DES** s3, 4

 See why it's important to adjust the head restraint correctly, and how to do it, in this video.

➲ **youtube.com/ watch?v=wlYlPuRvwtM**

Lights

If you're driving in poor visibility, such as fog or heavy rain, use dipped headlights. It's important for other road users to see you. If there's thick fog, use your fog lights but remember to switch them off when visibility improves.

HC r113–115, 226

When leaving your car on a two-way road at night, park in the direction of the traffic. If the speed limit is more than 30 mph (46 km/h), switch on your parking lights.

DES s12

Hazard warning lights are fitted so that you can warn road users of a hazard ahead, such as

- when you've broken down
- queuing traffic on a dual carriageway or motorway.

Don't use them as an excuse to park illegally, even for a short time.

HC r116, 274, 277–278 **DES** s3, 11

❯ Security

Although it's impossible to make a car completely secure, the harder you make it for a potential thief to break in and steal your property or your car, the less likely you are to be targeted.

Make it as difficult as you can for a thief to either break into your car or steal it.

Use a steering lock.

Remove the car keys and lock your car, even if you're only leaving it for a short time.

Make it as difficult as you can for a thief to either break into your car or steal it.

 Lock any contents, especially valuables, out of sight, or take them with you if you can.

 Don't leave the vehicle registration documents in the car: these documents would make it easy for a thief to sell the vehicle.

 At night, park in a well-lit area.

HC p131 **DES** s20

To make it more difficult for an opportunist thief, you can

- fit an anti-theft alarm or immobiliser
- use a visible security device such as a steering lock or handbrake lock
- have the vehicle registration number etched on the windows: this makes it harder for a thief to sell a vehicle.

Stereos and other forms of in-car entertainment are prime targets for thieves. Install a security-coded stereo to deter thieves, or a removable one so you can lock it away or take it with you.

 Always lock away valuable items, or anything that looks valuable, out of sight or take them with you.

You **MUST NOT** leave your vehicle unattended with the engine running.

HC r123

Always switch off the engine and lock your car before leaving it.

Consider joining a Vehicle Watch scheme if there's one in your area. Contact the crime prevention officer at your local police station to find out more.

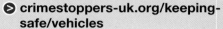

Use this link to find out more about thefts from vehicles.

➲ **crimestoppers-uk.org/keeping-safe/vehicles**

➲ Parking safely

Where you park your car can affect the safety of other road users. Avoid parking where your car would block access or visibility for others, such as

- in front of a property entrance
- at or near a bus stop
- near the brow of a hill where the limited view of the road ahead makes it difficult to see whether it's safe to pass the obstruction
- at a dropped kerb, as this is a place for wheelchair and mobility scooter users to get onto the road or pavement.

HC r243

You **MUST NOT** stop or park on the zigzag lines at a pedestrian crossing. This would block the view of pedestrians and road users, and endanger people trying to use the crossing.

HC r239–250, 291 **DES** s9

❯ Being aware of the environment

Most cars burn petrol or diesel, which are both fossil fuels. Burning these fuels causes air pollution and damages the environment, while using up natural resources that can't be replaced.

You can help the environment by driving in an ecosafe way: you'll help to improve road safety, reduce exhaust emissions and reduce your fuel consumption, which will save you money.

DES s17

Ecosafe driving

Follow these guidelines to make your driving ecosafe.

Reduce your speed. Vehicles travelling at 70 mph (112 km/h) use up to 30% more fuel than those travelling at 50 mph (80 km/h).

Plan well ahead so that you can drive smoothly. Avoiding rapid acceleration and heavy braking can cut your fuel bill by up to 15%.

Use selective gear changing: miss out some gears when you're accelerating. This can help by reducing the amount of time you're accelerating, which is the time when your vehicle uses the most fuel.

Have your vehicle regularly serviced and tuned properly.

Make sure your tyres are correctly inflated.

`DES` `s17`

Avoid

- carrying unnecessary loads or leaving an empty roof rack on your car
- over-revving the engine in lower gears
- leaving the engine running unnecessarily – if your vehicle is stationary and likely to remain so for some time, switch off the engine.

`HC` `r123` `DES` `s17`

Try not to use your car to make a lot of short journeys: consider walking or cycling instead. Using public transport or sharing a car can reduce the volume of traffic and vehicle emissions.

`DES` `s17`

In an automatic car, 'kick-down' is a mechanism that gives quick acceleration when needed; for example, to overtake. Excessive use of this will burn more fuel.

`DES` `s22`

Keeping your car in good condition

Having your car serviced regularly will help you to maintain the fuel economy of your car, and reduce its exhaust emissions. If your vehicle is over three years old (over four years old in Northern Ireland), it will have to pass an emissions test as part of the MOT test.

`DES` `s17`

The amount of road tax you'll need to pay depends on the amount of carbon dioxide emitted by your car. Use this website to calculate vehicle tax rates.

❯ **www.gov.uk**

If you service your own vehicle, dispose of old engine oil and batteries responsibly. Take them to a local authority site or a garage. Don't pour oil down the drain.

Make sure your fuel filler cap is securely fastened. If it's loose, it could spill fuel, which wastes both fuel and money. Spilt diesel fuel makes the road slippery for other road users.

HC p130 **DES** s14

Noise pollution

Don't make excessive noise with your vehicle. In built-up areas, you **MUST NOT** use your car horn between 11.30 pm and 7.00 am unless another vehicle poses a danger.

HC r112 **DES** s3

❯ Avoiding congestion

Sometimes it's impossible to avoid road congestion, but if you can it will make driving less stressful for you.

Always try to

* plan your route before starting out
* avoid driving at times when roads will be busy, if possible
* allow plenty of time for your journey, especially if you have an appointment to keep or a connection to make.

DES s18

Plan your route by

- looking at a map
- using satellite navigation equipment
- checking for roadworks or major events with a motoring organisation
- using a route planner on the internet.

In some towns and cities you may see red lines on the side of the road, which indicate 'Red Routes'. They help the traffic flow by restricting stopping on these routes.
HC p115 **DES** s6

If you're travelling on a new or unfamiliar route, it's a good idea to print out or write down the route, and also to plan an alternative route in case there's a problem with your original route.

If you can avoid travelling at busy times, you'll

- be less likely to be delayed
- help to ease congestion for those who have to travel at these times.

In some areas, you may have to pay a congestion charge to use congested road space. In London, those exempt from paying include

- disabled people who hold a Blue Badge
- riders of two-wheeled vehicles
- people living within the area.

DES s18

Find out more about congestion charging in London using this website.

> **tfl.gov.uk/roadusers/ congestioncharging**

Meeting the standards

You must be able to

check that all lights and reflectors are

- legal
- clean
- in good working order

make sure that all tyres (including any spare)

- are at the right pressure
- have enough tread depth

get to know the vehicle if it's the first time you've driven it

carry out pre-start checks on

- doors
- parking brake
- seat
- steering
- seat belt
- mirrors.

You must know and understand

that these must be kept clean at all times

- lights
- indicators
- reflectors
- number plates

how to check that tyres

- are correctly fitted
- are correctly inflated
- have enough tread depth
- are legal to use

how to check what sort of fuel your vehicle uses.

Notes

You can use this page to make your own notes or diagrams about the key points you need to remember.

Think about

- What maintenance does your car need each week, month and year?
- What should you do if a warning light appears on your dashboard while you're driving?
- Which security features does your car have? How could you improve your car's security?
- Are there more efficient alternative forms of transport available for your journey?
- How can you find out about local traffic congestion? (For example, local radio stations, websites and mobile phone apps.)

Your notes

Things to discuss and practise with your instructor

These are just a few examples of what you could discuss and practise with your instructor. Read more about safety and your vehicle to come up with your own ideas.

Discuss with your instructor

- the importance of the state of your tyres, eg on safety, fuel consumption, vehicle handling, etc
- what the seat belt requirements are for different age groups and who's responsible for them
- how to keep your car and belongings safe while parked.

Practise with your instructor

- driving through built-up areas to get used to different methods of traffic calming
- parking in safe areas, both in daylight and at night
- planning your journey. Do this with your lesson route and see how you can avoid busy times and places. Prepare an alternative route as well.

3.1   Mark two answers   DES s12, 14, HC p129

Which TWO are badly affected if the tyres are under-inflated?

☐ Braking

☐ Steering

☐ Changing gear

☐ Parking

Your tyres are your only contact with the road so it is very important to ensure that they are free from defects, have sufficient tread depth and are correctly inflated. Correct tyre pressures help reduce the risk of skidding and provide a safer and more comfortable drive or ride.

3.2   Mark one answer   DES s3, HC r112

You must NOT sound your horn

☐ between 10 pm and 6 am in a built-up area

☐ at any time in a built-up area

☐ between 11.30 pm and 7 am in a built-up area

☐ between 11.30 pm and 6 am on any road

Vehicles can be noisy. Every effort must be made to prevent excessive noise, especially in built-up areas at night. Don't

• rev the engine

• sound the horn

unnecessarily.

It is illegal to sound your horn in a built-up area between 11.30 pm and 7 am, except when another vehicle poses a danger.

3.3   Mark three answers   DES s17

The pictured vehicle is 'environmentally friendly' because it

Trams are powered by electricity and therefore do not emit exhaust fumes. They are also much quieter than petrol or diesel engined vehicles and can carry a large number of passengers.

☐ reduces noise pollution

☐ uses diesel fuel

☐ uses electricity

☐ uses unleaded fuel

☐ reduces parking spaces

☐ reduces town traffic

3.4

Mark one answer

DES s18, HC p115

'Red routes' in major cities have been introduced to

☐ raise the speed limits

☐ help the traffic flow

☐ provide better parking

☐ allow lorries to load more freely

Traffic jams today are often caused by the volume of traffic. However, inconsiderate parking can lead to the closure of an inside lane or traffic having to wait for oncoming vehicles. Driving slowly in traffic increases fuel consumption and causes a build-up of exhaust fumes.

3.5

Mark one answer

DES s6, HC r153

Road humps, chicanes and narrowings are

☐ always at major road works

☐ used to increase traffic speed

☐ at toll-bridge approaches only

☐ traffic calming measures

Traffic calming measures help keep vehicle speeds low in congested areas where there are pedestrians and children. A pedestrian is much more likely to survive a collision with a vehicle travelling at 20 mph than at 40 mph.

3.6

Mark one answer

DES s17

The purpose of a catalytic converter is to reduce

☐ fuel consumption

☐ the risk of fire

☐ toxic exhaust gases

☐ engine wear

Catalytic converters are designed to reduce a large percentage of toxic emissions. They work more efficiently when the engine has reached its normal working temperature.

3.7

Mark one answer

DES s12, 14, HC p129

It is essential that tyre pressures are checked regularly. When should this be done?

☐ After any lengthy journey

☐ After travelling at high speed

☐ When tyres are hot

☐ When tyres are cold

When you check the tyre pressures do so when the tyres are cold. This will give you a more accurate reading. The heat generated from a long journey will raise the pressure inside the tyre.

Mark one answer

You will use more fuel if your tyres are

☐ under-inflated

☐ of different makes

☐ over-inflated

☐ new and hardly used

Check your tyre pressures frequently – normally once a week. If pressures are lower than those recommended by the manufacturer, there will be more 'rolling resistance'. The engine will have to work harder to overcome this, leading to increased fuel consumption.

Mark two answers

How should you dispose of a used battery?

☐ Take it to a local authority site

☐ Put it in the dustbin

☐ Break it up into pieces

☐ Leave it on waste land

☐ Take it to a garage

☐ Burn it on a fire

Batteries contain acid which is hazardous and must be disposed of safely.

Mark one answer

What is most likely to cause high fuel consumption?

☐ Poor steering control

☐ Accelerating around bends

☐ Staying in high gears

☐ Harsh braking and accelerating

Accelerating and braking gently and smoothly will help to save fuel, reduce wear on your vehicle and is better for the environment.

Mark one answer

The fluid level in your battery is low. What should you top it up with?

☐ Battery acid

☐ Distilled water

☐ Engine oil

☐ Engine coolant

Some modern batteries are maintenance-free. Check your vehicle handbook and, if necessary, make sure that the plates in each battery cell are covered.

3.12 Mark one answer DES s13

You are parked on the road at night. Where must you use parking lights?

☐ Where there are continuous white lines in the middle of the road

☐ Where the speed limit exceeds 30 mph

☐ Where you are facing oncoming traffic

☐ Where you are near a bus stop

When parking at night, park in the direction of the traffic. This will enable other road users to see the reflectors on the rear of your vehicle. Use your parking lights if the speed limit is over 30 mph.

3.13 Mark three answers DES s17

Motor vehicles can harm the environment. This has resulted in

☐ air pollution

☐ damage to buildings

☐ less risk to health

☐ improved public transport

☐ less use of electrical vehicles

☐ using up of natural resources

Exhaust emissions are harmful to health. Together with vibration from heavy traffic this can result in damage to buildings. Most petrol and diesel fuels come from a finite and non-renewable source. Anything you can do to reduce your use of these fuels will help the environment.

3.14 Mark three answers DES s14, HC p129

Excessive or uneven tyre wear can be caused by faults in which THREE of the following?

☐ The gearbox

☐ The braking system

☐ The accelerator

☐ The exhaust system

☐ Wheel alignment

☐ The suspension

Regular servicing will help to detect faults at an early stage and this will avoid the risk of minor faults becoming serious or even dangerous.

3.15 Mark one answer DES s14

You need to top up your battery. What level should you fill to?

☐ The top of the battery

☐ Half-way up the battery

☐ Just below the cell plates

☐ Just above the cell plates

Top up the battery with distilled water and make sure each cell plate is covered.

Before starting a journey it is wise to plan your route. How can you do this?

☐ Look at a map

☐ Contact your local garage

☐ Look in your vehicle handbook

☐ Check your vehicle registration document

Planning your journey before you set out can help to make it much easier, more pleasant and may help to ease traffic congestion. Look at a map to help you to do this. You may need different scale maps depending on where and how far you're going. Printing or writing out the route can also help.

Why is it a good idea to plan your journey to avoid busy times?

☐ You will have an easier journey

☐ You will have a more stressful journey

☐ Your journey time will be longer

☐ It will cause more traffic congestion

No one likes to spend time in traffic queues. Try to avoid busy times related to school or work travel. As well as moving vehicles you should also consider congestion caused by parked cars, buses and coaches around schools.

It is a good idea to plan your journey to avoid busy times. This is because

☐ your vehicle will use more fuel

☐ you will see less road works

☐ it will help to ease congestion

☐ you will travel a much shorter distance

Avoiding busy times means that you are not adding needlessly to traffic congestion. Other advantages are that you will use less fuel and feel less stressed.

It can help to plan your route before starting a journey. Why should you also plan an alternative route?

☐ Your original route may be blocked

☐ Your maps may have different scales

☐ You may find you have to pay a congestion charge

☐ Because you may get held up by a tractor

It can be frustrating and worrying to find your planned route is blocked by roadworks or diversions. If you have planned an alternative you will feel less stressed and more able to concentrate fully on your driving or riding. If your original route is mostly on motorways it's a good idea to plan an alternative using non-motorway roads. Always carry a map with you just in case you need to refer to it.

3.20 — Mark one answer — DES s18

You are making an appointment and will have to travel a long distance. You should

- [ ] allow plenty of time for your journey
- [ ] plan to go at busy times
- [ ] avoid all national speed limit roads
- [ ] prevent other drivers from overtaking

Always allow plenty of time for your journey in case of unforeseen problems. Anything can happen: punctures, breakdowns, road closures, diversions, etc. You will feel less stressed and less inclined to take risks if you are not 'pushed for time'.

3.21 — Mark one answer — DES s17

Rapid acceleration and heavy braking can lead to

- [ ] reduced pollution
- [ ] increased fuel consumption
- [ ] reduced exhaust emissions
- [ ] increased road safety

Using the controls smoothly can reduce fuel consumption by about 15% as well as reducing wear and tear on your vehicle. Plan ahead and anticipate changes of speed well in advance. This will reduce the need to accelerate rapidly or brake sharply.

3.22 — Mark one answer — DES s17

What percentage of all emissions does road transport account for?

- [ ] 10%
- [ ] 20%
- [ ] 30%
- [ ] 40%

Transport is an essential part of modern life but it does have environmental effects. In heavily populated areas traffic is the biggest source of air pollution. Ecosafe driving and riding will reduce emissions and can make a surprising difference to local air quality.

3.23 — Mark one answer — HC p130

Which of these, if allowed to get low, could cause you to crash?

- [ ] Anti-freeze level
- [ ] Brake fluid level
- [ ] Battery water level
- [ ] Radiator coolant level

You should carry out frequent checks on all fluid levels but particularly brake fluid. As the brake pads or shoes wear down the brake fluid level will drop. If it drops below the minimum mark on the fluid reservoir, air could enter the hydraulic system and lead to a loss of braking efficiency or complete brake failure.

3.24   Mark two answers   DES s14, HC p129

Excessive or uneven tyre wear can be caused by faults in the

- ☐ gearbox
- ☐ braking system
- ☐ suspension
- ☐ exhaust system

Uneven wear on your tyres can be caused by the condition of your vehicle. Having it serviced regularly will ensure that the brakes, steering and wheel alignment are maintained in good order.

3.25   Mark one answer   DES s7

The main cause of brake fade is

- ☐ the brakes overheating
- ☐ air in the brake fluid
- ☐ oil on the brakes
- ☐ the brakes out of adjustment

If your vehicle is fitted with drum brakes they can get hot and lose efficiency. This happens when they're used continually, such as on a long, steep, downhill stretch of road. Using a lower gear will assist the braking and help prevent the vehicle gaining momentum.

3.26   Mark one answer   DES s14

Your anti-lock brakes warning light stays on. You should

- ☐ check the brake fluid level
- ☐ check the footbrake free play
- ☐ check that the handbrake is released
- ☐ have the brakes checked immediately

Consult the vehicle handbook or garage before driving the vehicle. Only drive to a garage if it is safe to do so. If you're not sure get expert help.

3.27   Mark one answer   DES s3, HC p128

While driving, this warning light on your dashboard comes on. It means

- ☐ a fault in the braking system
- ☐ the engine oil is low
- ☐ a rear light has failed
- ☐ your seat belt is not fastened

Don't ignore this warning light. A fault in your braking system could have dangerous consequences.

3.28 Mark one answer | DES s1, HC r97

It is important to wear suitable shoes when you are driving. Why is this?

- ☐ To prevent wear on the pedals
- ☐ To maintain control of the pedals
- ☐ To enable you to adjust your seat
- ☐ To enable you to walk for assistance if you break down

When you're going to drive, ensure that you're wearing suitable clothing.

Comfortable shoes will ensure that you have proper control of the foot pedals.

3.29 Mark one answer | DES s3, HC r97

What will reduce the risk of neck injury resulting from a collision?

- ☐ An air-sprung seat
- ☐ Anti-lock brakes
- ☐ A collapsible steering wheel
- ☐ A properly adjusted head restraint

If you're involved in a collision, head restraints will reduce the risk of neck injury. They must be properly adjusted. Make sure they aren't positioned too low, in a crash this could cause damage to the neck.

3.30 Mark one answer | DES s14, HC p130

You are testing your suspension. You notice that your vehicle keeps bouncing when you press down on the front wing. What does this mean?

- ☐ Worn tyres
- ☐ Tyres under-inflated
- ☐ Steering wheel not located centrally
- ☐ Worn shock absorbers

If you find that your vehicle bounces as you drive around a corner or bend in the road, the shock absorbers might be worn. Press down on the front wing and, if the vehicle continues to bounce, take it to be checked by a qualified mechanic.

3.31 Mark one answer | DES s17

A roof rack fitted to your car will

- ☐ reduce fuel consumption
- ☐ improve the road handling
- ☐ make your car go faster
- ☐ increase fuel consumption

If you are carrying anything on a roof rack, make sure that any cover is securely fitted and does not flap about while driving. Aerodynamically designed roof boxes are available which reduce wind resistance and, in turn, fuel consumption.

3.32 — Mark one answer — DES s14, HC p129

It is illegal to drive with tyres that

☐ have been bought second-hand

☐ have a large deep cut in the side wall

☐ are of different makes

☐ are of different tread patterns

When checking your tyres for cuts and bulges in the side walls, don't forget the inner walls (ie those facing each other under the vehicle).

3.33 — Mark one answer — DES s14, HC p129

The legal minimum depth of tread for car tyres over three quarters of the breadth is

☐ 1 mm

☐ 1.6 mm

☐ 2.5 mm

☐ 4 mm

Tyres must have sufficient depth of tread to give them a good grip on the road surface. The legal minimum for cars is 1.6 mm.

This depth should be across the central three quarters of the breadth of the tyre and around the entire circumference.

3.34 — Mark one answer — DES s2, HC r100

You are carrying two 13-year-old children and their parents in your car. Who is responsible for seeing that the children wear seat belts?

☐ The children's parents

☐ You, the driver

☐ The front-seat passenger

☐ The children

Seat belts save lives and reduce the risk of injury. If you are carrying passengers under 14 years of age it's your responsibility as the driver to ensure that their seat belts are fastened or they are seated in an approved child restraint.

3.35 — Mark three answers — DES s17

How can you, as a driver, help the environment?

☐ By reducing your speed

☐ By gentle acceleration

☐ By using leaded fuel

☐ By driving faster

☐ By harsh acceleration

☐ By servicing your vehicle properly

Rapid acceleration and heavy braking lead to greater fuel consumption. They also increase wear and tear on your vehicle.

Having your vehicle regularly serviced means your engine will maintain its efficiency, produce cleaner emissions and lengthen its life.

3.36 — Mark three answers — DES s17

To help the environment, you can avoid wasting fuel by

☐ having your vehicle properly serviced

☐ making sure your tyres are correctly inflated

☐ not over-revving in the lower gears

☐ driving at higher speeds where possible

☐ keeping an empty roof rack properly fitted

☐ servicing your vehicle less regularly

If you don't have your vehicle serviced regularly, the engine will not burn all the fuel efficiently. This will cause excess gases to be discharged into the atmosphere.

3.37 — Mark three answers — DES s17

To reduce the volume of traffic on the roads you could

☐ use public transport more often

☐ share a car when possible

☐ walk or cycle on short journeys

☐ travel by car at all times

☐ use a car with a smaller engine

☐ drive in a bus lane

Walking or cycling are good ways to get exercise. Using public transport also gives the opportunity for exercise if you walk to the railway station or bus stop. Leave the car at home whenever you can.

3.38 — Mark three answers — DES s17

Which THREE of the following are most likely to waste fuel?

☐ Reducing your speed

☐ Carrying unnecessary weight

☐ Using the wrong grade of fuel

☐ Under-inflated tyres

☐ Using different brands of fuel

☐ A fitted, empty roof rack

Wasting fuel costs you money and also causes unnecessary pollution. Ensuring your tyres are correctly inflated, avoiding carrying unnecessary weight, and removing a roof rack that is not in use will all help to reduce your fuel consumption.

3.39 Mark three answers DES s2, 14, HC p128

Which THREE does the law require you to keep in good condition?

☐ Gears

☐ Transmission

☐ Headlights

☐ Windscreen

☐ Seat belts

Other things to check include lights, get someone to help you check the brake lights and indicators. Battery, a lot of these are now maintenance-free. Steering, check for play in the steering. Oil, water and suspension also need checking. Always check that the speedometer is working once you've moved off.

3.40 Mark one answer DES s17

Driving at 70 mph uses more fuel than driving at 50 mph by up to

☐ 10%

☐ 30%

☐ 75%

☐ 100%

Your vehicle will use less fuel if you avoid heavy acceleration. The higher the engine revs, the more fuel you will use. Using the same gear, a vehicle travelling at 70 mph will use up to 30% more fuel to cover the same distance than a vehicle travelling at 50 mph. However, don't travel so slowly that you inconvenience or endanger other road users.

3.41 Mark one answer DES s14

Your vehicle pulls to one side when braking. You should

☐ change the tyres around

☐ consult your garage as soon as possible

☐ pump the pedal when braking

☐ use your handbrake at the same time

The brakes on your vehicle must be effective and properly adjusted. If your vehicle pulls to one side when braking, take it to be checked by a qualified mechanic. Don't take risks.

3.42 Mark one answer DES s14

Unbalanced wheels on a car may cause

☐ the steering to pull to one side

☐ the steering to vibrate

☐ the brakes to fail

☐ the tyres to deflate

If your wheels are out of balance it will cause the steering to vibrate at certain speeds. It is not a fault that will rectify itself. You will have to take your vehicle to a garage or tyre fitting firm as this is specialist work.

3.43   **Mark two answers**   **DES s3**

Turning the steering wheel while your car is stationary can cause damage to the

- ☐ gearbox
- ☐ engine
- ☐ brakes
- ☐ steering
- ☐ tyres

Turning the steering wheel when the car is not moving can cause unnecessary wear to the tyres and steering mechanism. This is known as 'dry' steering.

3.44   **Mark one answer**   **DES s20, HC p131**

You have to leave valuables in your car. It would be safer to

- ☐ put them in a carrier bag
- ☐ park near a school entrance
- ☐ lock them out of sight
- ☐ park near a bus stop

If you have to leave valuables in your car, always lock them out of sight. If you can see them, so can a thief.

3.45   **Mark one answer**   **DES s20, HC p131**

Which of the following may help to deter a thief from stealing your car?

- ☐ Always keeping the headlights on
- ☐ Fitting reflective glass windows
- ☐ Always keeping the interior light on
- ☐ Etching the car number on the windows

Having your car registration number etched on all your windows is a cheap and effective way to deter professional car thieves.

3.46   **Mark one answer**   **DES s20, HC p131**

Which of the following should not be kept in your vehicle?

- ☐ A first aid kit
- ☐ A road atlas
- ☐ The tax disc
- ☐ The vehicle documents

Never leave the vehicle's documents inside it. They would help a thief dispose of the vehicle more easily.

When leaving your vehicle parked and unattended you should

☐ park near a busy junction

☐ park in a housing estate

☐ remove the key and lock it

☐ leave the left indicator on

An unlocked car is an open invitation to thieves. Leaving the keys in the ignition not only makes your car easy to steal, it could also invalidate your insurance.

Which TWO of the following will improve fuel consumption?

☐ Reducing your road speed

☐ Planning well ahead

☐ Late and harsh braking

☐ Driving in lower gears

☐ Short journeys with a cold engine

☐ Rapid acceleration

Harsh braking, constant gear changes and harsh acceleration increase fuel consumption. An engine uses less fuel when travelling at a constant low speed.

You need to look well ahead so you are able to anticipate hazards early. Easing off the accelerator and timing your approach, at junctions, for example, could actually improve the fuel consumption of your vehicle.

You service your own vehicle. How should you get rid of the old engine oil?

☐ Take it to a local authority site

☐ Pour it down a drain

☐ Tip it into a hole in the ground

☐ Put it into your dustbin

It is illegal to pour engine oil down any drain. Oil is a pollutant and harmful to wildlife. Dispose of it safely at an authorised site.

3.50 · Mark one answer · DES s17

Why do MOT tests include a strict exhaust emission test?

- ☐ To recover the cost of expensive garage equipment
- ☐ To help protect the environment against pollution
- ☐ To discover which fuel supplier is used the most
- ☐ To make sure diesel and petrol engines emit the same fumes

Emission tests are carried out to ensure your vehicle engine is operating efficiently. This ensures the pollution produced by the engine is kept to a minimum. If your vehicle is not serviced regularly, it may fail the annual MOT test.

3.51 · Mark three answers · DES s17

To reduce the damage your vehicle causes to the environment you should

- ☐ use narrow side streets
- ☐ avoid harsh acceleration
- ☐ brake in good time
- ☐ anticipate well ahead
- ☐ use busy routes

By looking well ahead and recognising hazards early you can avoid last-minute harsh braking. Watch the traffic flow and look well ahead for potential hazards so you can control your speed accordingly. Avoid over-revving the engine and accelerating harshly as this increases wear to the engine and uses more fuel.

3.52 · Mark two answers · DES s5

A properly serviced vehicle will give

- ☐ lower insurance premiums
- ☐ you a refund on your road tax
- ☐ better fuel economy
- ☐ cleaner exhaust emissions

When you purchase your vehicle, check at what intervals you should have it serviced. This can vary depending on model and manufacturer. Use the service manual and keep it up to date. The cost of a service may well be less than the cost of running a poorly maintained vehicle.

You enter a road where there are road humps. What should you do?

The humps are there for a reason – to reduce the speed of the traffic. Don't accelerate harshly between them as this means you will only have to brake harshly to negotiate the next hump. Harsh braking and accelerating uses more fuel.

☐ Maintain a reduced speed throughout

☐ Accelerate quickly between each one

☐ Always keep to the maximum legal speed

☐ Drive slowly at school times only

When should you especially check the engine oil level?

☐ Before a long journey

☐ When the engine is hot

☐ Early in the morning

☐ Every 6000 miles

During long journeys an engine can use more oil than on shorter trips. Insufficient oil is potentially dangerous: it can lead to excessive wear and expensive repairs.

Most cars have a dipstick to allow the oil level to be checked. If not, you should refer to the vehicle handbook. Also make checks on

• fuel

• water

• tyres.

You are having difficulty finding a parking space in a busy town. You can see there is space on the zigzag lines of a zebra crossing. Can you park there?

It's an offence to park there. You will be causing an obstruction by obscuring the view of both pedestrians and drivers.

☐ No, unless you stay with your car

☐ Yes, in order to drop off a passenger

☐ Yes, if you do not block people from crossing

☐ No, not in any circumstances

3.56

Mark one answer

DES s20, HC p131

When leaving your car unattended for a few minutes you should

☐ leave the engine running

☐ switch the engine off but leave the key in

☐ lock it and remove the key

☐ park near a traffic warden

Always switch off the engine, remove the key and lock your car, even if you are only leaving it for a few minutes.

3.57

Mark one answer

DES s20, HC p131

When leaving your vehicle where should you park if possible?

☐ Opposite a traffic island

☐ In a secure car park

☐ On a bend

☐ At or near a taxi rank

Whenever possible leave your car in a secure car park. This will help stop thieves.

3.58

Mark three answers

HC r243

In which THREE places would parking your vehicle cause danger or obstruction to other road users?

☐ In front of a property entrance

☐ At or near a bus stop

☐ On your driveway

☐ In a marked parking space

☐ On the approach to a level crossing

Don't park your vehicle where parking restrictions apply. Think carefully before you slow down and stop. Look at road markings and signs to ensure that you aren't parking illegally.

3.59

Mark one answer

DES s3, HC r97

The most important reason for having a properly adjusted head restraint is to

☐ make you more comfortable

☐ help you to avoid neck injury

☐ help you to relax

☐ help you to maintain your driving position

The restraint should be adjusted so that it gives maximum protection to the head and neck. This will help in the event of a rear-end collision.

3.60 — Mark two answers — DES s17

As a driver you can cause more damage to the environment by

☐ choosing a fuel-efficient vehicle

☐ making a lot of short journeys

☐ driving in as high a gear as possible

☐ accelerating as quickly as possible

☐ having your vehicle regularly serviced

For short journeys it may be quicker to walk, or cycle, which is far better for your health. Time spent stationary in traffic with the engine running is damaging to health, the environment and expensive in fuel costs.

3.61 — Mark one answer — DES s17

As a driver, you can help reduce pollution levels in town centres by

☐ driving more quickly

☐ over-revving in a low gear

☐ walking or cycling

☐ driving short journeys

Using a vehicle for short journeys means the engine does not have time to reach its normal running temperature. When an engine is running below its normal running temperature it produces increased amounts of pollution. Walking and cycling do not create pollution and have health benefits as well.

3.62 — Mark one answer — DES s20, HC p131

How can you reduce the chances of your car being broken into when leaving it unattended?

☐ Take all valuables with you

☐ Park near a taxi rank

☐ Place any valuables on the floor

☐ Park near a fire station

When leaving your car take all valuables with you if you can, otherwise lock them out of sight.

3.63 — Mark one answer — DES s20

How can you help to prevent your car radio being stolen?

☐ Park in an unlit area

☐ Hide the radio with a blanket

☐ Park near a busy junction

☐ Install a security-coded radio

A security-coded radio can deter thieves as it is likely to be of little use when removed from the vehicle.

3.64 — Mark one answer — DES s20

How can you lessen the risk of your vehicle being broken into at night?

☐ Leave it in a well-lit area

☐ Park in a quiet side road

☐ Don't engage the steering lock

☐ Park in a poorly lit area

Having your vehicle broken into or stolen can be very distressing and inconvenient. Avoid leaving your vehicle unattended in poorly lit areas.

3.65 — Mark one answer — DES s20

To help keep your car secure you could join a

☐ vehicle breakdown organisation

☐ vehicle watch scheme

☐ advanced driver's scheme

☐ car maintenance class

The vehicle watch scheme helps reduce the risk of having your car stolen. By displaying high visibility vehicle watch stickers in your car you are inviting the police to stop your vehicle if seen in use between midnight and 5 am.

3.66 — Mark one answer — DES s17

On a vehicle, where would you find a catalytic converter?

☐ In the fuel tank

☐ In the air filter

☐ On the cooling system

☐ On the exhaust system

Although carbon dioxide is still produced, a catalytic converter reduces the toxic and polluting gases by up to 90%. Unleaded fuel must be used in vehicles fitted with a catalytic converter.

3.67 — Mark one answer — DES s17

You will find that driving smoothly can

☐ reduce journey times by about 15%

☐ increase fuel consumption by about 15%

☐ reduce fuel consumption by about 15%

☐ increase journey times by about 15%

Not only will you save about 15% of your fuel by driving smoothly, but you will also reduce the amount of wear and tear on your vehicle as well as reducing pollution. You will also feel more relaxed and have a more pleasant journey.

3.68 **Mark one answer** DES s17

You can save fuel when conditions allow by

☐ using lower gears as often as possible

☐ accelerating sharply in each gear

☐ using each gear in turn

☐ missing out some gears

Missing out intermediate gears when appropriate, helps to reduce the amount of time spent accelerating and decelerating – the time when your vehicle uses most fuel.

3.69 **Mark one answer** DES s17, HC r123

How can driving in an ecosafe manner help protect the environment?

☐ Through the legal enforcement of speed regulations

☐ By increasing the number of cars on the road

☐ Through increased fuel bills

☐ By reducing exhaust emissions

Ecosafe driving is all about becoming a more environmentally friendly driver. This will make your journeys more comfortable as well as considerably reducing your fuel bills and reducing emissions that can damage the environment.

3.70 **Mark one answer** DES s17

What does ecosafe driving achieve?

☐ Increased fuel consumption

☐ Improved road safety

☐ Damage to the environment

☐ Increased exhaust emissions

The emphasis is on hazard awareness and planning ahead. By looking well ahead you will have plenty of time to deal with hazards safely and won't need to brake sharply. This will also reduce damage to the environment.

3.71 **Mark one answer** DES s14, HC p129

You are checking your trailer tyres. What is the legal minimum tread depth over the central three quarters of its breadth?

☐ 1 mm

☐ 1.6 mm

☐ 2 mm

☐ 2.6 mm

Trailers and caravans may be left in storage over the winter months and tyres can deteriorate. It's important to check their tread depth and also the pressures and general condition. The legal tread depth applies to the central three quarters of its breadth over its entire circumference.

3.72 — Mark one answer — DES s17

Fuel consumption is at its highest when you are

☐ braking

☐ coasting

☐ accelerating

☐ steering

Always try to use the accelerator smoothly. Taking your foot off the accelerator allows the momentum of the car to take you forward, especially when going downhill. This can save a considerable amount of fuel without any loss of control over the vehicle.

3.73 — Mark one answer — DES s2, HC r99

Car passengers MUST wear a seat belt/ restraint if one is available, unless they are

☐ under 14 years old

☐ under 1.5 metres (5 feet) in height

☐ sitting in the rear seat

☐ exempt for medical reasons

If you have adult passengers it is their responsibility to wear a seat belt, but you should still remind them to use them as they get in the car. It is your responsibility to ensure that all children in your car are secured with an appropriate restraint.

3.74 — Mark one answer — DES s2, HC r100

You are driving the children of a friend home from school. They are both under 14 years old. Who is responsible for making sure they wear a seat belt or approved child restraint where required?

☐ An adult passenger

☐ The children

☐ You, the driver

☐ Your friend

Passengers should always be secured and safe. Children should be encouraged to fasten their seat belts or approved restraints themselves from an early age so that it becomes a matter of routine. As the driver you must check that they are fastened securely. It's your responsibility.

3.75 — Mark one answer — DES s14

You have too much oil in your engine. What could this cause?

☐ Low oil pressure

☐ Engine overheating

☐ Chain wear

☐ Oil leaks

Too much oil in the engine will create excess pressure and could damage engine seals and cause oil leaks. Any excess oil should be drained off.

You are carrying a five-year-old child in the back seat of your car. They are under 1.35 metres (4 feet 5 inches). A correct child restraint is NOT available. They MUST

☐ sit behind the passenger seat

☐ use an adult seat belt

☐ share a belt with an adult

☐ sit between two other children

Usually a correct child restraint MUST be used. In a few exceptional cases if one is not available an adult seat belt MUST be used. In a collision unrestrained objects and people can cause serious injury or even death.

You are carrying an 11-year-old child in the back seat of your car. They are under 1.35 metres (4 feet 5 inches) in height. You MUST make sure that

☐ they sit between two belted people

☐ they can fasten their own seat belt

☐ a suitable child restraint is available

☐ they can see clearly out of the front window

It is your responsibility as a driver to ensure that children are secure and safe in your vehicle. Make sure you are familiar with the rules. In a few very exceptional cases when a child restraint is not available, an adult seat belt MUST be used. Child restraints and seat belts save lives!

You are parked at the side of the road. You will be waiting for some time for a passenger. What should you do?

☐ Switch off the engine

☐ Apply the steering lock

☐ Switch off the radio

☐ Use your headlights

If your vehicle is stationary and is likely to remain so for some time, switch off the engine. We should all try to reduce global warming and pollution.

3.79 | Mark one answer | DES s2, HC r101

You are using a rear-facing baby seat. You want to put it on the front passenger seat which is protected by a frontal airbag. What MUST you do before setting off?

☐ Deactivate the airbag

☐ Turn the seat to face sideways

☐ Ask a passenger to hold the baby

☐ Put the child in an adult seat belt

If the airbag activates near a baby seat, it could cause serious injury or even death to the child. It is illegal to fit a rear-facing baby seat into a passenger seat protected by an active frontal airbag. You MUST secure it in a different seat or deactivate the relevant airbag. Follow the manufacturer's advice when fitting a baby seat.

3.80 | Mark one answer | DES s17, HC r123

You are leaving your vehicle parked on a road unattended. When may you leave the engine running?

☐ If you will be parking for less than five minutes

☐ If the battery keeps going flat

☐ When parked in a 20 mph zone

☐ Never if you are away from the vehicle

When you leave your vehicle parked on a road, switch off the engine and secure the vehicle. Make sure there aren't any valuables visible, shut all the windows, lock the vehicle, set the alarm if it has one and use an anti-theft device such as a steering wheel lock.

Case study practice – 3
Safety and your vehicle

Jeff drives through the city centre, choosing to travel outside the rush hour.

In the city, there are double red lines along the roadside.

Later, Jeff reaches a major junction. The traffic lights aren't working but there are very few vehicles on the road.

At work, Jeff has to park on the roadside. When parking, his steering feels a little heavy.

He picks up his laptop to take to work and locks the car. He leaves his camera on the back seat.

3.1 What effect could Jeff's choice of travel time have on his journey?

Mark **one** answer

- ☐ Increased delays
- ☐ Decreased mileage
- ☐ Higher traffic volume
- ☐ Shorter travel time

DES s1, 18

3.2 What do these red lines mean?

Mark **one** answer

- ☐ No stopping at peak time
- ☐ No stopping at lunch time
- ☐ No stopping at any time
- ☐ No stopping at night time

HC r240, 247, p115 **DES** s18

3.3 What should Jeff do at these traffic lights?

Mark one answer

- ☐ Stop and wait for the signals to start working again
- ☐ Proceed with care as with an unmarked junction
- ☐ Continue on and assume he has right of way
- ☐ Drive as quickly as possible over the junction

HC r176

3.4 What could be affecting Jeff's steering?

Mark one answer

- ☐ Tyres that are over-inflated
- ☐ Tyres that are low on tread
- ☐ Tyres that are under-inflated
- ☐ Tyres that are non-matching

HC p129 **DES** s7

3.5 What should Jeff do with his camera?

Mark one answer

- ☐ Leave it lying on the back seat
- ☐ Put it in a bag on the front seat
- ☐ Lock it away securely out of sight
- ☐ Cover it up with a thick blanket

HC p131 **DES** s20

Section four
Safety margins

In this section, you'll learn about

- keeping yourself and others safe by staying within safety margins
- stopping, thinking and braking distances
- risks caused by different weather conditions and road surfaces
- the risk of skidding
- contraflow systems.

Safety margins

It's essential that you always keep your safety, and that of your passengers and other road users, in mind as you're driving.

You can reduce your chances of being involved in an incident on the road by knowing the safety margins and what can happen if you don't drive within them. Never take risks.

Keep control of your car by using the correct procedures. For instance, when you're travelling on a long downhill stretch of road, control your speed by selecting a lower gear and using your brakes carefully. Excessive braking on hills can cause your brakes to overheat and become less effective.

HC r160 **DES** s5, 7

Don't 'coast' – this means travelling in neutral or with the clutch disengaged (pressed down) – as this can reduce your control over the car.

HC r122

> Stopping distance

Leave enough room between your vehicle and the one in front so that you can pull up safely if it slows down or stops suddenly.

Your overall stopping distance is the distance your car travels from the moment that you realise you must brake to the moment your car stops.

HC r126 **DES** s7

Thinking distance		**Braking distance**		**Stopping distance**
(distance travelled in the time it takes to react to a situation)	**+**	(distance travelled from when you start to use the brakes to when your car completely stops)	**=**	

> Typical stopping distances

Look at the typical stopping, thinking and braking distances given in *The Official Highway Code*. Remember that these are based on vehicles travelling

- with good tyres and brakes
- on a dry road
- in good conditions.

HC r126 **DES** s7

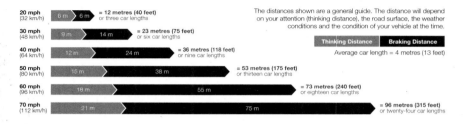

20 mph (32 km/h)	6 m	6 m	= 12 metres (40 feet) or three car lengths
30 mph (48 km/h)	9 m	14 m	= 23 metres (75 feet) or six car lengths
40 mph (64 km/h)	12 m	24 m	= 36 metres (118 feet) or nine car lengths
50 mph (80 km/h)	15 m	38 m	= 53 metres (175 feet) or thirteen car lengths
60 mph (96 km/h)	18 m	55 m	= 73 metres (240 feet) or eighteen car lengths
70 mph (112 km/h)	21 m	75 m	= 96 metres (315 feet) or twenty-four car lengths

The distances shown are a general guide. The distance will depend on your attention (thinking distance), the road surface, the weather conditions and the condition of your vehicle at the time.

| Thinking Distance | Braking Distance |

Average car length = 4 metres (13 feet)

To help you learn and understand more about stopping distances, try the interactive exercise at this link.

> **safedrivingforlife.info/stoppingdistances**

Watch the 'How fast can you stop?' video at this link.

> **youtu.be/JUd1vBee9SY**

Don't just learn the stopping distance figures: you need to be able to judge the distance when you're driving.

HC r126 **DES** s12

In good conditions, leave a two-second gap between your car and the vehicle in front. Use a fixed point, like a road sign, to measure the time gap between your vehicle and the one in front. You can measure two seconds by saying the sentence 'Only a fool breaks the two-second rule.'

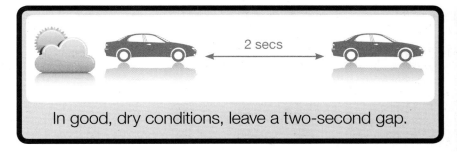

In good, dry conditions, leave a two-second gap.

In other conditions, you need to increase this distance.

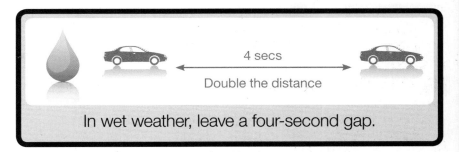

In wet weather, leave a four-second gap.

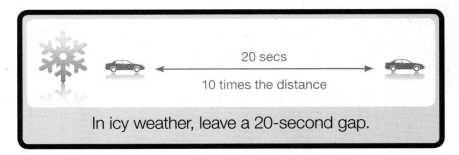

In icy weather, leave a 20-second gap.

Keeping a safe distance from the vehicle in front will help to lower your risk of having a collision. If someone overtakes you and pulls into the gap in front, drop back to keep a safe distance from them.

HC r126 DES s12

❯ Weather conditions

Weather conditions have a major effect on your safety margins. If there's bad weather, such as snow, ice or thick fog, think about whether you really need to make your journey. Never underestimate the dangers.

`HC r228–231`

Find more information about winter driving at this website.

❯ **highways.gov.uk/traffic-information/seasonal-advice**

Weather	Actions to take

Heavy rain 	When there's heavy rainfall, water can collect on the road surface and may cause aquaplaning. This is where the tyres lift off the road surface and skate on a film of water. The steering becomes light.
	
	If this happens,
	• ease off the accelerator
	• don't brake until your steering feels normal again.
	`HC r131, 227` `DES s5, 7`
	
	If you've driven through deep water, such as a ford or a flood, test your brakes. You may need to dry them out by pressing lightly on the brake pedal as you drive.
	`HC r121` `DES s5, 7`

Hot and/or bright 	Hot weather can also be dangerous. The road surface can become soft and may begin to melt. This could affect your braking and steering. Bright sunlight can dazzle. Other drivers might not be able to see your indicators flashing. Give an arm signal if you think it will be helpful. `HC r237` `DES s12`

Weather	Actions to take
Freezing 	Freezing conditions can make roads very slippery, which will make your car harder to control. Before starting a journey, clear ice and snow from your windows, lights, mirrors and number plates. **DES** 7 When driving, • keep your speed down • brake gently and in plenty of time • be prepared to stop and clean your windscreen by hand if the wipers can't keep the windscreen clear. **HC** r228–231
Foggy 	Fog reduces your visibility. Remember to • allow more time for your journey • slow down, because you can't see as far ahead as usual • increase the gap between your vehicle and the one in front of you • use dipped headlights, even in daylight. If visibility falls below 100 metres (328 feet), use fog lights if you've got them. You **MUST** switch them off when the fog lifts. **HC** r234–236 **DES** 12
Windy 	High winds can blow you off course, especially on an open stretch of road. They have an even greater effect on • high-sided vehicles • vehicles towing trailers or caravans • motorcyclists • cyclists. Take care and allow extra room if you pass these road users, as they may be blown off course by a sudden gust of wind. Check your left side as you pass them. **HC** r232–233 **DES** s12

❯ Skidding

Skidding is when the tyres lose grip on the road, and it's caused by the driver. Road surface and tyre conditions can increase the risk of skidding, but skids are the result of how the driver controls acceleration, braking, speed and steering.

There's a greater risk of skidding in wet or icy conditions. Black ice can be a hazard in very cold weather and it isn't obvious until you feel the steering becoming light.

HC r119, 231 **DES** s5, 12

To reduce the risk of skidding in slippery conditions, drive

- at a low speed
- in the highest gear you can use effectively.

If you brake too hard and start to skid,

- take your foot off the brake, then press it again gently
- steer in the direction of the skid; for example, if the back of the car skids to the right, steer to the right.

DES s5

To reduce the risk of skidding, scan the road ahead for clues such as road signs and markings. You can then plan your driving so that you can

- slow down gradually before you reach a hazard, such as a bend
- avoid sudden steering movements.

HC r119, 231 **DES** s5

Anti-lock braking systems

An anti-lock braking system (ABS) is designed to prevent skidding caused by excessive braking. Wheel speed sensors anticipate when a wheel is about to lock, which could lead to skidding.

If you have to brake suddenly when you're driving a vehicle with ABS,

- press the footbrake quickly and firmly
- don't release the brake pedal until your vehicle has stopped.

HC r120 **DES** s5, 12

ABS doesn't necessarily reduce your stopping distance, but you can keep steering while braking because the wheels are prevented from locking. It may not work as well if there's

- surface water, such as when there's been heavy rainfall
- a loose road surface, such as gravel.

ABS will help prevent skidding caused by braking too hard for the conditions; it won't reduce your car's stopping distance.

> Contraflow systems

contraflow system

where one or more lanes have a direction of traffic against that of the rest of the carriageway

When you enter a **contraflow system**, you should

- reduce your speed in good time
- choose a suitable lane in good time: look for signs advising you to use a particular lane if you want to take an exit that will be coming up soon, or if you have a wide vehicle
- keep a safe distance behind the vehicle in front.

HC r290 DES s11

Meeting the standards

You must be able to

keep a safe distance from the vehicle in front

use the accelerator and brakes correctly to

- regulate your speed
- bring the vehicle to a stop safely

always use a safe, systematic approach to keep you and other road users safe.
For example, **mirrors, signal, manoeuvre, position, speed, look.**

You must know and understand

the importance of keeping a safe separation distance in all weather and traffic conditions

about skidding

- why a skid may occur
- how to avoid skids
- how to correct them if they do occur

the distance that a vehicle needs to stop

- from different speeds
- in different road conditions
- in different weather conditions

how traffic and weather conditions may affect other road users and what to do.
For example, their visibility may be reduced.

Notes

You can use this page to make your own notes or diagrams about the key points you need to remember.

Think about

- What are typical stopping distances and how do wet or icy roads affect them?
- What extra considerations or precautions might you need to take if the weather is
  - snowy or icy
  - wet
  - foggy
  - hot
  - bright and dazzling
  - windy?
- Does the car you're driving have ABS? How can you reduce the risk of skidding and what should you do if you start to skid?
- Picture yourself entering a contraflow system. What actions can you take to reduce risk?

Your notes

Things to discuss and practise with your instructor

These are just a few examples of what you could discuss and practise with your instructor. Read more about safety margins to come up with your own ideas.

Discuss with your instructor

- the causes of skidding and how to avoid it
- how to use your brakes and gears in snowy and icy weather
- stopping distances on dry, wet and icy roads.

Practise with your instructor

- driving in different weather conditions to practise vehicle handling
- driving up and down steep hills to practise your gear selection and control of the brakes
- driving through a ford to see how it will affect your brakes.

Braking distances on ice can be

☐ twice the normal distance

☐ five times the normal distance

☐ seven times the normal distance

☐ ten times the normal distance

In icy and snowy weather, your stopping distance will increase by up to ten times compared to good, dry conditions.

Take extra care when braking, accelerating and steering, to cut down the risk of skidding.

Freezing conditions will affect the distance it takes you to come to a stop. You should expect stopping distances to increase by up to

☐ two times

☐ three times

☐ five times

☐ ten times

Your tyre grip is greatly reduced on icy roads and you need to allow up to ten times the normal stopping distance.

In windy conditions you need to take extra care when

☐ using the brakes

☐ making a hill start

☐ turning into a narrow road

☐ passing pedal cyclists

You should always give cyclists plenty of room when overtaking. When it's windy, a sudden gust could blow them off course.

When approaching a right-hand bend you should keep well to the left. Why is this?

Doing this will give you an earlier view around the bend and enable you to see any hazards sooner.

It also reduces the risk of collision with an oncoming vehicle that may have drifted over the centre line while taking the bend.

☐ To improve your view of the road

☐ To overcome the effect of the road's slope

☐ To let faster traffic from behind overtake

☐ To be positioned safely if you skid

4.5   Mark two answers   DES s12, HC r237

In very hot weather the road surface can become soft. Which TWO of the following will be most affected?

☐ The suspension

☐ The grip of the tyres

☐ The braking

☐ The exhaust

Only a small part of your tyres is in contact with the road. This is why you must consider the surface on which you're travelling, and alter your speed to suit the road conditions.

4.6   Mark one answer   DES s12, HC r232

Where are you most likely to be affected by a side wind?

☐ On a narrow country lane

☐ On an open stretch of road

☐ On a busy stretch of road

☐ On a long, straight road

In windy conditions, care must be taken on exposed roads. A strong gust of wind can blow you off course. Watch out for other road users who are particularly likely to be affected, such as cyclists, motorcyclists, high-sided lorries and vehicles towing trailers.

4.7   Mark one answer   HC r126

In good conditions, what is the typical stopping distance at 70 mph?

☐ 53 metres (175 feet)

☐ 60 metres (197 feet)

☐ 73 metres (240 feet)

☐ 96 metres (315 feet)

Note that this is the typical stopping distance. It will take at least this distance to think, brake and stop in good conditions. In poor conditions it will take much longer.

4.8   Mark one answer   HC r126

What is the shortest overall stopping distance on a dry road at 60 mph?

☐ 53 metres (175 feet)

☐ 58 metres (190 feet)

☐ 73 metres (240 feet)

☐ 96 metres (315 feet)

This distance is the equivalent of 18 car lengths. Try pacing out 73 metres and then look back. It's probably further than you think.

You are following a vehicle at a safe distance on a wet road. Another driver overtakes you and pulls into the gap you have left. What should you do?

☐ Flash your headlights as a warning

☐ Try to overtake safely as soon as you can

☐ Drop back to regain a safe distance

☐ Stay close to the other vehicle until it moves on

Wet weather will affect the time it takes for you to stop and can affect your control. Your speed should allow you to stop safely and in good time. If another vehicle pulls into the gap you've left, ease back until you've regained your stopping distance.

You are travelling at 50 mph on a good, dry road. What is your typical overall stopping distance?

☐ 36 metres (118 feet)

☐ 53 metres (175 feet)

☐ 75 metres (245 feet)

☐ 96 metres (315 feet)

Even in good conditions it will usually take you further than you think to stop. Don't just learn the figures, make sure you understand how far the distance is.

You are on a good, dry, road surface. Your brakes and tyres are good. What is the typical overall stopping distance at 40 mph?

☐ 23 metres (75 feet)

☐ 36 metres (118 feet)

☐ 53 metres (175 feet)

☐ 96 metres (315 feet)

Stopping distances are affected by a number of variable factors. These include the type, model and condition of your vehicle, road and weather conditions, and your reaction time. Look well ahead for hazards and leave enough space between you and the vehicle in front. This should allow you to pull up safely if you have to, without braking sharply.

What should you do when overtaking a motorcyclist in strong winds?

☐ Pass close

☐ Pass quickly

☐ Pass wide

☐ Pass immediately

In strong winds riders of two-wheeled vehicles are particularly vulnerable. When you overtake them allow plenty of room. Always check to the left as you pass.

4.13 Mark one answer HC r126

Overall stopping distance is made up of thinking and braking distance. You are on a good, dry road surface with good brakes and tyres. What is the typical BRAKING distance from 50 mph?

☐ 14 metres (46 feet)

☐ 24 metres (80 feet)

☐ 38 metres (125 feet)

☐ 55 metres (180 feet)

Be aware this is just the braking distance. You need to add the thinking distance to this to give the OVERALL STOPPING DISTANCE. At 50 mph the typical thinking distance will be 15 metres (50 feet), plus a braking distance of 38 metres (125 feet), giving an overall stopping distance of 53 metres (175 feet). The distance could be greater than this depending on your attention and response to any hazards. These figures are a general guide.

4.14 Mark one answer DES s11, HC r126

In heavy motorway traffic the vehicle behind you is following too closely. How can you lower the risk of a collision?

☐ Increase your distance from the vehicle in front

☐ Operate the brakes sharply

☐ Switch on your hazard lights

☐ Move onto the hard shoulder and stop

On busy roads traffic may still travel at high speeds despite being close together. Don't follow too closely to the vehicle in front. If a driver behind seems to be 'pushing' you, gradually increase your distance from the vehicle in front by slowing down gently. This will give you more space in front if you have to brake, and lessen the risk of a collision involving several vehicles.

4.15 Mark one answer DES s12, HC r235

You are following other vehicles in fog. You have your lights on. What else can you do to reduce the chances of being in a collision?

☐ Keep close to the vehicle in front

☐ Use your main beam instead of dipped headlights

☐ Keep up with the faster vehicles

☐ Reduce your speed and increase the gap in front

When it's foggy use dipped headlights. This will help you see and be seen by other road users. If visibility is seriously reduced consider using front and rear fog lights. Keep a sensible speed and don't follow the vehicle in front too closely. If the road is wet and slippery you'll need to allow twice the normal stopping distance.

4.16

Mark three answers

DES s11, HC r290

To avoid a collision when entering a contraflow system, you should

☐ reduce speed in good time

☐ switch lanes at any time to make progress

☐ choose an appropriate lane in good time

☐ keep the correct separation distance

☐ increase speed to pass through quickly

☐ follow other motorists closely to avoid long queues

In a contraflow system you will be travelling close to oncoming traffic and sometimes in narrow lanes. You should obey the temporary speed limit signs, get into the correct lane at the proper time and keep a safe separation distance from the vehicle ahead. When traffic is at a very low speed, merging in turn is recommended if it's safe and appropriate.

4.17

Mark one answer

DES s5, 12, HC r231

You are driving on an icy road. How can you avoid wheelspin?

☐ Drive at a slow speed in as high a gear as possible

☐ Use the handbrake if the wheels start to slip

☐ Brake gently and repeatedly

☐ Drive in a low gear at all times

If you're travelling on an icy road extra caution will be required to avoid loss of control. Keeping your speed down and using the highest gear possible will reduce the risk of the tyres losing their grip on this slippery surface.

4.18

Mark one answer

DES s5, HC r119

Skidding is mainly caused by

☐ the weather

☐ the driver

☐ the vehicle

☐ the road

You should always consider the conditions and drive accordingly.

4.19

Mark two answers

DES s12, HC r231

You are driving in freezing conditions. What should you do when approaching a sharp bend?

☐ Slow down before you reach the bend

☐ Gently apply your handbrake

☐ Firmly use your footbrake

☐ Coast into the bend

☐ Avoid sudden steering movements

Harsh use of the accelerator, brakes or steering are likely to lead to skidding, especially on slippery surfaces. Avoid steering and braking at the same time.

In icy conditions it's very important that you constantly assess what's ahead, so that you can take appropriate action in plenty of time.

4.20 — Mark one answer — DES s12, HC r231

You are turning left on a slippery road. The back of your vehicle slides to the right. You should

- ☐ brake firmly and not turn the steering wheel
- ☐ steer carefully to the left
- ☐ steer carefully to the right
- ☐ brake firmly and steer to the left

Steer into the skid but be careful not to overcorrect with too much steering. Too much movement may lead to a skid in the opposite direction. Skids don't just happen, they are caused. The three important factors in order are the driver, the vehicle and the road conditions.

4.21 — Mark four answers — DES s12, HC p128

Before starting a journey in freezing weather you should clear ice and snow from your vehicle's

- ☐ aerial
- ☐ windows
- ☐ bumper
- ☐ lights
- ☐ mirrors
- ☐ number plates

Don't travel unless you have no choice. Making unnecessary journeys in bad weather can increase the risk of having a collision. It's important that you can see and be seen. Make sure any snow or ice is cleared from lights, mirrors, number plates and windows.

4.22 — Mark one answer — DES s12, HC r231

You are trying to move off on snow. You should use

- ☐ the lowest gear you can
- ☐ the highest gear you can
- ☐ a high engine speed
- ☐ the handbrake and footbrake together

If you attempt to move off in a low gear, such as first, the engine will rev at a higher speed. This could cause the wheels to spin and dig further into the snow.

4.23 — Mark one answer — DES s12, HC r230

When driving in falling snow you should

- ☐ brake firmly and quickly
- ☐ be ready to steer sharply
- ☐ use sidelights only
- ☐ brake gently in plenty of time

Braking on snow can be extremely dangerous. Be gentle with both the accelerator and brake to prevent wheel-spin.

The MAIN benefit of having four-wheel drive is to improve

☐ road holding

☐ fuel consumption

☐ stopping distances

☐ passenger comfort

By driving all four wheels there is improved grip, but this does not replace the skills you need to drive safely. The extra grip helps road holding when travelling on slippery or uneven roads.

You are about to go down a steep hill. To control the speed of your vehicle you should

☐ select a high gear and use the brakes carefully

☐ select a high gear and use the brakes firmly

☐ select a low gear and use the brakes carefully

☐ select a low gear and avoid using the brakes

When going down a steep hill your vehicle will speed up. This will make it more difficult for you to stop. Select a lower gear to give you more engine braking and control. Use this in combination with careful use of the brakes.

You wish to park facing DOWNHILL. Which TWO of the following should you do?

☐ Turn the steering wheel towards the kerb

☐ Park close to the bumper of another car

☐ Park with two wheels on the kerb

☐ Put the handbrake on firmly

☐ Turn the steering wheel away from the kerb

Turning the wheels towards the kerb will allow it to act as a chock, preventing any forward movement of the vehicle. It will also help to leave it in gear, or select Park if you have an automatic.

4.27
Mark one answer DES s6, HC r153

You are driving in a built-up area. You approach a speed hump. You should

- ☐ move across to the left-hand side of the road
- ☐ wait for any pedestrians to cross
- ☐ slow your vehicle right down
- ☐ stop and check both pavements

Many towns have speed humps to slow down traffic. Slow down when driving over them. If you go too fast they may affect your steering and suspension, causing you to lose control or even damaging it. Be aware of pedestrians in these areas.

4.28
Mark one answer DES s3, 5, 12, HC r120

Anti-lock brakes reduce the chances of a skid occurring particularly when

- ☐ driving down steep hills
- ☐ braking during normal driving
- ☐ braking in an emergency
- ☐ driving on good road surfaces

The anti-lock braking system will operate when the brakes have been applied harshly.

It will reduce the chances of your car skidding, but it is not a miracle cure for careless driving.

4.29
Mark two answers DES s5

Anti-lock brakes may not work as effectively if the road surface is

- ☐ dry
- ☐ loose
- ☐ wet
- ☐ good
- ☐ firm

Poor contact with the road surface could cause one or more of the tyres to lose grip on the road. This is more likely to happen when braking in poor weather conditions, when the road surface is uneven or has loose chippings.

4.30
Mark one answer DES s3, 5, HC r120

Anti-lock brakes are of most use when you are

- ☐ braking gently
- ☐ driving on worn tyres
- ☐ braking excessively
- ☐ driving normally

Anti-lock brakes will not be required when braking normally. Looking well down the road and anticipating possible hazards could prevent you having to brake late and harshly. Knowing that you have anti-lock brakes is not an excuse to drive in a careless or reckless way.

Mark one answer

Driving a vehicle fitted with anti-lock brakes allows you to

☐ brake harder because it is impossible to skid

☐ drive at higher speeds

☐ steer and brake at the same time

☐ pay less attention to the road ahead

When stopping in an emergency anti-lock brakes will help you continue to steer when braking. In poor weather conditions this may be less effective. You need to depress the clutch pedal to prevent the car stalling as most power steering systems use an engine-driven pump and will only operate when the engine is running. Look in your vehicle handbook for the correct method when stopping in an emergency.

Mark one answer

You are driving a vehicle fitted with anti-lock brakes. You need to stop in an emergency. You should apply the footbrake

☐ slowly and gently

☐ slowly but firmly

☐ rapidly and gently

☐ rapidly and firmly

Look well ahead down the road as you drive and give yourself time and space to react safely to any hazards. You may have to stop in an emergency due to a misjudgement by another driver or a hazard arising suddenly such as a child running out into the road. In this case, if your vehicle has anti-lock brakes, you should apply the brakes immediately and keep them firmly applied until you stop.

Mark two answers

Your vehicle has anti-lock brakes, but they may not always prevent skidding. This is most likely to happen when driving

☐ in foggy conditions

☐ on surface water

☐ on loose road surfaces

☐ on dry tarmac

☐ at night on unlit roads

In very wet weather water can build up between the tyre and the road surface. As a result your vehicle actually rides on a thin film of water and your tyres will not grip the road. Gravel or shingle surfaces also offer less grip and can present problems when braking. An anti-lock braking system may be ineffective in these conditions.

4.34 Mark one answer DES s12, HC r121

You are driving along a country road. You see this sign. AFTER dealing safely with the hazard you should always

☐ check your tyre pressures

☐ switch on your hazard warning lights

☐ accelerate briskly

☐ test your brakes

Deep water can affect your brakes, so you should check that they're working properly before you build up speed again. Before you do this, remember to check your mirrors and consider what's behind you.

4.35 Mark two answers DES s12, HC r231

How can you tell if you are driving on ice?

☐ The tyres make a rumbling noise

☐ The tyres make hardly any noise

☐ The steering becomes heavier

☐ The steering becomes lighter

Drive extremely carefully when the roads are icy. When travelling on ice, tyres make virtually no noise and the steering feels unresponsive.

In icy conditions, avoid harsh braking, acceleration and steering.

4.36 Mark one answer DES s12, HC r227

You are driving along a wet road. How can you tell if your vehicle's tyres are losing their grip on the surface?

☐ The engine will stall

☐ The steering will feel very heavy

☐ The engine noise will increase

☐ The steering will feel very light

If you drive at speed in very wet conditions your steering may suddenly feel lighter than usual. This means that the tyres have lifted off the surface of the road and are skating on the surface of the water. This is known as aquaplaning. Reduce speed but don't brake until your steering returns to a normal feel.

4.37
Mark one answer — DES s12, HC r126

Your overall stopping distance will be much longer when driving

☐ in the rain
☐ in fog
☐ at night
☐ in strong winds

Extra care should be taken in wet weather as, on wet roads, your stopping distance could be double that necessary for dry conditions.

4.38
Mark one answer — DES s7, HC r126

You are on a fast, open road in good conditions. For safety, the distance between you and the vehicle in front should be

☐ a two-second time gap
☐ one car length
☐ 2 metres (6 feet 6 inches)
☐ two car lengths

One useful method of checking that you've allowed enough room between you and the vehicle in front is the two-second rule.

To check for a two-second time gap, choose a stationary object ahead, such as a bridge or road sign. When the car in front passes the object say 'Only a fool breaks the two-second rule'. If you reach the object before you finish saying it you're too close.

4.39
Mark one answer — DES s7, HC r122, 160

How can you use your vehicle's engine as a brake?

☐ By changing to a lower gear
☐ By selecting reverse gear
☐ By changing to a higher gear
☐ By selecting neutral gear

When driving on downhill stretches of road selecting a lower gear gives increased engine braking. This will prevent excess use of the brakes, which become less effective if they overheat.

4.40
Mark one answer — DES s5, HC r120

Anti-lock brakes are most effective when you

☐ keep pumping the foot brake to prevent skidding
☐ brake normally, but grip the steering wheel tightly
☐ brake promptly and firmly until you have slowed down
☐ apply the handbrake to reduce the stopping distance

Releasing the brake before you have slowed right down will disable the system. If you have to brake in an emergency ensure that you keep your foot firmly on the brake pedal until the vehicle has stopped.

4.41 — Mark one answer — DES s5, HC r120

Anti-lock brakes will take effect when

☐ you do not brake quickly enough

☐ maximum brake pressure has been applied

☐ you have not seen a hazard ahead

☐ speeding on slippery road surfaces

If your car is fitted with anti-lock brakes they will take effect when you use them very firmly in an emergency. The system will only activate when it senses the wheels are about to lock.

4.42 — Mark one answer — DES s12, HC r227

You are on a wet motorway with surface spray. You should use

☐ hazard flashers

☐ dipped headlights

☐ rear fog lights

☐ sidelights

When surface spray reduces visibility switch on your dipped headlights. This will help other road users to see you.

4.43 — Mark one answer — DES s5, HC r122

Travelling for long distances in neutral (known as coasting)

☐ improves the driver's control

☐ makes steering easier

☐ reduces the driver's control

☐ uses more fuel

Coasting is the term used when the clutch is held down, or the gear lever is in neutral, and the vehicle is allowed to freewheel. This reduces the driver's control of the vehicle. When you coast, the engine can't drive the wheels to pull you through a corner. Coasting also removes the assistance of engine braking that helps to slow the car.

4.44 — Mark three answers — DES s12, HC r226, 235

When driving in fog, which THREE of these are correct?

☐ Use dipped headlights

☐ Position close to the centre line

☐ Allow more time for your journey

☐ Keep close to the car in front

☐ Slow down

☐ Use side lights only

Don't venture out if your journey is not necessary. If you have to travel and someone is expecting you at the other end, let them know that you will be taking longer than usual for your journey. This will stop them worrying if you don't turn up on time and will also take the pressure off you, so you don't feel you have to rush.

> Case study practice – 4 Safety margins

You have a short but essential journey to make.

It's early morning and the roads are icy in places. It's very cold and snow is falling.

Your tyres are making almost no sound. On turning left, the back of your vehicle slides a little to the right.

Further on there's a slow-moving vehicle spreading salt on the road surface.

4.1 What should you do in such weather conditions?
Mark **two** answers

- ☐ Allow more distance
- ☐ Allow more time
- ☐ Allow more fuel
- ☐ Allow more money

HC r228 **DES** s12

4.2 How should you brake under the conditions described?
Mark **one** answer

- ☐ Quickly and heavily
- ☐ Gently and quickly
- ☐ Slowly and heavily
- ☐ Gently and slowly

HC r231 **DES** s12

4.3 What might your tyres be telling you?
Mark **one** answer

☐ There could be grit
☐ There's new tarmac
☐ The road could be icy
☐ The road surface is worn

HC r231 **DES** s12

4.4 What should you do in the skid described?
Mark **one** answer

☐ Ease off the brake pedal and keep the wheels straight
☐ Ease off the accelerator but don't turn the steering wheel
☐ Ease off the brake pedal and then steer gently to the left
☐ Ease off the accelerator then steer carefully to the right

HC r119

4.5 What colour beacon would this slow-moving vehicle have?
Mark **one** answer

☐ Green
☐ Amber
☐ Blue
☐ White

HC r225

Section five
Hazard awareness

In this section, you'll learn about

- static hazards, eg parked cars, junctions, roundabouts
- moving hazards, eg pedestrians, cyclists, drivers
- road and weather conditions
- physical conditions that make someone unfit to drive.

Hazard awareness

When you start learning to drive, you'll be concentrating on the basic controls of the car. As your skills improve, so will your ability to recognise hazards on the road.

A hazard is a situation that may require you, as a driver, to respond by taking action, such as braking or steering.

Hazards can be …

static, such as parked cars, junctions or roundabouts

moving, such as pedestrians, cyclists or drivers

road and weather conditions

you, if you aren't alert and fit to drive

> Static hazards

There are many types of static hazard, including

- bends
- junctions
- roundabouts
- parked vehicles and obstructions in the road
- roadworks
- road surfaces
- different types of crossings
- traffic lights.

HC r153 **DES** s7, 8, 10

All of these may require you to respond in some way, so

- be aware that they're there
- slow down and be ready to stop if necessary.

At level crossings with traffic light signals, you **MUST stop before the barrier when the red lights are flashing, even if the barrier isn't yet down.**

HC r293

Road signs

Road signs and markings are there to give you clues about possible hazards, so it's vital that you learn their meanings. You can find them in *The Official Highway Code* (book, eBook, interactive CD-ROM, app and online) and *Know Your Traffic Signs* (book and online).

Watch out for signs and markings so that you can slow down in good time and are prepared for any action you may need to take. For example, if you see a sign for a bend, ask yourself, 'What if there's a pedestrian or an obstruction around the bend – could I stop in time? Could I do it safely?'

HC p106–116 **DES** s6, 7, 10 **KYTS** p10–71, 77–93

Parked vehicles

In busy areas, parked cars can cause a hazard – especially if they're parked illegally, for example on the zigzag lines by a pedestrian crossing.

Watch out for

- children running out from between vehicles
- vehicle doors opening
- vehicles moving away.

Would you be able to stop, or safely avoid them, in time?

HC r205–206 **DES** s7, 10

Junctions

Your view is often reduced at junctions, especially in built-up areas (for example, in towns). Take extra care and pull forward slowly until you can see down the road. You may also be able to see reflections of traffic in the windows of buildings, such as shops.

Be careful not to block a junction: leave it clear so that other vehicles can enter and emerge.

Where lanes are closed, be ready for vehicles cutting in front of you and keep a safe distance from the vehicle in front.

HC r151 **DES** s8, 10, 11

At a traffic light-controlled junction where the lights aren't working, treat it as an unmarked junction and be prepared to stop. There may be police officers controlling traffic in these circumstances – make sure that you know and understand their signals.

HC r105, 176, p104 **DES** s6

Motorways and dual carriageways

If you're driving on a motorway or dual carriageway and see a hazard or obstruction ahead, such as a traffic jam, you may use your hazard warning lights briefly to warn the traffic behind.

HC r116

Slow-moving or stationary vehicles with a large arrow displayed on the back show where you need to change lanes when approaching roadworks.

Breakdowns

If your vehicle breaks down and is causing an obstruction, switch on your hazard warning lights to warn other road users.

HC r116 **DES** s11

Find out more about what to do if you break down on a motorway at this link.

⊖ survivegroup.org/pages/safety-information/stopping-on-the-hard-shoulder

Moving hazards

Moving hazards tend to be hazards caused by other types of road user.

Road user	What to do
Pedestrians 	If you see pedestrians in the road, be patient and wait for them to finish crossing. On country roads there may be no pavement, so look out for pedestrians in the road. They may be walking towards you on your side of the road. **HC** r205–206 **DES** s7, 10
Cyclists 	Be aware of cyclists and give them plenty of room. They may wobble or swerve to avoid drains or potholes. At junctions or traffic lights, give cyclists time to turn or pull away. When travelling in slow traffic, before you turn left, check for cyclists filtering through the traffic on your left. **HC** r211–213 **DES** s10
Motorcyclists 	Look out for motorcyclists, especially when you're • emerging from a junction • turning into a road on your right • changing lanes or moving out to overtake. **HC** r211–213 **DES** s10
Horse riders 	Horses can be unpredictable and easily spooked. Reduce your speed and give them plenty of room when overtaking. **HC** r215 **DES** s10

Road user	What to do

Drivers of large vehicles

If you see a bus at a bus stop, remember that

- people may get off and then cross the road
- the bus may be about to move off.

`HC` `r223` `DES` `s10`

School buses might stop at places other than bus stops.

At some bridges, high vehicles may need to use the centre of the road to be able to pass underneath.

`HC` `r221` `DES` `s10`

Large goods vehicles over 13 metres long have red and yellow markings at the back of the vehicle.

`HC` `p117`

Drivers of vehicles carrying hazardous loads

Some vehicles have information signs on the back, to show that they contain a hazardous load. Learn what the signs mean.

`HC` `p117`

Drivers overtaking you

Watch out for vehicles, especially motorcyclists, overtaking and cutting in front of you.

If you need to, drop back to keep a safe distance from the vehicle in front.

When turning right, don't forget to check to your right for overtaking vehicles before making the turn.

`HC` `r211–213` `DES` `s10`

Road user	What to do
Disabled people using powered vehicles 	Reduce your speed and be careful. These small vehicles are extremely vulnerable on the road because • they're difficult to see • they travel slowly.
Older drivers 	Older drivers may not react very quickly, so be patient with them. **HC** **r216** **DES** **s10**

 Find out about the hazard perception test on DSA's YouTube channel.

❯ **youtube.com/dsagov**

❯ # Road and weather conditions

Different types of weather – rain, ice, fog and even bright sunlight – can create extra hazards by making it harder to see the road or affecting your control of the vehicle. Change the way you drive to suit the weather conditions, and be aware of the added dangers.

In these conditions ...	remember to do this
Rain	Double your distance from the vehicle in front to four seconds.
Ice	Increase your distance from the vehicle in front to 20 seconds.
Fog	Slow down and use dipped headlights.
Bright sunlight	Be aware that sunlight can dazzle you or other drivers.

HC r227 DES s11

❯ Yourself

Don't allow yourself to become a hazard on the road. You need to be alert and concentrate on your driving at all times.

Awareness

Make sure you use your mirrors so that you're aware of what's going on around you at all times. These may be convex (curved outwards slightly) to give a wider field of vision.

HC r161

Tiredness

Don't drive if you're tired. Plan your journey so that you have enough rest and refreshment breaks. Try to stop at least once every two hours. Open a window so you have plenty of fresh air.

If you feel tired,

- pull over at a safe and legal place to rest
- on a motorway, leave at the next exit or services.

HC r91 DES s1, 11

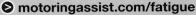

See the GEM Motoring Assist website for more information about driving and tiredness.

❯ **motoringassist.com/fatigue**

Distractions

Your concentration can be affected by

- using a mobile phone
- listening to loud music
- looking at a map or navigation system
- how you're feeling.

It's important to avoid being distracted by these things while you're driving.

- Turn off your mobile phone or switch it to voicemail.
- Keep music at a reasonable volume.
- Before looking at a map, find somewhere safe and legal to stop.
- If you're upset or angry, take time to calm down before you begin driving.

HC r91, 148–150 **DES** s1, 11

Take the Think! 'Driving Challenge' and learn more about distractions.

❯ **http://think.direct.gov.uk/drivingchallenge**

Alcohol

Never drive if you've been drinking alcohol: it's not worth taking a chance. If you're driving, don't drink. If you've had a drink, find another way to get home, such as public transport, taxi, walking or getting a lift.

HC r95

Did you know?

Alcohol can

- reduce your concentration, coordination and control
- give you a false sense of confidence
- reduce your judgement of speed
- slow down your reactions.

See the Think! road safety information on drink-driving.

❯ **http://think.direct.gov.uk/ drink-driving.html**

Medicines and drugs

You must be fit to drive. Some medicines can make you sleepy: check the label or ask your doctor or pharmacist if it's safe to drive after taking medication.

HC r90, 95–96 **DES** s1

Using illegal drugs is highly dangerous and the effects of some can last up to 72 hours. Never take them before driving.

If you've been convicted of driving while unfit through drink or drugs, the cost of your insurance will rise considerably. Driving while under the influence of drink or drugs may even invalidate your insurance.

DES s1

See the Think! road safety information on drug driving.

❯ **http://drugdrive.direct.gov.uk**

Eyesight

Your eyesight **MUST** be of the required legal standard to drive; if you need glasses or contact lenses to bring your eyesight up to this standard, you **MUST** wear them every time you drive. Tinted glasses can restrict your vision, so you mustn't wear them for driving at night.

You **MUST** tell the licensing authority if you suffer from any medical condition that may affect your driving.

HC r90, 92–94 **DES** s1

 Find out about the eyesight rules for driving at this website.

❯ **www.gov.uk**

Meeting the standards

You must be able to

use visual clues to prepare you for possible hazards. For example, reflections in shop windows

judge which possible hazards are most likely to affect you, so that you can plan what to do

respond to hazards safely.

You must know and understand

methods that you can use to scan around your vehicle, both close by and into the distance

which kinds of hazard you may find on different roads. For example

- tractors on country roads
- deer on forest roads
- children crossing near schools.

Notes

You can use this page to make your own notes or diagrams about the key points you need to remember.

Think about

- What are some examples of static hazards and why are they potentially dangerous?
- What kinds of moving hazards do you need to look out for when driving?
- What kinds of weather conditions can be hazardous and what can you do to reduce the risks?
- Think of the physical conditions that can make you unfit to drive. Have you experienced any? How did it affect you?

Your notes

Things to discuss and practise with your instructor

These are just a few examples of what you could discuss and practise with your instructor. Read more about hazard awareness to come up with your own ideas.

Discuss with your instructor

- the effects that alcohol and drugs can have on your driving
- how your driving is affected by tiredness and what you can do to stay alert
- how to deal with other people's bad driving behaviour.

Practise with your instructor

- driving through a busy town centre and identifying all the potential hazards, eg wobbling cyclists, stationary buses, vans pulling out of junctions, etc
- driving
  - under low bridges
  - up to blind junctions
  - along roads where many vehicles are parked
- identifying road markings.

Where would you expect to see these markers?

These markers must be fitted to vehicles over 13 metres long, large goods vehicles, and rubbish skips placed in the road. They are reflective to make them easier to see in the dark.

☐ On a motorway sign

☐ At the entrance to a narrow bridge

☐ On a large goods vehicle

☐ On a builder's skip placed on the road

What is the main hazard shown in this picture?

Look at the picture carefully and try to imagine you're there. The cyclist in this picture appears to be trying to cross the road. You must be able to deal with the unexpected, especially when you're approaching a hazardous junction. Look well ahead to give yourself time to deal with any hazards.

☐ Vehicles turning right

☐ Vehicles doing U-turns

☐ The cyclist crossing the road

☐ Parked cars around the corner

Which road user has caused a hazard?

The car arrowed A is parked within the area marked by zigzag lines at the pedestrian crossing. Parking here is illegal. It also

• blocks the view for pedestrians wishing to cross the road

• restricts the view of the crossing for approaching traffic.

☐ The parked car (arrowed A)

☐ The pedestrian waiting to cross (arrowed B)

☐ The moving car (arrowed C)

☐ The car turning (arrowed D)

What should the driver of the car approaching the crossing do?

☐ Continue at the same speed

☐ Sound the horn

☐ Drive through quickly

☐ Slow down and get ready to stop

Look well ahead to see if any hazards are developing. This will give you more time to deal with them in the correct way. The man in the picture is clearly intending to cross the road. You should be travelling at a speed that allows you to check your mirror, slow down and stop in good time. You shouldn't have to brake harshly.

What THREE things should the driver of the grey car (arrowed) be especially aware of?

☐ Pedestrians stepping out between cars

☐ Other cars behind the grey car

☐ Doors opening on parked cars

☐ The bumpy road surface

☐ Cars leaving parking spaces

☐ Empty parking spaces

You need to be aware that other road users may not have seen you. Always be on the lookout for hazards that may develop suddenly and need you to take avoiding action.

You see this sign ahead. You should expect the road to

☐ go steeply uphill

☐ go steeply downhill

☐ bend sharply to the left

☐ bend sharply to the right

Adjust your speed in good time and select the correct gear for your speed. Going too fast into the bend could cause you to lose control.

Braking late and harshly while changing direction reduces your vehicle's grip on the road, and is likely to cause a skid.

Section five Questions

You are approaching this cyclist. You should

Keep well back and allow the cyclist room to take up the correct position for the turn. Don't get too close behind or try to squeeze past.

☐ overtake before the cyclist gets to the junction

☐ flash your headlights at the cyclist

☐ slow down and allow the cyclist to turn

☐ overtake the cyclist on the left-hand side

Why must you take extra care when turning right at this junction?

You may have to pull forward slowly until you can see up and down the road. Be aware that the traffic approaching the junction can't see you either. If you don't know that it's clear, don't go.

☐ Road surface is poor

☐ Footpaths are narrow

☐ Road markings are faint

☐ There is reduced visibility

When approaching this bridge you should give way to

A double-deck bus or high-sided lorry will have to take up a position in the centre of the road so that it can clear the bridge. There is normally a sign to indicate this.

Look well down the road, through the bridge and be aware you may have to stop and give way to an oncoming large vehicle.

☐ bicycles

☐ buses

☐ motorcycles

☐ cars

5.10 Mark one answer DES s6, 10, KYTS p24

What type of vehicle could you expect to meet in the middle of the road?

The highest point of the bridge is in the centre so a large vehicle might have to move to the centre of the road to allow it enough room to pass under the bridge.

☐ Lorry

☐ Bicycle

☐ Car

☐ Motorcycle

5.11 Mark one answer DES s8, 10, HC r171

At this blind junction you must stop

The 'stop' sign has been put here because there is a poor view into the main road. You must stop because it will not be possible to assess the situation on the move, however slowly you are travelling.

☐ behind the line, then edge forward to see clearly

☐ beyond the line at a point where you can see clearly

☐ only if there is traffic on the main road

☐ only if you are turning to the right

5.12 Mark one answer DES s1, HC r147

A driver pulls out of a side road in front of you. You have to brake hard. You should

☐ ignore the error and stay calm

☐ flash your lights to show your annoyance

☐ sound your horn to show your annoyance

☐ overtake as soon as possible

Where there are a number of side roads, be alert. Be especially careful if there are a lot of parked vehicles because they can make it more difficult for drivers emerging to see you. Try to be tolerant if a vehicle does emerge and you have to brake quickly. Don't react aggressively.

An elderly person's driving ability could be affected because they may be unable to

☐ obtain car insurance

☐ understand road signs

☐ react very quickly

☐ give signals correctly

Be tolerant of older drivers. Poor eyesight and hearing could affect the speed with which they react to a hazard and may cause them to be hesitant.

You have just passed these warning lights. What hazard would you expect to see next?

These lights warn that children may be crossing the road to a nearby school. Slow down so that you're ready to stop if necessary.

☐ A level crossing with no barrier

☐ An ambulance station

☐ A school crossing patrol

☐ An opening bridge

You are planning a long journey. Do you need to plan rest stops?

☐ Yes, you should plan to stop every half an hour

☐ Yes, regular stops help concentration

☐ No, you will be less tired if you get there as soon as possible

☐ No, only fuel stops will be needed

Try to plan your journey so that you can take rest stops. It's recommended that you take a break of at least 15 minutes after every two hours of driving. This should help to maintain your concentration.

5.16 — Mark one answer — DES s6, HC r291–299

The red lights are flashing. What should you do when approaching this level crossing?

At level crossings the red lights flash before and when the barrier is down. At most crossings an amber light will precede the red lights. You must stop behind the white line unless you have already crossed it when the amber light comes on. NEVER zigzag around half-barriers.

☐ Go through quickly

☐ Go through carefully

☐ Stop before the barrier

☐ Switch on hazard warning lights

5.17 — Mark one answer — DES s6, HC r176

You are approaching crossroads. The traffic lights have failed. What should you do?

☐ Brake and stop only for large vehicles

☐ Brake sharply to a stop before looking

☐ Be prepared to brake sharply to a stop

☐ Be prepared to stop for any traffic

When approaching a junction where the traffic lights have failed, you should proceed with caution. Treat the situation as an unmarked junction and be prepared to stop.

5.18 — Mark one answer — DES s10, HC r206–207

What should the driver of the red car (arrowed) do?

Some people might take longer to cross the road. They may be older or have a disability. Be patient and don't hurry them by showing your impatience. They might have poor eyesight or not be able to hear traffic approaching. If pedestrians are standing at the side of the road, don't signal or wave them to cross. Other road users may not have seen your signal and this could lead the pedestrians into a hazardous situation.

☐ Wave the pedestrians who are waiting to cross

☐ Wait for the pedestrian in the road to cross

☐ Quickly drive behind the pedestrian in the road

☐ Tell the pedestrian in the road she should not have crossed

Mark one answer

You are following a slower-moving vehicle on a narrow country road. There is a junction just ahead on the right. What should you do?

☐ Overtake after checking your mirrors and signalling

☐ Stay behind until you are past the junction

☐ Accelerate quickly to pass before the junction

☐ Slow down and prepare to overtake on the left

You should never overtake as you approach a junction. If a vehicle emerged from the junction while you were overtaking, a dangerous situation could develop very quickly.

Mark one answer

What should you do as you approach this overhead bridge?

☐ Move out to the centre of the road before going through

☐ Find another route, this is only for high vehicles

☐ Be prepared to give way to large vehicles in the middle of the road

☐ Move across to the right-hand side before going through

Oncoming large vehicles may need to move to the middle of the road so that they can pass safely under the bridge. There will not be enough room for you to continue and you should be ready to stop and wait.

Mark one answer

Why are mirrors often slightly curved (convex)?

☐ They give a wider field of vision

☐ They totally cover blind spots

☐ They make it easier to judge the speed of following traffic

☐ They make following traffic look bigger

Although a convex mirror gives a wide view of the scene behind, you should be aware that it will not show you everything behind or to the side of the vehicle. Before you move off you will need to check over your shoulder to look for anything not visible in the mirrors.

5.22 | **Mark one answer** | DES s11, HC p113, 117, KYTS p135

You see this sign on the rear of a slow-moving lorry that you want to pass. It is travelling in the middle lane of a three-lane motorway. You should

This sign is found on slow-moving or stationary works vehicles. If you wish to overtake, do so on the left, as indicated. Be aware that there might be workmen in the area.

☐ cautiously approach the lorry then pass on either side

☐ follow the lorry until you can leave the motorway

☐ wait on the hard shoulder until the lorry has stopped

☐ approach with care and keep to the left of the lorry

5.23 | **Mark one answer** | HC r104

You think the driver of the vehicle in front has forgotten to cancel their right indicator. You should

☐ flash your lights to alert the driver

☐ sound your horn before overtaking

☐ overtake on the left if there is room

☐ stay behind and not overtake

The driver may be unsure of the location of a junction and turn suddenly. Be cautious and don't attempt to overtake.

What is the main hazard the driver of the red car (arrowed) should be aware of?

☐ Glare from the sun may affect the driver's vision

☐ The black car may stop suddenly

☐ The bus may move out into the road

☐ Oncoming vehicles will assume the driver is turning right

If you can do so safely give way to buses signalling to move off at bus stops. Try to anticipate the actions of other road users around you. The driver of the red car should be prepared for the bus pulling out. As you approach a bus stop look to see how many passengers are waiting to board. If the last one has just got on, the bus is likely to move off.

This yellow sign on a vehicle indicates this is

☐ a broken-down vehicle

☐ a school bus

☐ an ice cream van

☐ a private ambulance

Buses which carry children to and from school may stop at places other than scheduled bus stops. Be aware that they might pull over at any time to allow children to get on or off. This will normally be when traffic is heavy during rush hour.

5.26 — Mark two answers — DES s10, HC r205–206

What TWO main hazards should you be aware of when going along this street?

- ☐ Glare from the sun
- ☐ Car doors opening suddenly
- ☐ Lack of road markings
- ☐ The headlights on parked cars being switched on
- ☐ Large goods vehicles
- ☐ Children running out from between vehicles

On roads where there are many parked vehicles you should take extra care. You might not be able to see children between parked cars and they may run out into the road without looking.

People may open car doors without realising the hazard this can create. You will also need to look well down the road for oncoming traffic.

5.27 — Mark one answer — DES s10, HC r213

What is the main hazard you should be aware of when following this cyclist?

- ☐ The cyclist may move to the left and dismount
- ☐ The cyclist may swerve out into the road
- ☐ The contents of the cyclist's carrier may fall onto the road
- ☐ The cyclist may wish to turn right at the end of the road

When following a cyclist be aware that they have to deal with the hazards around them. They may wobble or swerve to avoid a pothole in the road or see a potential hazard and change direction suddenly. Don't follow them too closely or rev your engine impatiently.

5.28

Mark one answer

DES s1, HC r147

A driver's behaviour has upset you. It may help if you

☐ stop and take a break

☐ shout abusive language

☐ gesture to them with your hand

☐ follow their car, flashing your headlights

Tiredness may make you more irritable than you would be normally. You might react differently to situations because of it. If you feel yourself becoming tense, take a break.

5.29

Mark one answer

DES s6, HC r153

In areas where there are 'traffic calming' measures you should

☐ travel at a reduced speed

☐ always travel at the speed limit

☐ position in the centre of the road

☐ only slow down if pedestrians are near

Traffic calming measures such as road humps, chicanes and narrowings are intended to slow you down. Maintain a reduced speed until you reach the end of these features. They are there to protect pedestrians. Kill your speed!

5.30

Mark two answers

DES s6, 10, HC r291–299, p108–109

When approaching this hazard why should you slow down?

☐ Because of the bend

☐ Because it's hard to see to the right

☐ Because of approaching traffic

☐ Because of animals crossing

☐ Because of the level crossing

There are two hazards clearly signed in this picture. You should be preparing for the bend by slowing down and selecting the correct gear. You might also have to stop at the level crossing, so be alert and be prepared to stop if necessary.

5.31

Mark one answer

DES s6, HC p116, KYTS p70–71

Why are place names painted on the road surface?

☐ To restrict the flow of traffic

☐ To warn you of oncoming traffic

☐ To enable you to change lanes early

☐ To prevent you changing lanes

The names of towns and cities may be painted on the road at busy junctions and complex road systems. Their purpose is to let you move into the correct lane in good time, allowing traffic to flow more freely.

5.32 | Mark one answer | HC r135

Some two-way roads are divided into three lanes. Why are these particularly dangerous?

☐ Traffic in both directions can use the middle lane to overtake

☐ Traffic can travel faster in poor weather conditions

☐ Traffic can overtake on the left

☐ Traffic uses the middle lane for emergencies only

If you intend to overtake you must consider that approaching traffic could be planning the same manoeuvre. When you have considered the situation and have decided it is safe, indicate your intentions early. This will show the approaching traffic that you intend to pull out.

5.33 | Mark one answer | DES s10, HC r220

You are on a dual carriageway. Ahead you see a vehicle with an amber flashing light. What could this be?

☐ An ambulance

☐ A fire engine

☐ A doctor on call

☐ A disabled person's vehicle

An amber flashing light on a vehicle indicates that it is slow-moving. Battery powered vehicles used by disabled people are limited to 8 mph. It's not advisable for them to be used on dual carriageways where the speed limit exceeds 50 mph. If they are then an amber flashing light must be used.

5.34 | Mark one answer | HC p104

What does this signal from a police officer mean to oncoming traffic?

Police officers may need to direct traffic, for example, at a junction where the traffic lights have broken down. Check your copy of The Highway Code for the signals that they use.

☐ Go ahead

☐ Stop

☐ Turn left

☐ Turn right

Why should you be especially cautious when going past this stationary bus?

A stationary bus at a bus stop can hide pedestrians just in front of it who might be about to cross the road. Only go past at a speed that will enable you to stop safely if you need to.

- ☐ There is traffic approaching in the distance
- ☐ The driver may open the door
- ☐ It may suddenly move off
- ☐ People may cross the road in front of it
- ☐ There are bicycles parked on the pavement

Overtaking is a major cause of collisions. In which THREE of these situations should you NOT overtake?

You should not overtake unless it is really necessary. Arriving safely is more important than taking risks. Also look out for road signs and markings that show it is illegal or would be unsafe to overtake. In many cases overtaking is unlikely to significantly improve journey times.

- ☐ If you are turning left shortly afterwards
- ☐ When you are in a one-way street
- ☐ When you are approaching a junction
- ☐ If you are travelling up a long hill
- ☐ When your view ahead is blocked

Which THREE result from drinking alcohol?

You must understand the serious dangers of mixing alcohol with driving or riding. Alcohol will severely reduce your ability to drive or ride safely. Just one drink could put you over the limit. Don't risk people's lives – DON'T DRINK AND DRIVE OR RIDE!

- ☐ Less control
- ☐ A false sense of confidence
- ☐ Faster reactions
- ☐ Poor judgement of speed
- ☐ Greater awareness of danger

5.38 | Mark one answer | HC p114, KYTS p65

What does the solid white line at the side of the road indicate?

The continuous white line shows the edge of the carriageway. It can be especially useful when visibility is restricted, for example at night or in bad weather. It is discontinued where it crosses junctions, lay-bys etc.

- ☐ Traffic lights ahead
- ☐ Edge of the carriageway
- ☐ Footpath on the left
- ☐ Cycle path

5.39 | Mark one answer | DES s6, HC r293, KYTS p27

You are driving towards this level crossing. What would be the first warning of an approaching train?

The steady amber light will be followed by twin flashing red lights that mean you must stop. An alarm will also sound to alert you to the fact that a train is approaching.

- ☐ Both half barriers down
- ☐ A steady amber light
- ☐ One half barrier down
- ☐ Twin flashing red lights

    Mark one answer

You are behind this cyclist. When the traffic lights change, what should you do?

Hold back and allow the cyclist to move off. In some towns, junctions have special areas marked across the front of the traffic lane. These allow cyclists to wait for the lights to change and move off ahead of other traffic.

☐ Try to move off before the cyclist

☐ Allow the cyclist time and room

☐ Turn right but give the cyclist room

☐ Tap your horn and drive through first

    Mark one answer

When the traffic lights change to green the white car should

If you are waiting at traffic lights, check all around you before you move away, as cyclists often filter through waiting traffic. Allow the cyclist to move off safely.

☐ wait for the cyclist to pull away

☐ move off quickly and turn in front of the cyclist

☐ move close up to the cyclist to beat the lights

☐ sound the horn to warn the cyclist

5.42 | Mark one answer | DES s10, HC r178, 211–213

You intend to turn left at the traffic lights. Just before turning you should

☐ check your right mirror
☐ move close up to the white car
☐ straddle the lanes
☐ check for bicycles on your left

Check your nearside for cyclists before moving away. This is especially important if you have been in a stationary queue of traffic and are about to move off, as cyclists often try to filter past on the nearside of stationary vehicles.

5.43 | Mark one answer | DES s8, HC p108, KYTS p10

You should reduce your speed when driving along this road because

☐ there is a staggered junction ahead
☐ there is a low bridge ahead
☐ there is a change in the road surface
☐ the road ahead narrows

Traffic could be turning off ahead of you, to the left or right.

Vehicles turning left will be slowing down before the junction and any vehicles turning right may have to stop to allow oncoming traffic to clear. Be prepared for this as you might have to slow down or stop behind them.

5.44 | Mark one answer | DES s10, HC r134, p113, KYTS p129

What might you expect to happen in this situation?

☐ Traffic will move into the right-hand lane
☐ Traffic speed will increase
☐ Traffic will move into the left-hand lane
☐ Traffic will not need to change position

Be courteous and allow the traffic to merge into the left-hand lane.

You are driving on a road with several lanes. You see these signs above the lanes. What do they mean?

If you see a red cross above your lane it means that there is an obstruction ahead. You will have to move into one of the lanes which is showing the green light. If all the lanes are showing a red cross, then you must stop.

☐ The two right lanes are open

☐ The two left lanes are open

☐ Traffic in the left lanes should stop

☐ Traffic in the right lanes should stop

You are invited to a pub lunch. You know that you will have to drive in the evening. What is your best course of action?

Alcohol will stay in the body for several hours and may make you unfit to drive later in the day. Drinking during the day will also affect your performance at work or study.

☐ Avoid mixing your alcoholic drinks

☐ Not drink any alcohol at all

☐ Have some milk before drinking alcohol

☐ Eat a hot meal with your alcoholic drinks

You have been convicted of driving whilst unfit through drink or drugs. You will find this is likely to cause the cost of one of the following to rise considerably. Which one?

You have shown that you are a risk to yourself and others on the road. For this reason insurance companies may charge you a higher premium.

☐ Road fund licence

☐ Insurance premiums

☐ Vehicle test certificate

☐ Driving licence

5.48

What advice should you give to a driver who has had a few alcoholic drinks at a party?

☐ Have a strong cup of coffee and then drive home

☐ Drive home carefully and slowly

☐ Go home by public transport

☐ Wait a short while and then drive home

Drinking black coffee or waiting a few hours won't make any difference. Alcohol takes time to leave the body.

A driver who has been drinking should go home by public transport or taxi. They might even be unfit to drive the following morning.

5.49

You have been taking medicine for a few days which made you feel drowsy. Today you feel better but still need to take the medicine. You should only drive

☐ if your journey is necessary

☐ at night on quiet roads

☐ if someone goes with you

☐ after checking with your doctor

Take care – it's not worth taking risks. Always check with your doctor to be really sure. You may not feel drowsy now, but the medicine could have an effect on you later in the day.

5.50

You are about to return home from holiday when you become ill. A doctor prescribes drugs which are likely to affect your driving. You should

☐ drive only if someone is with you

☐ avoid driving on motorways

☐ not drive yourself

☐ never drive at more than 30 mph

Find another way to get home even if this proves to be very inconvenient. You must not put other road users, your passengers or yourself at risk.

5.51

During periods of illness your ability to drive may be impaired. You MUST

☐ see your doctor each time before you drive

☐ only take smaller doses of any medicines

☐ be medically fit to drive

☐ not drive after taking certain medicines

☐ take all your medicines with you when you drive

Be responsible and only drive if you are fit to do so. Some medication can affect your concentration and judgement when dealing with hazards. It may also cause you to become drowsy or even fall asleep. Driving while taking such medication is highly dangerous.

You feel drowsy when driving. You should

☐ stop and rest as soon as possible

☐ turn the heater up to keep you warm and comfortable

☐ make sure you have a good supply of fresh air

☐ continue with your journey but drive more slowly

☐ close the car windows to help you concentrate

You will be putting other road users at risk if you continue to drive when drowsy. Pull over and stop in a safe place. If you are driving a long distance, think about finding some accommodation so you can get some sleep before continuing your journey.

You are driving along a motorway and become tired. You should

☐ stop at the next service area and rest

☐ leave the motorway at the next exit and rest

☐ increase your speed and turn up the radio volume

☐ close all your windows and set heating to warm

☐ pull up on the hard shoulder and change drivers

If you have planned your journey properly, to include rest stops, you should arrive at your destination in good time.

You are about to drive home. You feel very tired and have a severe headache. You should

☐ wait until you are fit and well before driving

☐ drive home, but take a tablet for headaches

☐ drive home if you can stay awake for the journey

☐ wait for a short time, then drive home slowly

All your concentration should be on your driving. Any pain you feel will distract you and you should avoid driving when drowsy. The safest course of action is to wait until you have rested and feel better.

5.55 — Mark three answers — DES s1, HC r91

Driving long distances can be tiring. You can prevent this by

☐ stopping every so often for a walk

☐ opening a window for some fresh air

☐ ensuring plenty of refreshment breaks

☐ completing the journey without stopping

☐ eating a large meal before driving

Long-distance driving can be boring. This, coupled with a stuffy, warm vehicle, can make you feel tired. Make sure you take rest breaks to keep yourself awake and alert. Stop in a safe place before you get to the stage of fighting sleep.

5.56 — Mark one answer — DES s1, HC r96

You take some cough medicine given to you by a friend. What should you do before driving?

☐ Ask your friend if taking the medicine affected their driving

☐ Drink some strong coffee one hour before driving

☐ Check the label to see if the medicine will affect your driving

☐ Drive a short distance to see if the medicine is affecting your driving

Never drive if you have taken drugs, without first checking what the side effects might be. They might affect your judgement and perception, and therefore endanger lives.

5.57 — Mark one answer — DES s7, HC r143

You take the wrong route and find you are on a one-way street. You should

Never reverse or turn your vehicle around in a one-way street. This is highly dangerous. Carry on and find another route, checking the direction signs as you drive. If you need to check a map, first stop in a safe place.

☐ reverse out of the road

☐ turn round in a side road

☐ continue to the end of the road

☐ reverse into a driveway

177

Which THREE are likely to make you lose concentration while driving?

☐ Looking at road maps

☐ Listening to loud music

☐ Using your windscreen washers

☐ Looking in your wing mirror

☐ Using a mobile phone

Looking at road maps while driving is very dangerous. If you aren't sure of your route stop in a safe place and check the map. You must not allow anything to take your attention away from the road.

If you need to use a mobile phone, stop in a safe place before doing so.

You are driving along this road. The driver on the left is reversing from a driveway. You should

☐ move to the opposite side of the road

☐ drive through as you have priority

☐ sound your horn and be prepared to stop

☐ speed up and drive through quickly

White lights at the rear of a car show that it is about to reverse. Sound your horn to warn of your presence and reduce your speed as a precaution.

You have been involved in an argument before starting your journey. This has made you feel angry. You should

☐ start to drive, but open a window

☐ drive slower than normal and turn your radio on

☐ have an alcoholic drink to help you relax before driving

☐ calm down before you start to drive

If you are feeling upset or angry you should wait until you have calmed down before setting out on a journey.

5.61 Mark one answer DES s6, HC p113, KYTS p128–129

You are driving on this dual carriageway. Why may you need to slow down?

- [ ] There is a broken white line in the centre
- [ ] There are solid white lines either side
- [ ] There are roadworks ahead of you
- [ ] There are no footpaths

Look well ahead and read any road signs as you drive. They are there to inform you of what is ahead. In this case you may need to slow right down and change direction.

Make sure you can take whatever action is necessary in plenty of time. Check your mirrors so you know what is happening around you before you change speed or direction.

5.62 Mark one answer DES s10, HC r147

You have just been overtaken by this motorcyclist who is cutting in sharply. You should

- [ ] sound the horn
- [ ] brake firmly
- [ ] keep a safe gap
- [ ] flash your lights

If another vehicle cuts in too sharply, ease off the accelerator and drop back to allow a safe separation distance. Try not to overreact by braking sharply or swerving, as you could lose control. If vehicles behind you are too close or unprepared, it could lead to a crash.

5.63 Mark one answer DES s1, HC r92

You are about to drive home. You cannot find the glasses you need to wear. You should

- [ ] drive home slowly, keeping to quiet roads
- [ ] borrow a friend's glasses and use those
- [ ] drive home at night, so that the lights will help you
- [ ] find a way of getting home without driving

Don't be tempted to drive if you've lost or forgotten your glasses. You must be able to see clearly when driving.

Which THREE of these are likely effects of drinking alcohol?

☐ Reduced coordination

☐ Increased confidence

☐ Poor judgement

☐ Increased concentration

☐ Faster reactions

☐ Colour blindness

Alcohol can increase confidence to a point where a driver's behaviour might become 'out of character'. Someone who normally behaves sensibly suddenly takes risks and enjoys it. Never let yourself or your friends get into this situation.

Your doctor has given you a course of medicine. Why should you ask how it will affect you?

☐ Drugs make you a better driver by quickening your reactions

☐ You will have to let your insurance company know about the medicine

☐ Some types of medicine can cause your reactions to slow down

☐ The medicine you take may affect your hearing

Always check the label of any medication container. The contents might affect your driving. If you aren't sure, ask your doctor or pharmacist.

You find that you need glasses to read vehicle number plates at the required distance. When MUST you wear them?

☐ Only in bad weather conditions

☐ At all times when driving

☐ Only when you think it necessary

☐ Only in bad light or at night time

Have your eyesight tested before you start your practical training. Then, throughout your driving life, have checks periodically to ensure that your eyes haven't deteriorated.

Which of the following types of glasses should NOT be worn when driving at night?

☐ Half-moon

☐ Round

☐ Bi-focal

☐ Tinted

If you are driving at night or in poor visibility, tinted lenses will reduce the efficiency of your vision, by reducing the amount of available light reaching your eyes.

5.68 — Mark three answers — DES s1, HC r91, 95–96, 148

What else can seriously affect your concentration, other than alcoholic drinks?

☐ Drugs

☐ Tiredness

☐ Tinted windows

☐ Contact lenses

☐ Loud music

Even a slight distraction can allow your concentration to drift. Maintain full concentration at all times so you stay in full control of your vehicle.

5.69 — Mark one answer — DES s1, HC r90, 92

As a driver you find that your eyesight has become very poor. Your optician says they cannot help you. The law says that you should tell

☐ the licensing authority

☐ your own doctor

☐ the local police station

☐ another optician

This will have a serious effect on your judgement and concentration. If you cannot meet the eyesight requirements you must tell DVLA (or DVA in Northern Ireland).

5.70 — Mark one answer — DES s3, HC r116, 274

When should you use hazard warning lights?

☐ When you are double-parked on a two way road

☐ When your direction indicators are not working

☐ When warning oncoming traffic that you intend to stop

☐ When your vehicle has broken down and is causing an obstruction

Hazard warning lights are an important safety feature and should be used if you have broken down and are causing an obstruction. Don't use them as an excuse to park illegally such as when using a cash machine or post box. You may also use them on motorways to warn traffic behind you of danger ahead.

You want to turn left at this junction. The view of the main road is restricted. What should you do?

You should slow right down, and stop if necessary, at any junction where the view is restricted. Edge forward until you can see properly. Only then can you decide if it is safe to go.

☐ Stay well back and wait to see if something comes

☐ Build up your speed so that you can emerge quickly

☐ Stop and apply the handbrake even if the road is clear

☐ Approach slowly and edge out until you can see more clearly

When driving a car fitted with automatic transmission what would you use 'kick down' for?

'Kick down' selects a lower gear, enabling the vehicle to accelerate faster.

☐ Cruise control

☐ Quick acceleration

☐ Slow braking

☐ Fuel economy

You are driving along this motorway. It is raining. When following this lorry you should

The usual two second time gap will increase to four seconds when the roads are wet. If you stay well back you will

• be able to see past the vehicle

• be out of the spray thrown up by the lorry's tyres

• give yourself more time to stop if the need arises

• increase your chances of being seen by the lorry driver.

☐ allow at least a two-second gap

☐ move left and drive on the hard shoulder

☐ allow at least a four-second gap

☐ be aware of spray reducing your vision

☐ move right and stay in the right-hand lane

5.74   Mark one answer   HC r154

You are driving towards this left-hand bend. What dangers should you be aware of?

Pedestrians walking on a road with no pavement should walk against the direction of the traffic. You can't see around this bend: there may be hidden dangers. Always keep this in mind so you give yourself time to react if a hazard does arise.

☐ A vehicle overtaking you

☐ No white lines in the centre of the road

☐ No sign to warn you of the bend

☐ Pedestrians walking towards you

5.75   Mark two answers   DES s10, HC r126, 146

The traffic ahead of you in the left-hand lane is slowing. You should

Allow the traffic to merge into the nearside lane. Leave enough room so that your separation distance is not reduced drastically if a vehicle pulls in ahead of you.

☐ be wary of cars on your right cutting in

☐ accelerate past the vehicles in the left-hand lane

☐ pull up on the left-hand verge

☐ move across and continue in the right-hand lane

☐ slow down, keeping a safe separation distance

5.76   Mark two answers   DES s2, HC r253, p123

As a provisional licence holder, you must not drive a motor car

☐ at more than 40 mph

☐ on your own

☐ on the motorway

☐ under the age of 18 years at night

☐ with passengers in the rear seats

When you have passed your practical test you will be able to drive on a motorway. It is recommended that you have instruction on motorway driving before you venture out on your own. Ask your instructor about this.

For which of these may you use hazard warning lights?

☐ When driving on a motorway to warn traffic behind of a hazard ahead

☐ When you are double-parked on a two-way road

☐ When your direction indicators are not working

☐ When warning oncoming traffic that you intend to stop

Hazard warning lights are an important safety feature. Use them when driving on a motorway to warn traffic behind you of danger ahead.

You should also use them if your vehicle has broken down and is causing an obstruction.

You are waiting to emerge at a junction. Your view is restricted by parked vehicles. What can help you to see traffic on the road you are joining?

☐ Looking for traffic behind you

☐ Reflections of traffic in shop windows

☐ Making eye contact with other road users

☐ Checking for traffic in your interior mirror

When your view is restricted into the new road you must still be completely sure it is safe to emerge. Try to look for traffic through the windows of the parked cars or the reflections in shop windows. Keep looking in all directions as you slowly edge forwards until you can see it is safe.

After passing your driving test, you suffer from ill health. This affects your driving. You MUST

☐ inform your local police station

☐ avoid using motorways

☐ always drive accompanied

☐ inform the licensing authority

The licensing authority won't automatically take away your licence without investigation. For advice, contact the Driver and Vehicle Licensing Agency (or DVA in Northern Ireland).

Why should the junction on the left be kept clear?

You should always try to keep junctions clear. If you are in queuing traffic make sure that when you stop you leave enough space for traffic to flow in and out of the junction.

- ☐ To allow vehicles to enter and emerge
- ☐ To allow the bus to reverse
- ☐ To allow vehicles to make a U-turn
- ☐ To allow vehicles to park

Your motorway journey seems boring and you feel drowsy. What should you do?

- ☐ Stop on the hard shoulder for a sleep
- ☐ Open a window and stop as soon as it's safe and legal
- ☐ Speed up to arrive at your destination sooner
- ☐ Slow down and let other drivers overtake

Never stop on the hard shoulder to rest. If there is no service station for several miles, leave the motorway at the next exit and find somewhere safe and legal to pull over.

Case study practice – 5
Hazard awareness

Andrea is waiting to turn right in the town centre. Cars are parked along the roadside, obstructing Andrea's view.

There are many shop windows. The area is busy with traffic and pedestrians.

Further on, a vehicle is unloading on the left and there are several oncoming cars.

At inactive traffic lights a police officer is directing traffic. He's facing Andrea with one hand straight up, his palm showing.

There's a bus lane, but no signs showing periods of operation or permitted use by other vehicles.

5.1 How could Andrea use the shop windows?

Mark **one** answer

☐ To check for reflections of any vehicles approaching
☐ To check to ensure the vehicle's indicator is working
☐ To check for any good bargains, sales or promotions
☐ To check the number of cars parked on the main road

DES s7

5.2 What could happen because of these parked cars?

Mark **one** answer

☐ Empty parking spaces may be available
☐ The road surface could be bumpy and uneven
☐ Pedestrians or cyclists could be stepping out
☐ Traffic wardens may be working in the area

HC r205–206 DES s10

5.3 What should Andrea do about the delivery vehicle?

Mark **one** answer

- ☐ Stop and wait until the vehicle pulls away
- ☐ Speed up and quickly pass the vehicle
- ☐ Stop and wait until the way is clear ahead
- ☐ Rev the engine and press the horn repeatedly

`HC` r163 `DES` s7, 10

5.4 What MUST Andrea do in response to the officer's signal?

Mark **one** answer

- ☐ Travel as quickly as possible through the junction
- ☐ Drive carefully and slowly past the police officer
- ☐ Slow to a crawl, while flashing the headlights
- ☐ Stop and wait patiently till signalled to go on

`HC` r105, p104

5.5 In the bus lane, what's indicated by the absence of signs?

Mark **one** answer

- ☐ Other vehicles can use the bus lane at any time
- ☐ Only certain vehicles can use the bus lane
- ☐ The lane can only be used by buses at all times
- ☐ There hasn't been enough time to erect a sign

`HC` r141 `DES` s6, 7

> Section six
Vulnerable road users

In this section, you'll learn about

- who is particularly vulnerable on the road
- how to help keep other road users safe.

Vulnerable road users

As a car driver, you'll share the road with many other road users. Some of these are more vulnerable than you, because of their

- inexperience or lack of judgement
- size
- speed
- unpredictable behaviour.

In a car you're also surrounded by bodywork that's designed to protect you in a crash. Among the most vulnerable road users are

- pedestrians – especially children and older people
- cyclists
- motorcyclists
- horse riders.

Remember to treat all road users with courtesy and consideration. It's particularly important to be patient when there are children, older or disabled people using the road.

The most vulnerable drivers and riders are those who are still learning, inexperienced or older. Keep calm and make allowances for them.

❯ Pedestrians

People walking on or beside the road – pedestrians – are vulnerable because they move more slowly than other road users and have no protection if they're involved in a collision. Everybody is a pedestrian at some time, but not every pedestrian has the understanding of how to use roads safely.

Pedestrians normally use a pavement or footpath. Take extra care if they have to walk in the road – for example, when the pavement is closed for repairs or on country roads where there's no pavement. Always check for road signs that indicate people may be walking in the road.

HC **r206** **DES** **s10** **KYTS** **p13**

189

On country roads, it's usually safest for pedestrians to walk on the right-hand side of the road, so that they're facing oncoming traffic and can see the vehicles approaching.

HC r2

A large group of people, such as those on an organised walk, may walk on the left-hand side. At night, the person at the front of the group should show a white light while the person at the back of the group should show a bright red light to help approaching drivers to see them.

HC r5

Watch out for pedestrians already crossing when you're turning into a side road. They have priority, so allow them to finish crossing.

HC r170 **DES** s8

When you see a bus stopped on the other side of the road, watch out for pedestrians who may come from behind the bus and cross the road, or dash across the road from your left to catch the bus.

HC r223 **DES** s10

Pedestrian crossings

Pedestrian crossings allow people to cross the road safely: be ready to slow down and stop as you approach them. Make sure you know how different types of crossing work. See section 2, Attitude, for more details.

Remember that you should never park on or near a pedestrian crossing; for example, on the zigzag lines either side of a zebra crossing.

HC r195–199 **DES** s7

Look for tell-tale signs that someone is going to cross the road between parked cars, such as

- seeing their feet when looking between the wheels of the parked cars
- a ball bouncing out into the road
- a bicycle wheel sticking out between cars.

Slow down and be prepared to stop.

HC r205 **DES** s10

Children

Children are particularly vulnerable as road users because they can be unpredictable. They're less likely than other pedestrians to look before stepping into the road.

See this link for information on teaching road safety to children.

> **http://think.direct.gov.uk/ education/early-years-and- primary**

Drive carefully near schools.

There may be flashing amber lights under a school warning sign, to show that children are likely to be crossing the road on their way to or from school. Slow down until you're clear of the area.

Be prepared for a school crossing patrol to stop the traffic by stepping out into the road with a stop sign. You **MUST** obey the stop signal given by a school crossing patrol.

Don't wait or park on yellow zigzag lines outside a school. A clear view of the crossing area outside the school is needed by

- drivers and riders on the road
- pedestrians on the pavement.

HC r208–210, 238 **DES** s6, 10 **KYTS** p56

Buses and coaches carrying schoolchildren show a special sign in the back. This tells you that they may stop often, and not just at normal bus stops.

HC r209, p117 **DES** s10

➤ Older and disabled pedestrians

If you see older people about to cross the road ahead, be careful as they may have misjudged your speed.

If they're crossing, be patient and allow them to cross in their own time: they may need extra time to cross the road.

HC r207 **DES** s10

A pedestrian with hearing difficulties may have a dog with a distinctive yellow or burgundy coloured coat.

Take extra care as they may not be aware of vehicles approaching.

A person carrying a white stick with a red band is both deaf and blind. They may also have a guide dog with a red and white checked harness.

HC r207 **DES** s10

> Cyclists

Cyclists should normally follow the same rules of the road as drivers, but they're slower and more vulnerable than other vehicles.

Find out about cycling safely at this link.

> **dft.gov.uk/bikeability**

Cycle routes

In some areas there may be special cycle or shared cycle and pedestrian routes, which are marked by signs.

KYTS p35–36

At traffic lights, advanced stop lines are sometimes marked on the road so that cyclists can stop in front of other traffic. When the lights are red or about to become red, you should stop at the first white line.

HC r178

Overtaking cyclists

If you're overtaking a cyclist, give them as much room as you would a car. They may swerve

- to avoid an uneven road surface
- if a gust of wind blows them off course.

HC r211–213 **DES** s7, 10

A cyclist travelling at a low speed, or glancing over their shoulder to check for traffic, may be planning to turn right. Stay behind and give them plenty of room.

Never overtake a slow-moving vehicle just before you turn left. Hold back and wait until it has passed the junction before you turn.

Cyclists at junctions

When you're emerging from a junction, look carefully for cyclists. They're not as easy to see as larger vehicles. Also look out for cyclists emerging from junctions.

HC r77, 187 **DES** s8

Be aware of cyclists at a roundabout. They may decide to stay in the left-hand lane, whichever direction they're planning to take. Hold back and give them plenty of room.

> Motorcyclists

Motorcyclists can be hard to see because their vehicles are smaller than cars. They're usually fast-moving too, so they can be very vulnerable in a collision.

Remember to leave enough room while overtaking a motorcycle; the rider may swerve to avoid an uneven surface or be affected by a gust of wind. Look carefully for motorcyclists at junctions too, as they may be easily hidden by other vehicles, **street furniture** or other roadside features, such as trees.

Definition

street furniture
objects and pieces of equipment on roads and pavements; for example, street lights and signs, bus stops, benches, bollards, etc.

Before you turn right, always check for other traffic, especially motorcyclists, who may be overtaking.

HC r180

When you're moving in queues of traffic, be aware that motorcyclists may

- filter between lanes
- cut in just in front of you
- pass very close to you.

Keep checking your mirrors for motorcycles approaching from behind and give them space if possible.

If there's a slow-moving motorcyclist ahead and you're not sure what the rider is going to do, stay behind them in case they change direction suddenly.

HC r180

To improve their visibility, motorcyclists often wear bright clothing and ride with dipped headlights, even during the day.

HC r86

Motorcyclists also wear safety equipment, such as a helmet, to protect themselves. If there's been an accident and you find a motorcyclist has been injured, get medical assistance. Don't remove their helmet unless it's essential.

HC r283 **DES** s16

If you have a collision, you **MUST** stop. By law, you **MUST** stop at the scene of the incident if damage or injury is caused to any other person, vehicle, animal or property.

HC r286 **DES** s16

> Animals

Horses and other animals can behave in unpredictable ways on the road because they get frightened by the noise and speed of vehicles. Always drive carefully if there are animals on the road.

- Stay well back.
- Don't rev your engine or sound your horn near horses as this may startle them.
- Go very slowly and be ready to stop.

When it's safe to overtake,

- drive past slowly
- leave plenty of room.

HC r214–215 **DES** s10

Take extra care when approaching a roundabout. Horse riders, like cyclists, may keep to the left, even if they're signalling right. Stay well back.

HC r187, 215 **DES** s8

See the Think! road safety advice about horses on the road.

> **http://think.direct.gov.uk/horses.html**

▶ Other drivers

Other drivers, especially those who are inexperienced or older, may not react as quickly as you to what's happening on the road. Learner drivers may make mistakes, such as stalling at a junction. Be patient and be ready to slow down or stop if necessary.

HC r216–217 **DES** s1

 A flashing amber beacon on the top of a vehicle means it's a slow-moving vehicle. A powered wheelchair or mobility scooter used by a disabled person **MUST** have a flashing amber light when travelling on a dual carriageway with a speed limit that exceeds 50 mph.

HC r220

If you find another vehicle is following you too closely in fast-moving traffic, slow down gradually to increase your distance from the vehicle in front. This gives you more room to slow down or stop if necessary, and so reduces the risk of the vehicle behind crashing into you because the driver hasn't left enough room to stop safely.

Learner drivers and newly qualified drivers

Statistics show that 17- to 25-year-olds are the most likely to be involved in a road traffic incident. Over-confidence and lack of experience and judgement are the main causes of incidents for young and new drivers and motorcyclists.

Anyone can teach you to drive providing they

- are over 21
- have held, and still hold, a full licence for that category of vehicle for at least three years
- don't charge – even petrol money – unless they're an approved driving instructor (ADI).

However, you're strongly advised to take lessons with an ADI to make sure you're taught the correct procedures from the start.

DES s1

For more information, read *The Official DSA Guide to Learning to Drive*, which includes lots of advice for those helping learners to practise.

 Find driving schools and lessons using this website.

➔ **www.gov.uk**

Meeting the standards

You must be able to

look out for the effect of starting your engine near vulnerable road users. Passing cyclists or pedestrians may be affected

look for vulnerable road users at junctions, roundabouts and crossings.
For example

- cyclists
- motorcyclists
- horse riders.

You must know and understand

when other road users are vulnerable and how to allow for them

the rules that apply to vulnerable road users, like cyclists and motorcyclists, and the position that they may select on the road as a result

how vulnerable road users may act on the road. For example

- cyclists may wobble
- children may run out
- older people may take longer to cross the road.

Notes

You can use this page to make your own notes or diagrams about the key points you need to remember.

Think about

- Which types of pedestrian crossing might you see, and what are the differences between them?
- When might you need to watch out for children near the road?
- Which disability might a person have if they're walking with a dog that has a red and white checked harness?
- What might a cyclist or motorcyclist be about to do if they're checking over their shoulder?
- What mustn't you do when driving near horses or other animals on the road?

Your notes

Things to discuss and practise with your instructor

These are just a few examples of what you could discuss and practise with your instructor. Read more about vulnerable road users to come up with your own ideas.

Discuss with your instructor

- which sticks are used by people with different disabilities, eg a white stick with a red band
- the times when motorcyclists may be particularly vulnerable and how you should behave towards them
- what you think a cyclist's experience of driving through traffic may be. How can you make them feel safer?

Practise with your instructor

- driving near schools at times when students and parents are likely to be arriving or leaving
- driving down country lanes where you may encounter horse riders or pedestrians walking along the road
- identifying the signs warning you of vulnerable road users, eg a red triangle with a picture of a bicycle.

Which sign means that there may be people walking along the road?

Always check the road signs. Triangular signs are warning signs and they'll keep you informed of hazards ahead and help you to anticipate any problems. There are a number of different signs showing pedestrians. Learn the meaning of each one.

You are turning left at a junction. Pedestrians have started to cross the road. You should

☐ go on, giving them plenty of room

☐ stop and wave at them to cross

☐ blow your horn and proceed

☐ give way to them

If you're turning into a side road, pedestrians already crossing the road have priority and you should give way to them. Don't wave them across the road, sound your horn, flash your lights or give any other misleading signal. Other road users may misinterpret your signal and this may lead the pedestrians into a dangerous situation. If a pedestrian is slow or indecisive be patient and wait. Don't hurry them across by revving your engine.

You are turning left from a main road into a side road. People are already crossing the road into which you are turning. You should

☐ continue, as it is your right of way

☐ signal to them to continue crossing

☐ wait and allow them to cross

☐ sound your horn to warn them of your presence

Always check the road into which you are turning. Approaching at the correct speed will allow you enough time to observe and react.

Give way to any pedestrians already crossing the road.

6.4 Mark one answer DES s8, HC r170

You are turning left into a side road. What hazards should you be especially aware of?

☐ One way street

☐ Pedestrians

☐ Traffic congestion

☐ Parked vehicles

Make sure that you have reduced your speed and are in the correct gear for the turn. Look into the road before you turn and always give way to any pedestrians who are crossing.

6.5 Mark one answer DES s10, HC r211

You intend to turn right into a side road. Just before turning you should check for motorcyclists who might be

☐ overtaking on your left

☐ following you closely

☐ emerging from the side road

☐ overtaking on your right

Never attempt to change direction to the right without first checking your right-hand mirror. A motorcyclist might not have seen your signal and could be hidden by the car behind you. This action should become a matter of routine.

6.6 Mark one answer DES s7, HC r25

A toucan crossing is different from other crossings because

☐ moped riders can use it

☐ it is controlled by a traffic warden

☐ it is controlled by two flashing lights

☐ cyclists can use it

Toucan crossings are shared by pedestrians and cyclists and they are shown the green light together. Cyclists are permitted to cycle across.

The signals are push-button operated and there is no flashing amber phase.

6.7 Mark one answer DES s10, HC r210

How will a school crossing patrol signal you to stop?

☐ By pointing to children on the opposite pavement

☐ By displaying a red light

☐ By displaying a stop sign

☐ By giving you an arm signal

If a school crossing patrol steps out into the road with a stop sign you must stop. Don't wave anyone across the road and don't get impatient or rev your engine.

Where would you see this sign?

Vehicles that are used to carry children to and from school will be travelling at busy times of the day. If you're following a vehicle with this sign be prepared for it to make frequent stops. It might pick up or set down passengers in places other than normal bus stops.

☐ In the window of a car taking children to school

☐ At the side of the road

☐ At playground areas

☐ On the rear of a school bus or coach

What does this sign mean?

This sign shows a shared route for pedestrians and cyclists: when it ends, the cyclists will be rejoining the main road.

☐ No route for pedestrians and cyclists

☐ A route for pedestrians only

☐ A route for cyclists only

☐ A route for pedestrians and cyclists

You see a pedestrian with a white stick and red band. This means that the person is

☐ physically disabled

☐ deaf only

☐ blind only

☐ deaf and blind

If someone is deaf as well as blind, they may be carrying a white stick with a red reflective band. You can't see if a pedestrian is deaf. Don't assume everyone can hear you approaching.

6.11
Mark one answer — DES s10, HC r207

What action would you take when elderly people are crossing the road?

Be aware that older people might take a long time to cross the road. They might also be hard of hearing and not hear you approaching. Don't hurry older people across the road by getting too close to them or revving your engine.

- ☐ Wave them across so they know that you have seen them
- ☐ Be patient and allow them to cross in their own time
- ☐ Rev the engine to let them know that you are waiting
- ☐ Tap the horn in case they are hard of hearing

6.12
Mark one answer — DES s8, HC r187

You are coming up to a roundabout. A cyclist is signalling to turn right. What should you do?

If you're following a cyclist who's signalling to turn right at a roundabout leave plenty of room. Give them space and time to get into the correct lane.

- ☐ Overtake on the right
- ☐ Give a horn warning
- ☐ Signal the cyclist to move across
- ☐ Give the cyclist plenty of room

6.13
Mark two answers — DES s10, HC r163

Which TWO should you allow extra room when overtaking?

Don't pass riders too closely as this may cause them to lose balance. Always leave as much room as you would for a car, and don't cut in.

- ☐ Motorcycles
- ☐ Tractors
- ☐ Bicycles
- ☐ Road-sweeping vehicles

Why should you look particularly for motorcyclists and cyclists at junctions?

☐ They may want to turn into the side road

☐ They may slow down to let you turn

☐ They are harder to see

☐ They might not see you turn

Cyclists and motorcyclists are smaller than other vehicles and so are more difficult to see. They can easily become hidden from your view by cars parked near a junction.

In daylight, an approaching motorcyclist is using a dipped headlight. Why?

☐ So that the rider can be seen more easily

☐ To stop the battery overcharging

☐ To improve the rider's vision

☐ The rider is inviting you to proceed

A motorcycle can be lost from sight behind another vehicle. The use of the headlight helps to make it more conspicuous and therefore more easily seen.

Motorcyclists should wear bright clothing mainly because

☐ they must do so by law

☐ it helps keep them cool in summer

☐ the colours are popular

☐ drivers often do not see them

Motorcycles are small vehicles and can be difficult to see. If the rider wears bright clothing it can make it easier for other road users to see them approaching, especially at junctions.

There is a slow-moving motorcyclist ahead of you. You are unsure what the rider is going to do. You should

☐ pass on the left

☐ pass on the right

☐ stay behind

☐ move closer

If a motorcyclist is travelling slowly it may be that they are looking for a turning or entrance. Be patient and stay behind them in case they need to make a sudden change of direction.

6.18 — Mark one answer — HC r212

Motorcyclists will often look round over their right shoulder just before turning right. This is because

☐ they need to listen for following traffic

☐ motorcycles do not have mirrors

☐ looking around helps them balance as they turn

☐ they need to check for traffic in their blind area

If you see a motorcyclist take a quick glance over their shoulder, this could mean they are about to change direction. Recognising a clue like this helps you to be prepared and take appropriate action, making you safer on the road.

6.19 — Mark three answers — DES s8, 10, HC r207, 211

At road junctions which of the following are most vulnerable?

☐ Cyclists

☐ Motorcyclists

☐ Pedestrians

☐ Car drivers

☐ Lorry drivers

Pedestrians and riders on two wheels can be harder to see than other road users. Make sure you keep a look-out for them, especially at junctions. Good effective observation, coupled with appropriate action, can save lives.

6.20 — Mark two answers — DES s10, HC r187, 215

You are approaching a roundabout. There are horses just ahead of you. You should

☐ be prepared to stop

☐ treat them like any other vehicle

☐ give them plenty of room

☐ accelerate past as quickly as possible

☐ sound your horn as a warning

Horse riders often keep to the outside of the roundabout even if they are turning right. Give them plenty of room and remember that they may have to cross lanes of traffic.

6.21 — Mark one answer — DES s10, HC r207

As you approach a pelican crossing the lights change to green. Elderly people are halfway across. You should

☐ wave them to cross as quickly as they can

☐ rev your engine to make them hurry

☐ flash your lights in case they have not heard you

☐ wait because they will take longer to cross

Even if the lights turn to green, wait for them to clear the crossing. Allow them to cross the road in their own time, and don't try to hurry them by revving your engine.

There are flashing amber lights under a school warning sign. What action should you take?

☐ Reduce speed until you are clear of the area

☐ Keep up your speed and sound the horn

☐ Increase your speed to clear the area quickly

☐ Wait at the lights until they change to green

The flashing amber lights are switched on to warn you that children may be crossing near a school. Slow down and take extra care as you may have to stop.

These road markings must be kept clear to allow

The markings are there to show that the area must be kept clear to allow an unrestricted view for

• approaching drivers and riders
• children wanting to cross the road.

☐ schoolchildren to be dropped off

☐ for teachers to park

☐ schoolchildren to be picked up

☐ a clear view of the crossing area

Where would you see this sign?

Watch out for children crossing the road from the other side of the bus.

☐ Near a school crossing

☐ At a playground entrance

☐ On a school bus

☐ At a 'pedestrians only' area

6.25 | Mark one answer | DES s8, 10, HC r77, 187

You are following two cyclists. They approach a roundabout in the left-hand lane. In which direction should you expect the cyclists to go?

☐ Left
☐ Right
☐ Any direction
☐ Straight ahead

Cyclists approaching a roundabout in the left-hand lane may be turning right but may not have been able to get into the correct lane due to the heavy traffic. They may also feel safer keeping to the left all the way round the roundabout. Be aware of them and give them plenty of room.

6.26 | Mark one answer | DES s8, HC r187, 211

You are travelling behind a moped. You want to turn left just ahead. You should

☐ overtake the moped before the junction
☐ pull alongside the moped and stay level until just before the junction
☐ sound your horn as a warning and pull in front of the moped
☐ stay behind until the moped has passed the junction

Passing the moped and turning into the junction could mean that you cut across the front of the rider. This might force them to slow down, stop or even lose control. Slow down and stay behind the moped until it has passed the junction and you can then turn safely.

6.27 | Mark one answer | DES s8, HC r187, 215

You see a horse rider as you approach a roundabout. They are signalling right but keeping well to the left. You should

Allow the horse rider to enter and exit the roundabout in their own time. They may feel safer keeping to the left all the way around the roundabout. Don't get up close behind or alongside them. This is very likely to upset the horse and create a dangerous situation.

☐ proceed as normal
☐ keep close to them
☐ cut in front of them
☐ stay well back

Mark one answer

How would you react to drivers who appear to be inexperienced?

☐ Sound your horn to warn them of your presence

☐ Be patient and prepare for them to react more slowly

☐ Flash your headlights to indicate that it is safe for them to proceed

☐ Overtake them as soon as possible

Learners might not have confidence when they first start to drive. Allow them plenty of room and don't react adversely to their hesitation. We all learn from experience, but new drivers will have had less practice in dealing with all the situations that might occur.

Mark one answer

You are on a country road. What should you expect to see coming towards you on YOUR side of the road?

☐ Motorcycles

☐ Bicycles

☐ Pedestrians

☐ Horse riders

On a quiet country road always be aware that there may be a hazard just around the next bend, such as a slow-moving vehicle or pedestrians. Pedestrians are advised to walk on the right-hand side of the road if there is no pavement, so they may be walking towards you on your side of the road.

Mark one answer

You are following a car driven by an elderly driver. You should

☐ expect the driver to drive badly

☐ flash your lights and overtake

☐ be aware that the driver's reactions may not be as fast as yours

☐ stay very close behind but be careful

You must show consideration to other road users. The reactions of older drivers may be slower and they might need more time to deal with a situation. Be tolerant and don't lose patience or show your annoyance.

6.31 | Mark one answer | DES s8, HC r187, 212

You are following a cyclist. You wish to turn left just ahead. You should

Make allowances for cyclists. Allow them plenty of room. Don't try to overtake and then immediately turn left. Be patient and stay behind them until they have passed the junction.

☐ overtake the cyclist before the junction

☐ pull alongside the cyclist and stay level until after the junction

☐ hold back until the cyclist has passed the junction

☐ go around the cyclist on the junction

6.32 | Mark one answer | DES s8, HC r187, 215

A horse rider is in the left-hand lane approaching a roundabout. You should expect the rider to

☐ go in any direction

☐ turn right

☐ turn left

☐ go ahead

Horses and their riders will move more slowly than other road users. They might not have time to cut across heavy traffic to take up position in the offside lane. For this reason a horse and rider may approach a roundabout in the left-hand lane, even though they're turning right.

6.33 | Mark one answer | DES s10, HC r220

Powered vehicles used by disabled people are small and hard to see. How do they give early warning when on a dual carriageway?

☐ They will have a flashing red light

☐ They will have a flashing green light

☐ They will have a flashing blue light

☐ They will have a flashing amber light

Powered vehicles used by disabled people are small, low, hard to see and travel very slowly. On a dual carriageway a flashing amber light will warn other road users.

You should never attempt to overtake a cyclist

☐ just before you turn left
☐ on a left-hand bend
☐ on a one-way street
☐ on a dual carriageway

If you want to turn left and there's a cyclist in front of you, hold back. Wait until the cyclist has passed the junction and then turn left behind them.

Ahead of you there is a moving vehicle with a flashing amber beacon. This means it is

☐ slow moving
☐ broken down
☐ a doctor's car
☐ a school crossing patrol

As you approach the vehicle, assess the situation. Due to its slow progress you will need to judge whether it is safe to overtake.

What does this sign mean?

☐ Contraflow pedal cycle lane
☐ With-flow pedal cycle lane
☐ Pedal cycles and buses only
☐ No pedal cycles or buses

The picture of a cycle will also usually be painted on the road, sometimes with a different coloured surface. Leave these clear for cyclists and don't pass too closely when you overtake.

You notice horse riders in front. What should you do FIRST?

☐ Pull out to the middle of the road
☐ Slow down and be ready to stop
☐ Accelerate around them
☐ Signal right

Be particularly careful when approaching horse riders – slow down and be prepared to stop. Always pass wide and slowly and look out for signals given by horse riders. Horses are unpredictable: always treat them as potential hazards and take great care when passing them.

6.38 — Mark one answer — DES s6, HC r208, 238, KYTS p56

You must not stop on these road markings because you may obstruct

SCHOOL KEEP CLEAR

☐ children's view of the crossing area

☐ teachers' access to the school

☐ delivery vehicles' access to the school

☐ emergency vehicles' access to the school

These markings are found on the road outside schools. DO NOT stop (even to set down or pick up children) or park on them. The markings are to make sure that drivers, riders, children and other pedestrians have a clear view.

6.39 — Mark one answer — DES s10, HC r2, 206

The left-hand pavement is closed due to street repairs. What should you do?

☐ Watch out for pedestrians walking in the road

☐ Use your right-hand mirror more often

☐ Speed up to get past the roadworks quicker

☐ Position close to the left-hand kerb

Where street repairs have closed off pavements, proceed carefully and slowly as pedestrians might have to walk in the road.

6.40 — Mark one answer — DES s10, HC r213

You are following a motorcyclist on an uneven road. You should

☐ allow less room so you can be seen in their mirrors

☐ overtake immediately

☐ allow extra room in case they swerve to avoid potholes

☐ allow the same room as normal because road surfaces do not affect motorcyclists

Potholes and bumps in the road can unbalance a motorcyclist. For this reason the rider might swerve to avoid an uneven road surface. Watch out at places where this is likely to occur.

What does this sign tell you?

☐ No cycling

☐ Cycle route ahead

☐ Cycle parking only

☐ End of cycle route

With people's concern today for the environment, cycle routes are being created in our towns and cities. These are usually defined by road markings and signs.

Respect the presence of cyclists on the road and give them plenty of room if you need to pass.

You are approaching this roundabout and see the cyclist signal right. Why is the cyclist keeping to the left?

☐ It is a quicker route for the cyclist

☐ The cyclist is going to turn left instead

☐ The cyclist thinks The Highway Code does not apply to bicycles

☐ The cyclist is slower and more vulnerable

Cycling in today's heavy traffic can be hazardous. Some cyclists may not feel happy about crossing the path of traffic to take up a position in an outside lane. Be aware of this and understand that, although in the left-hand lane, the cyclist might be turning right.

You are approaching this crossing. You should

☐ prepare to slow down and stop

☐ stop and wave the pedestrians across

☐ speed up and pass by quickly

☐ continue unless the pedestrians step out

Be courteous and prepare to stop. Do not wave people across as this could be dangerous if another vehicle is approaching the crossing.

6.44
Mark one answer
DES s10, HC r207

You see a pedestrian with a dog. The dog has a yellow or burgundy coat. This especially warns you that the pedestrian is

- [ ] elderly
- [ ] dog training
- [ ] colour blind
- [ ] deaf

Take extra care as the pedestrian may not be aware of vehicles approaching.

6.45
Mark one answer
DES s7, HC r25

At toucan crossings

- [ ] you only stop if someone is waiting to cross
- [ ] cyclists are not permitted
- [ ] there is a continuously flashing amber beacon
- [ ] pedestrians and cyclists may cross

There are some crossings where cycle routes lead the cyclists to cross at the same place as pedestrians. These are called toucan crossings. Always look out for cyclists, as they're likely to be approaching faster than pedestrians.

6.46
Mark one answer
HC r178

Some junctions controlled by traffic lights have a marked area between two stop lines. What is this for?

- [ ] To allow taxis to position in front of other traffic
- [ ] To allow people with disabilities to cross the road
- [ ] To allow cyclists and pedestrians to cross the road together
- [ ] To allow cyclists to position in front of other traffic

These are known as advanced stop lines. When the lights are red (or about to become red) you should stop at the first white line. However if you have crossed that line as the lights change you must stop at the second line even if it means you are in the area reserved for cyclists.

6.47
Mark one answer
DES s7, 10, HC r211–213

When you are overtaking a cyclist you should leave as much room as you would give to a car. What is the main reason for this?

- [ ] The cyclist might speed up
- [ ] The cyclist might get off the bike
- [ ] The cyclist might swerve
- [ ] The cyclist might have to make a left turn

Before overtaking assess the situation. Look well ahead to see if the cyclist will need to change direction. Be especially aware of the cyclist approaching parked vehicles as they will need to alter course. Do not pass too closely or cut in sharply.

6.48   Mark three answers   DES s10, HC r214

Which THREE should you do when passing sheep on a road?

☐ Allow plenty of room

☐ Go very slowly

☐ Pass quickly but quietly

☐ Be ready to stop

☐ Briefly sound your horn

Slow down and be ready to stop if you see animals in the road ahead. Animals are easily frightened by noise and vehicles passing too close to them. Stop if signalled to do so by the person in charge.

6.49   Mark one answer   HC r5

At night you see a pedestrian wearing reflective clothing and carrying a bright red light. What does this mean?

☐ You are approaching roadworks

☐ You are approaching an organised walk

☐ You are approaching a slow-moving vehicle

☐ You are approaching a traffic danger spot

The people on the walk should be keeping to the left, but don't assume this. Pass slowly, make sure you have time to do so safely. Be aware that the pedestrians have their backs to you and may not know that you're there.

6.50   Mark one answer   DES s24, HC p134

You have just passed your test. How can you reduce your risk of being involved in a collision?

☐ By always staying close to the vehicle in front

☐ By never going over 40 mph

☐ By staying only in the left-hand lane on all roads

☐ By taking further training

New drivers and riders are often involved in a collision or incident early in their driving career. Due to a lack of experience they may not react to hazards as quickly as more experienced road users. Approved training courses are offered by driver and rider training schools. The Pass Plus scheme has been created by DSA for new drivers who would like to improve their basic skills and safely widen their driving experience.

6.51   Mark one answer   DES s9, HC r202

You want to reverse into a side road. You are not sure that the area behind your car is clear. What should you do?

☐ Look through the rear window only

☐ Get out and check

☐ Check the mirrors only

☐ Carry on, assuming it is clear

If you cannot be sure whether there is anything behind you, it is always safest to check before reversing. There may be a small child or a low obstruction close behind your car. The shape and size of your vehicle can restrict visibility.

6.52 Mark one answer DES s9, HC r202

You are about to reverse into a side road. A pedestrian wishes to cross behind you. You should

☐ wave to the pedestrian to stop

☐ give way to the pedestrian

☐ wave to the pedestrian to cross

☐ reverse before the pedestrian starts to cross

If you need to reverse into a side road try to find a place that's free from traffic and pedestrians. Look all around before and during the manoeuvre. Stop and give way to any pedestrians who want to cross behind you. Avoid waving them across, sounding the horn, flashing your lights or giving any misleading signals that could lead them into a dangerous situation.

6.53 Mark one answer DES s9, HC r202

Who is especially in danger of not being seen as you reverse your car?

☐ Motorcyclists

☐ Car drivers

☐ Cyclists

☐ Children

As you look through the rear of your vehicle you may not be able to see a small child. Be aware of this before you reverse. If there are children about, get out and check if it is clear before reversing.

6.54 Mark one answer DES s8, 10, HC r152

You want to turn right from a junction but your view is restricted by parked vehicles. What should you do?

☐ Move out quickly, but be prepared to stop

☐ Sound your horn and pull out if there is no reply

☐ Stop, then move slowly forward until you have a clear view

☐ Stop, get out and look along the main road to check

If you want to turn right from a junction and your view is restricted, STOP. Ease forward until you can see – there might be something approaching.

IF YOU DON'T KNOW, DON'T GO.

6.55 Mark one answer DES s8, HC r180

You are at the front of a queue of traffic waiting to turn right into a side road. Why is it important to check your right mirror just before turning?

☐ To look for pedestrians about to cross

☐ To check for overtaking vehicles

☐ To make sure the side road is clear

☐ To check for emerging traffic

There could be a motorcyclist riding along the outside of the queue. Always check your mirror before turning as situations behind you can change in the time you have been waiting to turn.

Mark one answer

What must a driver do at a pelican crossing when the amber light is flashing?

☐ Signal the pedestrian to cross

☐ Always wait for the green light before proceeding

☐ Give way to any pedestrians on the crossing

☐ Wait for the red-and-amber light before proceeding

The flashing amber light allows pedestrians already on the crossing to get to the other side before a green light shows to the traffic. Be aware that some pedestrians, such as elderly people and young children, need longer to cross. Let them do this at their own pace.

Mark two answers

You have stopped at a pelican crossing. A disabled person is crossing slowly in front of you. The lights have now changed to green. You should

☐ allow the person to cross

☐ drive in front of the person

☐ drive behind the person

☐ sound your horn

☐ be patient

☐ edge forward slowly

At a pelican crossing the green light means you may proceed as long as the crossing is clear. If someone hasn't finished crossing, be patient and wait for them.

Mark one answer

You are driving past a line of parked cars. You notice a ball bouncing out into the road ahead. What should you do?

Beware of children playing in the street and running out into the road. If a ball bounces out from the pavement, slow down and stop. Don't encourage anyone to retrieve it. Other road users may not see your signal and you might lead a child into a dangerous situation.

☐ Continue driving at the same speed and sound your horn

☐ Continue driving at the same speed and flash your headlights

☐ Slow down and be prepared to stop for children

☐ Stop and wave the children across to fetch their ball

6.59 Mark one answer DES s8, HC r180

You want to turn right from a main road into a side road. Just before turning you should

☐ cancel your right-turn signal

☐ select first gear

☐ check for traffic overtaking on your right

☐ stop and set the handbrake

Motorcyclists often overtake queues of vehicles. Make one last check in your mirror and your blind spot to avoid turning across their path.

6.60 Mark one answer DES s10, HC r211

You are driving in slow-moving queues of traffic. Just before changing lane you should

☐ sound the horn

☐ look for motorcyclists filtering through the traffic

☐ give a 'slowing down' arm signal

☐ change down to first gear

In this situation motorcyclists could be passing you on either side. Always check before you change lanes or change direction.

6.61 Mark one answer DES s10, HC r223

You are driving in town. There is a bus at the bus stop on the other side of the road. Why should you be careful?

☐ The bus may have broken down

☐ Pedestrians may come from behind the bus

☐ The bus may move off suddenly

☐ The bus may remain stationary

If you see a bus ahead watch out for pedestrians. They may not be able to see you if they're crossing from behind the bus.

6.62 Mark one answer DES s7, 10, HC r215

How should you overtake horse riders?

☐ Drive up close and overtake as soon as possible

☐ Speed is not important but allow plenty of room

☐ Use your horn just once to warn them

☐ Drive slowly and leave plenty of room

When you're on country roads be aware of particular dangers. Be prepared for farm animals, horses, pedestrians, farm vehicles and wild animals. Always be prepared to slow down or stop.

Why should you allow extra room when overtaking a motorcyclist on a windy day?

☐ The rider may turn off suddenly to get out of the wind

☐ The rider may be blown across in front of you

☐ The rider may stop suddenly

☐ The rider may be travelling faster than normal

If you're driving in high winds, be aware that the conditions might force a motorcyclist or cyclist to swerve or wobble. Take this into consideration if you're following or wish to overtake a two-wheeled vehicle.

Where should you take particular care to look out for motorcyclists and cyclists?

☐ On dual carriageways

☐ At junctions

☐ At zebra crossings

☐ On one-way streets

Motorcyclists and cyclists are often more difficult to see on the road. This is especially the case at junctions. You may not be able to see a motorcyclist approaching a junction if your view is blocked by other traffic. A motorcycle may be travelling as fast as a car, sometimes faster. Make sure that you judge speeds correctly before you emerge.

The road outside this school is marked with yellow zigzag lines. What do these lines mean?

Parking here would block the view of the school entrance and would endanger the lives of children on their way to and from school.

☐ You may park on the lines when dropping off schoolchildren

☐ You may park on the lines when picking schoolchildren up

☐ You must not wait or park your vehicle here at all

☐ You must stay with your vehicle if you park here

6.66   Mark one answer   DES s10, HC r211

You are driving past parked cars. You notice a bicycle wheel sticking out between them. What should you do?

☐ Accelerate past quickly and sound your horn

☐ Slow down and wave the cyclist across

☐ Brake sharply and flash your headlights

☐ Slow down and be prepared to stop for a cyclist

Scan the road as you drive. Try to anticipate hazards by being aware of the places where they are likely to occur. You'll then be able to react in good time, if necessary.

6.67   Mark one answer   DES s4

You are dazzled at night by a vehicle behind you. You should

☐ set your mirror to anti-dazzle

☐ set your mirror to dazzle the other driver

☐ brake sharply to a stop

☐ switch your rear lights on and off

The interior mirror of most vehicles can be set to the anti-dazzle position. You will still be able to see the lights of the traffic behind you, but the dazzle will be greatly reduced.

6.68   Mark one answer   DES s7, 10, HC r195, 207

You are driving towards a zebra crossing. A person in a wheelchair is waiting to cross. What should you do?

☐ Continue on your way

☐ Wave to the person to cross

☐ Wave to the person to wait

☐ Be prepared to stop

You should slow down and be prepared to stop as you would with an able-bodied person. Don't wave them across as other traffic may not stop.

6.69   Mark one answer   DES s6, HC p116, KYTS p56

What do these road markings outside a school mean?

SCHOOL KEEP CLEAR

☐ You may park here if you are a teacher

☐ Sound your horn before parking

☐ When parking, use your hazard warning lights

☐ You should not wait or park your vehicle here

These markings are used outside schools so that children can see and be seen clearly when crossing the road. Parking here would block people's view of the school entrance. This could endanger the lives of children on their way to and from school.

Case study practice – 6 Vulnerable road users

You're driving behind a cyclist and the road has potholes and cracks.

Further ahead there's a roundabout. A horse rider is approaching it in the left-hand lane.

In a built-up area with street lights, you see a school sign with a flashing amber signal. There are no speed limit signs.

Later, you stop at the red light of a pedestrian crossing. The person crossing carries a red-banded white stick and has a guide dog wearing a red and white checked harness.

6.1 What might the cyclist need to do on this road surface?

Mark **one** answer

☐ Swerve
☐ Speed up
☐ Turn left
☐ Turn round

HC r213 **DES** s10

6.2 What should you expect this horse rider to do next?

Mark **one** answer

- ☐ Make a right-hand turn
- ☐ Go in any direction
- ☐ Make a left-hand turn
- ☐ Proceed straight on

HC r187 **DES** s8, 10

6.3 What does this flashing amber signal mean?

Mark **one** answer

- ☐ Children may be playing in the road
- ☐ Parents may be standing in the road
- ☐ Children may be crossing the road
- ☐ Vehicles may be turning in the road

HC r208 **DES** s6, 7 **KYTS** p14

6.4 What would the speed limit be in the built-up area?

Mark **one** answer

- ☐ 10 mph
- ☐ 20 mph
- ☐ 30 mph
- ☐ 40 mph

HC r124, p40 **DES** s6

6.5 What's meant by the red and white harness and red-banded stick?

Mark **one** answer

- ☐ The pedestrian is partially deaf
- ☐ The pedestrian is blind and mute
- ☐ The pedestrian is partially blind
- ☐ The pedestrian is deaf and blind

HC r207 **DES** s10

Other types of vehicle

In this section, you'll learn about

> different types of vehicles
> safety when driving towards or following other types of vehicle.

Other types of vehicle

When you're driving towards or following another type of vehicle, such as a motorcycle or a lorry, you need to be aware of that vehicle's capabilities and how they're different to those of your car.

⊙ Motorcycles

Windy weather has a big effect on motorcyclists; they can be blown into your path, so

- if you're overtaking a motorcyclist, allow extra room
- if a motorcyclist in front of you is overtaking a high-sided vehicle, keep well back, as they could be blown off course
- be particularly aware of motorcyclists where there are crosswind warning signs.

HC r232–233, p109 **DES** s12

Crosswinds are likely to affect

- cyclists
- motorcyclists
- drivers towing caravans or trailers
- drivers of high-sided vehicles

more than car drivers. If you're following or overtaking, be aware that these vehicles might be blown off course, and give them extra room.

DES s12

Motorcyclists may swerve to avoid uneven or slippery surfaces, so if you're following a motorcyclist allow plenty of space. Metal drain covers in wet weather are particularly hazardous for two-wheeled vehicles.

HC r213 **DES** s10

See the Think! road safety information about driving safely near motorcyclists.

> **http://think.direct.gov.uk/ motorcycles.html**

> Large vehicles

Large vehicles can make it difficult for you to see the road ahead. Keep well back if you're following a large vehicle, especially if you're planning to overtake. If another vehicle fills the gap you've left, drop back further. This will improve your view of the road ahead.

HC r164, 222 **DES** s7

Overtaking a large vehicle is risky because it takes more time to overtake than a car.

Never begin to overtake unless you're sure that you can complete the manoeuvre safely.

Keep well back until you can see that the road ahead is clear. This also helps the driver of the large vehicle to see you in their mirrors.

HC r164 **DES** s7, 12

In wet weather, large vehicles throw up a lot of spray. This can make it difficult for you to see, so drop back further until you can see clearly. If the conditions make it difficult for you to be seen by other road users, use dipped headlights. If visibility is reduced to less than 100 metres (328 feet), you may use fog lights.

HC r226 **DES** s11, 12

TIP

If you're driving downhill and a large vehicle coming uphill needs to move out to pass a parked car, slow down and give way if possible. It's much more difficult for large vehicles to stop and then start up again if they're going uphill.

DES s7

Stay well back and give large vehicles plenty of room as they approach or negotiate

- road junctions
- crossroads
- mini-roundabouts.

To get around a corner, long vehicles may need to move in the opposite direction to the one they're indicating. If they want to turn left, they may indicate left but move over to the right before making the turn, and vice versa.

HC r221 **DES** s8

If you're waiting to turn left from a minor road and a large vehicle is approaching from the right, think. It may seem as if there's time to turn but there could be an overtaking vehicle hidden from view.

 # Buses

Bus drivers need to make frequent stops to pick up and set down passengers. If a bus pulls up at a bus stop, watch out for pedestrians who may get off and cross the road in front of or behind the bus. Be prepared to give way to a bus that's trying to move off from a bus stop, as long as it's safe to do so.

HC r223 **DES** s10

❯ Trams

Some cities have trams. Take extra care around them because they

- are very quiet
- move quickly
- can't steer to avoid you.

HC r223–224 **DES** s7

In these cities there may be extra white light signals at some traffic lights, which are for tram drivers.

❯ Powered vehicles used by disabled people

Powered vehicles used by disabled people, such as wheelchairs and mobility scooters, have a maximum speed limit of 8 mph (12 km/h) when used on the road.

HC r36, 220

Meeting the standards

You must be able to

look out for other road users and predict what they may do

monitor and manage your own reactions to other road users.

You must know and understand

the rules that apply to other road users and the positions they may select on the road as a result. For example

- drivers of large vehicles
- bus and coach drivers
- cyclists
- motorcyclists.

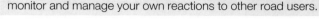

Notes

You can use this page to make your own notes or diagrams about the key points you need to remember.

Think about

- What conditions could make a motorcyclist swerve unexpectedly?
- When do you need to give large vehicles plenty of space?
- What should you watch out for when a bus has stopped at the side of the road?
- What do you need to be aware of when driving in an area that has trams?

Your notes

Things to discuss and practise with your instructor

These are just a few examples of what you could discuss and practise with your instructor. Read more about other types of vehicle to come up with your own ideas.

Discuss with your instructor

- how windy weather can affect the way motorcyclists ride. What can you do to allow for this?
- the maximum speed of powered wheelchairs and how you should behave when you need to overtake one
- how trams operate and what to look out for if you encounter a tram system.

Practise with your instructor

- driving around an industrial estate, or somewhere you're likely to encounter large vehicles
- overtaking large vehicles and noting how this differs from overtaking a car
- driving in different weather conditions and making sure that you can be seen by other road users, eg in the rain, in the fog, etc.

You are about to overtake a slow-moving motorcyclist. Which one of these signs would make you take special care?

In windy weather, watch out for motorcyclists and also cyclists as they can be blown sideways into your path. When you pass them, leave plenty of room and check their position in your mirror before pulling back in.

You are waiting to emerge left from a minor road. A large vehicle is approaching from the right. You have time to turn, but you should wait. Why?

☐ The large vehicle can easily hide an overtaking vehicle

☐ The large vehicle can turn suddenly

☐ The large vehicle is difficult to steer in a straight line

☐ The large vehicle can easily hide vehicles from the left

Large vehicles can hide other vehicles that are overtaking, especially motorcycles which may be filtering past queuing traffic. You need to be aware of the possibility of hidden vehicles and not assume that it is safe to emerge.

You are following a long vehicle. It approaches a crossroads and signals left, but moves out to the right. You should

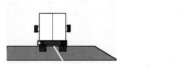

A lorry may swing out to the right as it approaches a left turn. This is to allow the rear wheels to clear the kerb as it turns. Don't try to filter through if you see a gap on the nearside.

☐ get closer in order to pass it quickly

☐ stay well back and give it room

☐ assume the signal is wrong and it is really turning right

☐ overtake as it starts to slow down

7.4 | **Mark one answer** | DES s8, HC r221

You are following a long vehicle approaching a crossroads. The driver signals right but moves close to the left-hand kerb. What should you do?

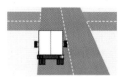

When a long vehicle is going to turn right it may need to keep close to the left-hand kerb. This is to prevent the rear end of the trailer cutting the corner. You need to be aware of how long vehicles behave in such situations. Don't overtake the lorry because it could turn as you're alongside. Stay behind and wait for it to turn.

☐ Warn the driver of the wrong signal

☐ Wait behind the long vehicle

☐ Report the driver to the police

☐ Overtake on the right-hand side

7.5 | **Mark one answer** | DES s7, HC r164, 222

Before overtaking a large vehicle you should keep well back. Why is this?

☐ To give acceleration space to overtake quickly on blind bends

☐ To get the best view of the road ahead

☐ To leave a gap in case the vehicle stops and rolls back

☐ To offer other drivers a safe gap if they want to overtake you

When following a large vehicle keep well back. If you're too close you won't be able to see the road ahead and the driver of the long vehicle might not be able to see you in their mirrors.

7.6 | **Mark two answers** | DES s10, HC r223

You are travelling behind a bus that pulls up at a bus stop. What should you do?

☐ Accelerate past the bus sounding your horn

☐ Watch carefully for pedestrians

☐ Be ready to give way to the bus

☐ Pull in closely behind the bus

There might be pedestrians crossing from in front of the bus. Look out for them if you intend to pass. Consider staying back and waiting.

How many people are waiting to get on the bus? Check the queue if you can. The bus might move off straight away if there is no one waiting to get on.

If a bus is signalling to pull out, give it priority as long as it is safe to do so.

You are following a large lorry on a wet road. Spray makes it difficult to see. You should

☐ drop back until you can see better

☐ put your headlights on full beam

☐ keep close to the lorry, away from the spray

☐ speed up and overtake quickly

Large vehicles may throw up a lot of spray when the roads are wet. This will make it difficult for you to see ahead. Dropping back further will

• move you out of the spray and allow you to see further

• increase your separation distance. It takes longer to stop when the roads are wet and you need to allow more room.

Don't

• follow the vehicle in front too closely

• overtake, unless you can see and are sure that the way ahead is clear.

You keep well back while waiting to overtake a large vehicle. A car fills the gap. You should

☐ sound your horn

☐ drop back further

☐ flash your headlights

☐ start to overtake

It's very frustrating when your separation distance is shortened by another vehicle. React positively, stay calm and drop further back.

When you approach a bus signalling to move off from a bus stop you should

☐ get past before it moves

☐ allow it to pull away, if it is safe to do so

☐ flash your headlights as you approach

☐ signal left and wave the bus on

Try to give way to buses if you can do so safely, especially when they signal to pull away from bus stops. Look out for people who've stepped off the bus or are running to catch it, and may try to cross the road without looking. Don't try to accelerate past before it moves away or flash your lights as other road users may be misled by this signal.

7.10
Mark one answer
DES s7, HC r164

You wish to overtake a long, slow-moving vehicle on a busy road. You should

☐ follow it closely and keep moving out to see the road ahead

☐ flash your headlights for the oncoming traffic to give way

☐ stay behind until the driver waves you past

☐ keep well back until you can see that it is clear

If you want to overtake a long vehicle, stay well back so that you can get a better view of the road ahead. The closer you get the less you will be able to see of the road ahead. Be patient, overtaking calls for sound judgement. DON'T take a gamble, only overtake when you are certain that you can complete the manoeuvre safely.

7.11
Mark one answer
DES s12, HC r232–233

Which of these is LEAST likely to be affected by crosswinds?

☐ Cyclists

☐ Motorcyclists

☐ High-sided vehicles

☐ Cars

Although cars are the least likely to be affected, crosswinds can take anyone by surprise. This is most likely to happen after overtaking a large vehicle, when passing gaps between hedges or buildings, and on exposed sections of road.

7.12
Mark one answer
DES s8, HC r221

What should you do as you approach this lorry?

When turning, long vehicles need much more room on the road than other vehicles. At junctions they may take up the whole of the road space, so be patient and allow them the room they need.

☐ Slow down and be prepared to wait

☐ Make the lorry wait for you

☐ Flash your lights at the lorry

☐ Move to the right-hand side of the road

You are following a large vehicle approaching crossroads. The driver signals to turn left. What should you do?

☐ Overtake if you can leave plenty of room

☐ Overtake only if there are no oncoming vehicles

☐ Do not overtake until the vehicle begins to turn

☐ Do not overtake when at or approaching a junction

Hold back and wait until the vehicle has turned before proceeding. Do not overtake because the vehicle turning left could hide a vehicle emerging from the same junction.

Powered vehicles, such as wheelchairs or scooters, used by disabled people have a maximum speed of

☐ 8 mph

☐ 12 mph

☐ 16 mph

☐ 20 mph

These are small battery powered vehicles and include wheelchairs and mobility scooters. Some are designed for use on the pavement only and have an upper speed limit of 4 mph (6 km/h). Others can go on the road as well and have a speed limit of 8 mph (12 km/h). They are now very common and are generally used by the elderly, disabled or infirm. Take great care as they are extremely vulnerable because of their low speed and small size.

Why is it more difficult to overtake a large vehicle than a car?

☐ It takes longer to pass one

☐ They may suddenly pull up

☐ Their brakes are not as good

☐ They climb hills more slowly

Depending on relevant speed, it will usually take you longer to pass a lorry than other vehicles. Some hazards to watch for include oncoming traffic, junctions ahead, bends or dips which could restrict your view, and signs or road markings that prohibit overtaking. Make sure you can see that it's safe to complete the manoeuvre before you start to overtake.

7.16
Mark one answer   DES s12, HC r232–233

It is very windy. You are behind a motorcyclist who is overtaking a high-sided vehicle. What should you do?

☐ Overtake the motorcyclist immediately

☐ Keep well back

☐ Stay level with the motorcyclist

☐ Keep close to the motorcyclist

Motorcyclists are affected more by windy weather than other vehicles. In windy conditions, high-sided vehicles cause air turbulence. You should keep well back as the motorcyclist could be blown off course.

7.17
Mark two answers   DES s10, HC r223

You are driving in town. Ahead of you a bus is at a bus stop. Which TWO of the following should you do?

☐ Be prepared to give way if the bus suddenly moves off

☐ Continue at the same speed but sound your horn as a warning

☐ Watch carefully for the sudden appearance of pedestrians

☐ Pass the bus as quickly as you possibly can

As you approach, look out for any signal the driver might make. If you pass the vehicle watch out for pedestrians attempting to cross the road from the other side of the bus. They will be hidden from view until the last moment.

7.18
Mark one answer   DES s8, HC r221

You are driving along this road. What should you be prepared to do?

☐ Sound your horn and continue

☐ Slow down and give way

☐ Report the driver to the police

☐ Squeeze through the gap

Sometimes large vehicles may need more space than other road users. If a vehicle needs more time and space to turn be prepared to stop and wait.

As a driver why should you be more careful where trams operate?

☐ Because they do not have a horn

☐ Because they do not stop for cars

☐ Because they do not have lights

☐ Because they cannot steer to avoid you

You should take extra care when you first encounter trams. You will have to get used to dealing with a different traffic system.

Be aware that they can accelerate and travel very quickly and that they cannot change direction to avoid obstructions.

You are towing a caravan. Which is the safest type of rear-view mirror to use?

☐ Interior wide-angle mirror

☐ Extended-arm side mirrors

☐ Ordinary door mirrors

☐ Ordinary interior mirror

Towing a large trailer or caravan can greatly reduce your view of the road behind. You need to use the correct equipment to make sure you can see clearly behind and down both sides of the caravan or trailer.

You are driving in heavy traffic on a wet road. Spray makes it difficult to be seen. You should use your

☐ full beam headlights

☐ rear fog lights if visibility is less than 100 metres (328 feet)

☐ rear fog lights if visibility is more than 100 metres (328 feet)

☐ dipped headlights

☐ sidelights only

You must ensure that you can be seen by others on the road. Use your dipped headlights during the day if the visibility is bad. If you use your rear fog lights, don't forget to turn them off when the visibility improves.

It is a very windy day and you are about to overtake a cyclist. What should you do?

☐ Overtake very closely

☐ Keep close as you pass

☐ Sound your horn repeatedly

☐ Allow extra room

Cyclists, and motorcyclists, are very vulnerable in crosswinds. They can easily be blown well off course and veer into your path. Always allow plenty of room when overtaking them. Passing too close could cause a draught and unbalance the rider.

Case study practice – 7
Other types of vehicle

It's dry but very windy. On the motorway, you see a car towing a large caravan in the middle lane.

You then move onto a long open stretch of single carriageway, where you pass a motorcyclist.

Later, you're travelling behind a long vehicle and want to overtake.

Once in town, there are trams directed by traffic light signals and you have to drive across their tracks.

Further on, a bus is signalling its intention to pull out from a bus stop.

7.1 What's the national motorway speed limit for the vehicle and caravan?

Mark **one** answer

☐　40 mph
☐　50 mph
☐　60 mph
☐　70 mph

HC p40

7.2 What could happen to the motorcyclist in these weather conditions?

Mark **one** answer

☐ They may have to turn around
☐ They may travel faster than usual
☐ They could be blown off course
☐ They could have engine trouble

HC r232–233 **DES** s12

7.3 What should you do when following the long vehicle?

Mark **one** answer

☐ Get closer so that you can overtake more quickly
☐ Drop back so you can see more of the road ahead
☐ Slow down until the long vehicle moves out of sight
☐ Keep pressing the horn to get the driver's attention

HC r164 **DES** s7

7.4 Why is it important not to obstruct these tracks?

Mark **one** answer

☐ Electric power to the tram may be disrupted
☐ The wheels of your vehicle could get stuck
☐ Your tyre treads could be seriously damaged
☐ Trams are unable to steer round obstructions

HC r224, 302 **DES** s7

7.5 What should you do about the bus?

Mark **one** answer

☐ Speed up and pass it before it pulls out
☐ Drive past slowly so the driver can see you
☐ Give way as long as it's safe to do so
☐ Stop and switch on hazard warning lights

HC r223 **DES** s10

Road conditions and vehicle handling

In this section, you'll learn about

- how to drive safely in different weather conditions
- driving at night
- keeping control of your vehicle
- traffic-calming measures and different road surfaces.

Road conditions and vehicle handling

As well as being aware of other road users, you need to think about the conditions you're driving in and how they might affect your safety. The weather, the time of day, hills, traffic calming and different road surfaces can all change the way you need to drive.

> Weather conditions

The weather makes a big difference to how you drive and how your vehicle handles.

Rain and wet conditions

When it's raining or the road is wet, leave at least double the normal stopping distance between you and the vehicle in front. If you're following a vehicle at a safe distance and another vehicle pulls into the gap you've left, drop back until you're at a safe distance again. See section 4, Safety margins, for more information on stopping distances.

If visibility is poor during the day, such as when it's raining or misty, use dipped headlights to help other road users see you. If visibility becomes seriously reduced, you **MUST** use dipped headlights. 'Seriously reduced' means you can't see for more than about 100 metres (328 feet).

HC r226 **DES** s12

When there's been heavy rainfall, a ford is likely to flood and become difficult to cross. There may be a depth gauge to help you decide whether you should go through. If you decide to cross it,

- use a low gear
- drive through slowly
- test your brakes afterwards: wet brakes are less effective.

HC r121 **DES** s12

243

Fog

When visibility is seriously reduced, you **MUST** use headlights and you may also use fog lights if you have them.

Remember to switch off your fog lights when conditions improve. Never use front or rear fog lights unless visibility is seriously reduced because

- they can dazzle other road users
- road users behind you won't be able to see your brake lights clearly
- road users behind you may mistake your fog lights for brake lights and slow unnecessarily
- road users behind you may mistake your brake lights for fog lights and not react in time to stop safely.

It's hard to see what's happening ahead in foggy weather, so always keep your speed down. Increase your distance from the vehicle in front in case it stops or slows suddenly.

HC r114, 126, 226 **DES** s12

Always allow more time for your journey in bad weather.

When driving on motorways in fog, reflective studs help you to see the road ahead.

- Red studs mark the left-hand edge of the carriageway.
- Amber studs mark the central reservation.

For more details, see section 9, Motorway driving.

HC r132 **DES** s6

If you're parking on the road in foggy conditions, leave the parking lights on.

Very bad weather

In very bad weather, such as heavy snow or thick fog, don't travel unless your journey is essential. If you must travel, take great care and allow plenty of time.

Before you start your journey, make sure

- your lights are working
- your windows are clean.

HC **r228–235** **DES** **s12**

In deep snow, it's a good idea to fit chains to your wheels to help grip and prevent skidding.

When you're on the road, keep well back from the vehicle in front in case it stops suddenly. In icy conditions your stopping distance can be 10 times what it would be in dry conditions.

 If the road looks wet and your tyres are making hardly any noise, you could be on black ice. Keep your speed down and use the highest gear possible to reduce the risk of skidding.

 See this website for winter driving advice.

motoringassist.com/winter

Windy weather

Windy weather can affect all vehicles, but high-sided vehicles, cyclists, motorcyclists and cars towing caravans are likely to be the worst affected: a sudden gust can blow them off course. Look out for these vehicles, particularly when they're

- passing a large vehicle on a dual carriageway or motorway
- driving on exposed stretches of road
- passing gaps between buildings or hedges.

HC r232 **DES** s11, 12

▷ Driving at night

When you're driving at night, you need to think about how clearly you can see and be seen, as well as how your lights might affect other road users.

Make sure that your headlights don't dazzle the vehicle you're following or any oncoming traffic. If you're dazzled by the headlights of an oncoming vehicle, slow down or stop if necessary.

HC r114–115 **DES** s13

If you meet other road users at night, including cyclists and pedestrians, dip your headlights so that you don't dazzle them.

When you overtake at night, you can't see a long way ahead and there may be bends in the road or other unseen hazards.

On a motorway, use

- dipped headlights, even if the road is well lit
- sidelights if you've broken down and are parked on the hard shoulder. This will help other road users to see you.

DES s11, 15

Keeping control of your vehicle

You need to have full control of your vehicle at all times. Driving with the clutch down or in neutral for any length of time (called coasting) reduces your control of the car, especially steering and braking. This is particularly dangerous when you're travelling downhill, as your vehicle will speed up when there's no **engine braking**.

HC r122 **DES** s5, 7

Definition

engine braking
using the engine's resistance to help slow the vehicle

You can use your vehicle's engine to help control your speed: for example, if you select a lower gear when you're driving down a steep hill, the engine will act as a brake. This helps avoid your brakes overheating and becoming less effective.

When you're driving up a steep hill, the engine has to work harder. If you take your foot off the accelerator to reduce speed, you'll slow down sooner than usual. Changing down to a lower gear will help prevent the engine struggling as it delivers the power needed to climb the hill.

DES s7

On single-track roads, be aware of the limited space available. If you see a vehicle coming towards you, pull into (or opposite) a passing place.

HC r155

See the Don't Risk It website for advice on driving on country roads.

➡ **dontriskit.info/country-roads**

Always match your driving to the road and weather conditions. Your stopping distance will be affected by several factors, including

- your speed
- the condition of your tyres
- the road surface
- the weather.

DES s10

In wet or icy conditions, try to avoid skidding: it can be hard to get your car back under control once you've started skidding. If you don't have anti-lock brakes and your vehicle begins to skid when you're braking on a wet road,

- release the footbrake
- if the rear wheels begin to skid, steer into the skid by turning the steering wheel in the same direction.

HC r119 **DES** s5

> Traffic calming and road surfaces

Traffic calming is used to slow traffic and make the roads safer for vulnerable road users, especially pedestrians. One of the most common measures is road humps (sometimes called speed humps). Make sure that you stay within the speed limit and don't overtake other moving vehicles within traffic-calmed areas.

HC r153 **DES** s6

Rumble devices (raised markings across the road) may be used to warn you of a hazard, such as a roundabout, and to encourage you to reduce your speed.

KYTS p68, 75

In cities where trams operate, the areas used by the trams may have a different surface texture or colour, which may be edged with white line markings.

HC r300 **KYTS** p31

If it rains after a long dry hot spell, the road surface can become unusually slippery. Loose chippings can also increase the risk of skidding, so slow down and be aware of the increased skid risk in these conditions.

HC r237 **DES** s12

Meeting the standards

You must be able to

use the accelerator smoothly to reach and keep to a suitable speed

change gear smoothly and in good time

coordinate the use of gears with braking and acceleration

steer the vehicle safely and responsibly in all road and traffic conditions.

You must know and understand

why it's best not to over-rev your engine when moving away and while stationary

the benefits of changing gear at the right time when going up and down hills

that different vehicles may have different numbers of gears with different ratios

how to keep control of the steering wheel.

Notes

You can use this page to make your own notes or diagrams about the key points you need to remember.

Think about

- By how much must visibility be reduced before you can use fog lights?
- Why must you make sure that your fog lights are turned off when visibility improves again?
- In which weather conditions should you increase the distance between your vehicle and the one in front?
- Which road users are most likely to be affected by very windy weather?
- When can you use engine braking, and why is it a good idea?
- What are rumble devices used for?

Your notes

Things to discuss and practise with your instructor

These are just a few examples of what you could discuss and practise with your instructor. Read more about road conditions and vehicle handling to come up with your own ideas.

Discuss with your instructor

- your stopping distances in different weather conditions
- when you may use your front fog lights
- the purpose of speed humps and how you should behave on the roads where they're found.

Practise with your instructor

- going out at night to get used to driving with reduced visibility
- using your brakes in heavy rain
- your gear selection and clutch control while driving downhill.

In which THREE of these situations may you overtake another vehicle on the left?

☐ When you are in a one-way street

☐ When approaching a motorway slip road where you will be turning off

☐ When the vehicle in front is signalling to turn right

☐ When a slower vehicle is travelling in the right-hand lane of a dual carriageway

☐ In slow-moving traffic queues when traffic in the right-hand lane is moving more slowly

At certain times of the day, traffic might be heavy. If traffic is moving slowly in queues and vehicles in the right-hand lane are moving more slowly, you may overtake on the left. Don't keep changing lanes to try and beat the queue.

You are travelling in very heavy rain. Your overall stopping distance is likely to be

☐ doubled

☐ halved

☐ up to ten times greater

☐ no different

As well as visibility being reduced, the road will be extremely wet. This will reduce the grip the tyres have on the road and increase the distance it takes to stop. Double your separation distance.

Which TWO of the following are correct? When overtaking at night you should

☐ wait until a bend so that you can see the oncoming headlights

☐ sound your horn twice before moving out

☐ be careful because you can see less

☐ beware of bends in the road ahead

☐ put headlights on full beam

Only overtake the vehicle in front if it's really necessary. At night the risks are increased due to the poor visibility. Don't overtake if there's a possibility of

- road junctions
- bends ahead
- the brow of a bridge or hill, except on a dual carriageway
- pedestrian crossings
- double white lines ahead
- vehicles changing direction
- any other potential hazard.

8.4
Mark one answer — DES s6, HC r174, KYTS p67

When may you wait in a box junction?

☐ When you are stationary in a queue of traffic

☐ When approaching a pelican crossing

☐ When approaching a zebra crossing

☐ When oncoming traffic prevents you turning right

The purpose of a box junction is to keep the junction clear by preventing vehicles from stopping in the path of crossing traffic.

You must not enter a box junction unless your exit is clear. But, you may enter the box and wait if you want to turn right and are only prevented from doing so by oncoming traffic.

8.5
Mark one answer — HC p109, KYTS p72

Which of these plates normally appear with this road sign?

☐ Humps for ½ mile

☐ Hump Bridge

☐ Low Bridge

☐ Soft Verge

Road humps are used to slow down the traffic. They are found in places where there are often pedestrians, such as

- in shopping areas
- near schools
- in residential areas.

Watch out for people close to the kerb or crossing the road.

8.6
Mark one answer — DES s6, HC r153

Traffic calming measures are used to

☐ stop road rage

☐ help overtaking

☐ slow traffic down

☐ help parking

Traffic calming measures are used to make the roads safer for vulnerable road users, such as cyclists, pedestrians and children. These can be designed as chicanes, road humps or other obstacles that encourage drivers and riders to slow down.

You are on a motorway in fog. The left-hand edge of the motorway can be identified by reflective studs. What colour are they?

☐ Green
☐ Amber
☐ Red
☐ White

Be especially careful if you're on a motorway in fog. Reflective studs are used to help you in poor visibility. Different colours are used so that you'll know which lane you are in. These are

• red on the left-hand side of the road
• white between lanes
• amber on the right-hand edge of the carriageway
• green between the carriageway and slip roads.

A rumble device is designed to

☐ give directions
☐ prevent cattle escaping
☐ alert you to low tyre pressure
☐ alert you to a hazard
☐ encourage you to reduce speed

A rumble device usually consists of raised markings or strips across the road. It gives an audible, visual and tactile warning of a hazard. These strips are found in places where traffic has constantly ignored warning or restriction signs. They are there for a good reason. Slow down and be ready to deal with a hazard.

You have to make a journey in foggy conditions. You should

☐ follow other vehicles' tail lights closely
☐ avoid using dipped headlights
☐ leave plenty of time for your journey
☐ keep two seconds behind other vehicles

If you're planning to make a journey when it's foggy, listen to the weather reports on the radio or television. Don't travel if visibility is very poor or your trip isn't necessary.

If you do travel, leave plenty of time for your journey. If someone is expecting you at the other end, let them know that you'll be taking longer than normal to arrive.

8.10 Mark one answer DES s13, HC r114–115

You are overtaking a car at night. You must be sure that

☐ you flash your headlights before overtaking

☐ you select a higher gear

☐ you have switched your lights to full beam before overtaking

☐ you do not dazzle other road users

To prevent your lights from dazzling the driver of the car in front, wait until you've overtaken before switching to full beam.

8.11 Mark one answer HC r153

You are on a road which has speed humps. A driver in front is travelling slower than you. You should

☐ sound your horn

☐ overtake as soon as you can

☐ flash your headlights

☐ slow down and stay behind

Be patient and stay behind the car in front. Normally you should not overtake other vehicles in traffic-calmed areas. If you overtake here your speed may exceed that which is safe along that road, defeating the purpose of the traffic calming measures.

8.12 Mark one answer KYTS p68

You see these markings on the road. Why are they there?

☐ To show a safe distance between vehicles

☐ To keep the area clear of traffic

☐ To make you aware of your speed

☐ To warn you to change direction

These lines may be painted on the road on the approach to a roundabout, village or a particular hazard. The lines are raised and painted yellow and their purpose is to make you aware of your speed. Reduce your speed in good time so that you avoid having to brake harshly over the last few metres before reaching the junction.

Areas reserved for trams may have

☐ metal studs around them

☐ white line markings

☐ zigzag markings

☐ a different coloured surface

☐ yellow hatch markings

☐ a different surface texture

Trams can run on roads used by other vehicles and pedestrians. The part of the road used by the trams is known as the reserved area and this should be kept clear. It has a coloured surface and is usually edged with white road markings. It might also have different surface texture.

You see a vehicle coming towards you on a single-track road. You should

☐ go back to the main road

☐ do an emergency stop

☐ stop at a passing place

☐ put on your hazard warning lights

You must take extra care when on single track roads. You may not be able to see around bends due to high hedges or fences. Proceed with caution and expect to meet oncoming vehicles around the next bend. If you do, pull into or opposite a passing place.

The road is wet. Why might a motorcyclist steer round drain covers on a bend?

☐ To avoid puncturing the tyres on the edge of the drain covers

☐ To prevent the motorcycle sliding on the metal drain covers

☐ To help judge the bend using the drain covers as marker points

☐ To avoid splashing pedestrians on the pavement

Other drivers or riders may have to change course due to the size or characteristics of their vehicle. Understanding this will help you to anticipate their actions. Motorcyclists and cyclists will be checking the road ahead for uneven or slippery surfaces, especially in wet weather. They may need to move across their lane to avoid surface hazards such as potholes and drain covers.

8.16

Mark one answer

DES s12, HC r121

After this hazard you should test your brakes. Why is this?

☐ You will be on a slippery road

☐ Your brakes will be soaking wet

☐ You will be going down a long hill

☐ You will have just crossed a long bridge

A ford is a crossing over a stream that's shallow enough to go through. After you've gone through a ford or deep puddle the water will affect your brakes. To dry them out apply a light brake pressure while moving slowly. Don't travel at normal speeds until you are sure your brakes are working properly again.

8.17

Mark one answer

DES s6, HC r234

Why should you always reduce your speed when travelling in fog?

☐ The brakes do not work as well

☐ You will be dazzled by other headlights

☐ The engine will take longer to warm up

☐ It is more difficult to see events ahead

You won't be able to see as far ahead in fog as you can on a clear day. You will need to reduce your speed so that, if a hazard looms out of the fog, you have the time and space to take avoiding action.

Travelling in fog is hazardous. If you can, try and delay your journey until it has cleared.

8.18

Mark two answers

DES s7

Hills can affect the performance of your vehicle. Which TWO apply when driving up steep hills?

☐ Higher gears will pull better

☐ You will slow down sooner

☐ Overtaking will be easier

☐ The engine will work harder

☐ The steering will feel heavier

The engine will need more power to pull the vehicle up the hill. When approaching a steep hill you should select a lower gear to help maintain your speed. You should do this without hesitation, so that you don't lose too much speed before engaging the lower gear.

Mark one answer

You are driving on the motorway in windy conditions. When passing high-sided vehicles you should

☐ increase your speed

☐ be wary of a sudden gust

☐ drive alongside very closely

☐ expect normal conditions

The draught caused by other vehicles could be strong enough to push you out of your lane. Keep both hands on the steering wheel to maintain full control.

Mark one answer

To correct a rear-wheel skid you should

☐ not steer at all

☐ steer away from it

☐ steer into it

☐ apply your handbrake

Prevention is better than cure, so it's important that you take every precaution to avoid a skid from starting.

If you feel the rear wheels of your vehicle beginning to skid, try to steer in the same direction to recover control. Don't brake suddenly – this will only make the situation worse.

Mark one answer

You are driving in fog. Why should you keep well back from the vehicle in front?

☐ In case it changes direction suddenly

☐ In case its fog lights dazzle you

☐ In case it stops suddenly

☐ In case its brake lights dazzle you

If you're following another road user in fog stay well back. The driver in front won't be able to see hazards until they're close and might brake suddenly. Another reason why it is important to maintain a good separation distance in fog is that the road surface is likely to be wet and slippery.

Mark one answer

You have to park on the road in fog. You should

☐ leave sidelights on

☐ leave dipped headlights and fog lights on

☐ leave dipped headlights on

☐ leave main beam headlights on

If you have to park your vehicle in foggy conditions it's important that it can be seen by other road users. Try to find a place to park off the road. If this isn't possible leave it facing in the same direction as the traffic. Make sure that your lights are clean and that you leave your sidelights on.

8.23

Mark one answer

DES s13, HC r115

You are travelling at night. You are dazzled by headlights coming towards you. You should

☐ pull down your sun visor

☐ slow down or stop

☐ switch on your main beam headlights

☐ put your hand over your eyes

You will have additional hazards to deal with at night. Visibility may be very limited and the lights of oncoming vehicles can often dazzle you. When this happens don't close your eyes, swerve or flash your headlights, as this will also distract other drivers. It may help to focus on the left kerb, verge or lane line.

8.24

Mark one answer

DES s12, HC r114, 226

Front fog lights may be used ONLY if

☐ visibility is seriously reduced

☐ they are fitted above the bumper

☐ they are not as bright as the headlights

☐ an audible warning device is used

Your vehicle should have a warning light on the dashboard which illuminates when the fog lights are being used. You need to be familiar with the layout of your dashboard so you are aware if they have been switched on in error, or you have forgotten to switch them off.

8.25

Mark one answer

DES s12, HC r114, 226

You are driving with your front fog lights switched on. Earlier fog has now cleared. What should you do?

Switch off your fog lights if the weather improves, but be prepared to use them again if visibility reduces to less than 100 metres (328 feet).

☐ Leave them on if other drivers have their lights on

☐ Switch them off as long as visibility remains good

☐ Flash them to warn oncoming traffic that it is foggy

☐ Drive with them on instead of your headlights

You forget to switch off your rear fog lights when the fog has cleared. This may

☐ dazzle other road users

☐ reduce battery life

☐ cause brake lights to be less clear

☐ be breaking the law

☐ seriously affect engine power

Don't forget to switch off your fog lights when the weather improves. You could be prosecuted for driving with them on in good visibility. The high intensity of the rear fog lights can look like brake lights, and on a high speed road this can cause other road users to brake unnecessarily.

Front fog lights should be used

☐ when visibility is reduced to 100 metres (328 feet)

☐ as a warning to oncoming traffic

☐ when driving during the hours of darkness

☐ in any conditions and at any time

When visibility is seriously reduced, switch on your fog lights if you have them fitted. It is essential not only that you can see ahead, but also that other road users are able to see you.

Using rear fog lights in clear daylight will

☐ be useful when towing a trailer

☐ give extra protection

☐ dazzle other drivers

☐ make following drivers keep back

Rear fog lights shine brighter than normal rear lights so that they show up in reduced visibility. When the weather is clear they could dazzle the driver behind, so switch them off.

Chains can be fitted to your wheels to help prevent

☐ damage to the road surface

☐ wear to the tyres

☐ skidding in deep snow

☐ the brakes locking

Snow chains can be fitted to your tyres during snowy conditions. They can help you to move off from rest or to keep moving in deep snow. You will still need to adjust your driving according to the road conditions at the time.

8.30 Mark one answer DES s5, 7

How can you use the engine of your vehicle to control your speed?

☐ By changing to a lower gear

☐ By selecting reverse gear

☐ By changing to a higher gear

☐ By selecting neutral

You should brake and slow down before selecting a lower gear. The gear can then be used to keep the speed low and help you control the vehicle. This is particularly helpful on long downhill stretches, where brake fade can occur if the brakes overheat.

8.31 Mark one answer DES s5, HC r122

Why could keeping the clutch down or selecting neutral for long periods of time be dangerous?

☐ Fuel spillage will occur

☐ Engine damage may be caused

☐ You will have less steering and braking control

☐ It will wear tyres out more quickly

Letting your vehicle roll or coast in neutral reduces your control over steering and braking. This can be dangerous on downhill slopes where your vehicle could pick up speed very quickly.

8.32 Mark one answer DES s12, HC r230

You are driving on an icy road. What distance should you drive from the car in front?

☐ four times the normal distance

☐ six times the normal distance

☐ eight times the normal distance

☐ ten times the normal distance

Don't travel in icy or snowy weather unless your journey is necessary.

Drive extremely carefully when roads are or may be icy. Stopping distances can be ten times greater than on dry roads.

Mark one answer DES s11

You are on a well-lit motorway at night. You must

☐ use only your sidelights

☐ always use your headlights

☐ always use rear fog lights

☐ use headlights only in bad weather

If you're driving on a motorway at night or in poor visibility, you must always use your headlights, even if the road is well-lit. The other road users in front must be able to see you in their mirrors.

Mark one answer DES s11

You are on a motorway at night with other vehicles just ahead of you. Which lights should you have on?

☐ Front fog lights

☐ Main beam headlights

☐ Sidelights only

☐ Dipped headlights

If you're driving behind other traffic at night on the motorway, leave a two-second time gap and use dipped headlights. Full beam will dazzle the other drivers. Your headlights' beam should fall short of the vehicle in front.

Mark three answers DES s7, HC r126

Which THREE of the following will affect your stopping distance?

☐ How fast you are going

☐ The tyres on your vehicle

☐ The time of day

☐ The weather

☐ The street lighting

There are several factors that can affect the distance it takes to stop your vehicle.

Adjust your driving to take account of how the weather conditions could affect your tyres' grip on the road.

Mark one answer DES s11, 15

You are on a motorway at night. You MUST have your headlights switched on unless

☐ there are vehicles close in front of you

☐ you are travelling below 50 mph

☐ the motorway is lit

☐ your vehicle is broken down on the hard shoulder

Always use your headlights at night on a motorway unless you have stopped on the hard shoulder. If you break down and have to stop on the hard shoulder, switch off the headlights but leave the sidelights on so that other road users can see your vehicle.

8.37 — Mark one answer — DES s5, 7

You will feel the effects of engine braking when you

☐ only use the handbrake

☐ only use neutral

☐ change to a lower gear

☐ change to a higher gear

When going downhill, prolonged use of the brakes can cause them to overheat and lose their effectiveness. Changing to a lower gear will assist your braking.

8.38 — Mark one answer — DES s11, 15, HC r115

Daytime visibility is poor but not seriously reduced. You should switch on

☐ headlights and fog lights

☐ front fog lights

☐ dipped headlights

☐ rear fog lights

Only use your fog lights when visibility is seriously reduced. Use dipped headlights in poor conditions.

8.39 — Mark one answer — DES s12

Why are vehicles fitted with rear fog lights?

☐ To be seen when driving at high speed

☐ To use if broken down in a dangerous position

☐ To make them more visible in thick fog

☐ To warn drivers following closely to drop back

Rear fog lights make it easier to spot a vehicle ahead in foggy conditions. Avoid the temptation to use other vehicles' lights as a guide, as they may give you a false sense of security.

8.40 — Mark one answer — DES s12, HC r114, 226

While you are driving in fog, it becomes necessary to use front fog lights. You should

☐ only turn them on in heavy traffic conditions

☐ remember not to use them on motorways

☐ only use them on dual carriageways

☐ remember to switch them off as visibility improves

It is an offence to have your fog lights on in conditions other than seriously reduced visibility, ie less than 100 metres (328 feet).

Mark one answer DES s12, HC r228

When snow is falling heavily you should

☐ only drive with your hazard lights on

☐ not drive unless you have a mobile phone

☐ only drive when your journey is short

☐ not drive unless it is essential

Consider if the increased risk is worth it. If the weather conditions are bad and your journey isn't essential, then stay at home.

Mark one answer DES s7

You are driving down a long steep hill. You suddenly notice your brakes are not working as well as normal. What is the usual cause of this?

☐ The brakes overheating

☐ Air in the brake fluid

☐ Oil on the brakes

☐ Badly adjusted brakes

This is more likely to happen on vehicles fitted with drum brakes but can apply to disc brakes as well. Using a lower gear will assist the braking and help you to keep control of your vehicle.

Mark two answers DES s12

You have to make a journey in fog. What are the TWO most important things you should do before you set out?

☐ Top up the radiator with anti-freeze

☐ Make sure that you have a warning triangle in the vehicle

☐ Check that your lights are working

☐ Check the battery

☐ Make sure that the windows are clean

Don't drive in fog unless you really have to. Adjust your driving to the conditions. You should always be able to pull up within the distance you can see ahead.

Mark one answer DES s12, HC r114, 226

You have just driven out of fog. Visibility is now good. You MUST

☐ switch off all your fog lights

☐ keep your rear fog lights on

☐ keep your front fog lights on

☐ leave fog lights on in case fog returns

You MUST turn off your fog lights if visibility is over 100 metres (328 feet). However, be prepared for the fact that the fog may be patchy.

8.45   Mark two answers   DES s12, HC r114, 226

Why is it dangerous to leave rear fog lights on when they are not needed?

☐ Brake lights are less clear

☐ Following drivers can be dazzled

☐ Electrical systems could be overloaded

☐ Direction indicators may not work properly

☐ The battery could fail

If your rear fog lights are left on when it isn't foggy, the glare they cause makes it difficult for road users behind to know whether you are braking or you have just forgotten to turn off your rear fog lights. This can be a particular problem on wet roads and on motorways. If you leave your rear fog lights on at night, road users behind you are likely to be dazzled and this could put them at risk.

8.46   Mark one answer   DES s5, HC r122

Holding the clutch pedal down or rolling in neutral for too long while driving will

☐ use more fuel

☐ cause the engine to overheat

☐ reduce your control

☐ improve tyre wear

Holding the clutch down or staying in neutral for too long will cause your vehicle to freewheel. This is known as 'coasting' and it is dangerous as it reduces your control of the vehicle.

8.47   Mark one answer   DES s5, HC r122

You are driving down a steep hill. Why could keeping the clutch down or rolling in neutral for too long be dangerous?

☐ Fuel consumption will be higher

☐ Your vehicle will pick up speed

☐ It will damage the engine

☐ It will wear tyres out more quickly

Driving in neutral or with the clutch down for long periods is known as 'coasting'. There will be no engine braking and your vehicle will pick up speed on downhill slopes. Coasting can be very dangerous because it reduces steering and braking control.

8.48   Mark two answers   DES s5, HC r122

What are TWO main reasons why coasting downhill is wrong?

☐ Fuel consumption will be higher

☐ The vehicle will get faster

☐ It puts more wear and tear on the tyres

☐ You have less braking and steering control

☐ It damages the engine

Coasting is when you allow the vehicle to freewheel in neutral or with the clutch pedal depressed. Doing this gives you less control over the vehicle. It's especially important not to let your vehicle coast when approaching hazards such as junctions and bends and when travelling downhill.

Which FOUR of the following may apply when dealing with this hazard?

During the winter the stream is likely to flood. It is also possible that in extremely cold weather it could ice over. Assess the situation carefully before you drive through. If you drive a vehicle with low suspension you may have to find a different route.

☐ It could be more difficult in winter

☐ Use a low gear and drive slowly

☐ Use a high gear to prevent wheelspin

☐ Test your brakes afterwards

☐ Always switch on fog lamps

☐ There may be a depth gauge

Why is travelling in neutral for long distances (known as coasting) wrong?

☐ It will cause the car to skid

☐ It will make the engine stall

☐ The engine will run faster

☐ There is no engine braking

Try to look ahead and read the road. Plan your approach to junctions and select the correct gear in good time. This will give you the control you need to deal with any hazards that occur.

You'll coast a little every time you change gear. This can't be avoided, but it should be kept to a minimum.

When MUST you use dipped headlights during the day?

☐ All the time

☐ Along narrow streets

☐ In poor visibility

☐ When parking

You MUST use dipped headlights and/or fog lights in fog when visibility is seriously reduced to 100 metres (328 feet) or less.

You should use dipped headlights, but NOT fog lights, when visibility is poor, such as in heavy rain.

Mark one answer

You are braking on a wet road. Your vehicle begins to skid. It does not have anti-lock brakes. What is the FIRST thing you should do?

☐ Quickly pull up the handbrake

☐ Release the footbrake

☐ Push harder on the brake pedal

☐ Gently use the accelerator

If the skid has been caused by braking too hard for the conditions, release the brake. You may then need to reapply and release the brake again. You may need to do this a number of times. This will allow the wheels to turn and so limit the skid. Skids are much easier to get into than they are to get out of. Prevention is better than cure. Stay alert to the road and weather conditions. Drive so that you can stop within the distance you can see to be clear.

Section eight Questions

Case study practice – 8 Road conditions and vehicle handling

Alan is driving in very thick fog and the road surface is also rather damp.

Alan is using fog lights as well as headlights.

He leaves a larger gap than normal between himself and the vehicle in front.

Later, a gutter drain is being unblocked and the pumping vehicle is obstructing the road on Alan's side.

Still further on, there are rumble devices on approach to a roundabout.

8.1 How might the road condition affect Alan's stopping distance?

Mark one answer

☐ It may be improved
☐ It could be doubled
☐ It remains unaffected
☐ It should be halved

DES s12

8.2 Why would Alan be using his fog lights?

Mark one answer

- ☐ Visibility is below 100 metres
- ☐ Visibility is below 150 metres
- ☐ Visibility is below 200 metres
- ☐ Visibility is below 250 metres

HC r226 DES s12

8.3 Why would Alan leave a larger gap between vehicles?

Mark one answer

- ☐ His vehicle may need to stop suddenly
- ☐ The other vehicle's lights may dazzle him
- ☐ The other vehicle may stop suddenly
- ☐ His vehicle's lights might cause glare

HC r235 DES s12

8.4 What should Alan do before overtaking the pumping vehicle?

Mark one answer

- ☐ Use the horn and drive past quickly
- ☐ Wait until the vehicle stops work
- ☐ Pass slowly with hazard lights on
- ☐ Wait until the road ahead is clear

HC r163 DES s7

8.5 What information would these devices provide, to help Alan?

Mark one answer

- ☐ A routine test of his car's suspension
- ☐ A caution to check his tyre pressures
- ☐ A reminder to make him aware of speed
- ☐ A warning about the road surface condition

DES s6 KYTS p75

> **Section nine**
Motorway driving

In this section, you'll learn about

- ⊘ how to drive safely on motorways
- ⊘ the speed limits that apply on motorways and how they're used to avoid congestion
- ⊘ the markings used on motorway lanes
- ⊘ what to do if your car breaks down on the motorway.

Motorway driving

Motorways are designed to help traffic travel at constant, higher speeds than single carriageways. Due to the traffic's speed, situations on motorways can change more quickly than on other roads, so you need to be especially alert at all times.

Check your vehicle thoroughly before starting a long motorway journey. Driving at high speeds for long periods of time may increase the risk of your vehicle breaking down. See section 3, Safety and your vehicle, for more information about what to check.

DES s11

As a learner you can't drive a car or ride a motorcycle on the motorway but you can drive or ride on dual carriageways.

HC r253

Pedestrians and horse riders can't use a motorway. The following vehicles can't be used on a motorway

- bicycles
- motorcycles under 50 cc
- most powered wheelchairs/mobility scooters
- agricultural vehicles
- some slow-moving vehicles.

HC r253

❯ Driving on the motorway

When you join the motorway,

- use the slip road to adjust your speed to match the traffic already on the motorway
- give way to traffic already on the motorway.

HC r259 **DES** s11

All traffic, whatever its speed, should normally use the left-hand lane of the motorway. Use the middle and right-hand lanes only for overtaking other vehicles and return to the left lane when you've finished overtaking.

HC r264, 267 **DES** s11

You should normally only overtake on the right. However, you may overtake on the left if traffic is moving slowly in queues and the queue on your right is moving more slowly than the one you're in.

HC r268 **DES** s11

Where the motorway goes uphill steeply, there may be a separate lane for slow-moving vehicles. This helps the faster-moving traffic to flow more easily.

HC r139 **DES** s11

If you're travelling in the left-hand lane and traffic is joining from a slip road, move to another lane if you're able to do so safely. This helps the flow of traffic joining the motorway, especially at peak times.

DES s11

Countdown markers on the left-hand verge show that you're approaching the next exit. If you want to leave the motorway, try to get into the left-hand lane in plenty of time. If you accidentally go past the exit you wanted, carry on to the next one. Never try to stop and reverse.

HC r272 **DES** s11

Improve your motorway driving by watching the Highways Agency's 'Stay safe keep moving' playlist on YouTube.

> **youtube.com/HighwaysAgency**

⊙ Speed limits

The national speed limit for cars and motorcycles on a motorway is 70 mph (112 km/h). This limit applies to all lanes. Obey any signs showing a lower speed limit.

HC r261, p40 **DES** s11

A vehicle towing a trailer

* is restricted to a lower speed limit of 60 mph (96 km/h)
* isn't allowed to travel in the right-hand lane of a motorway with three or more lanes, unless there are lane closures
* in Northern Ireland shouldn't use the right-hand lane of a three-lane motorway.

You can use your hazard lights to warn traffic behind you that the traffic ahead is slowing down or stopping suddenly. Switch them off as soon as following traffic has reacted to your signal.

HC r116 **DES** s11

When you're approaching roadworks, watch for lower speed limits, especially if there's a contraflow system. You should

* obey all speed limits
* keep a safe distance from the vehicle ahead.

HC r289–290 **DES** s11

See section 4, Safety margins, for more information about contraflow systems.

⊙ Reducing congestion

Active traffic management (ATM), also known as 'managed motorways', tries to reduce congestion and make journey times more reliable. Where this is in use, **mandatory speed limit** signs will show on the gantries. The speed limit helps to keep the traffic speed constant so that traffic is less likely to bunch up and journey times can be improved.

DES s18

Definition

mandatory speed limit
the maximum speed at which you may travel

In ATM areas, the hard shoulder is sometimes used as a normal traffic lane. You'll know when you can use this because a speed limit sign will be shown above all lanes, including the hard shoulder. A red cross showing above the hard shoulder means that you shouldn't travel in this lane and it should be used only in an emergency or breakdown.

Emergency refuge areas have been built in these areas for use in cases of emergency or breakdown.

Find out more about ATM here.

> **highways.gov.uk/our-road-network/managing-our-roads/improving-our-network/managed-motorways**

Highways Agency traffic officers operate on most motorways and some 'A' class roads throughout England. They

- can stop and direct anyone on a motorway or an 'A' road
- answer motorway emergency telephones, which are linked to Highways Agency control centres in some areas.

HC r105, 108 **DES** s18

> Lane markings

Reflective studs help you to see where you are on the carriageway, especially at night or in fog. Different colours are used in different places.

HC r132 **DES** s11

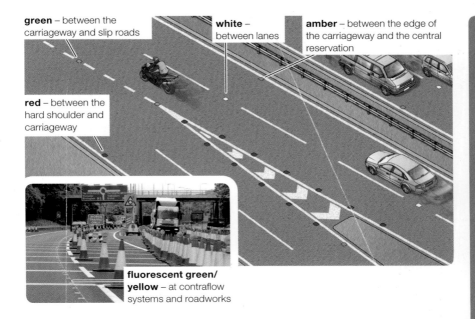

green – between the carriageway and slip roads

white – between lanes

amber – between the edge of the carriageway and the central reservation

red – between the hard shoulder and carriageway

fluorescent green/ yellow – at contraflow systems and roadworks

▶ Stopping and breakdowns

Motorways are designed to keep traffic moving, so you mustn't stop on the motorway unless you have to.

Only stop on the motorway

- if flashing red lights show above every lane
- when told to do so by the police, Vehicle and Operator Services Agency (VOSA) officers or Highways Agency traffic officers
- in a traffic jam
- in an emergency or breakdown.

Move over if signals on the overhead gantries advise you to do so.

HC r258, 270 **DES** s11 **KYTS** p90

Should you need to stop for any other reason, such as to have a rest, make a phone call or look at a map, either leave at the next exit or go to a service area.

HC r270 **DES** s11

If your vehicle breaks down or a tyre has a puncture, try to get onto the hard shoulder and call for help. If you can, use one of the emergency telephones. These are

- normally at one-mile intervals. Marker posts at 100-metre intervals point you in the direction of the nearest phone
- connected directly to Highways Agency control. They'll be able to find you easily.

HC r275 **DES** s15

When you're using an emergency phone, stand facing the oncoming traffic so that you can see any hazards approaching – for example, the draught from a large vehicle driving past could take you by surprise.

If you decide to use your mobile phone,

- make a note of your location (the number on the nearest marker post) before you make the call
- give this information to the emergency services.

HC r275 **DES** s15

Having parked your car on the hard shoulder,

- switch on your hazard lights to warn other drivers that you've broken down
- switch on the sidelights at night or if visibility is poor
- don't open the offside doors (those nearest the carriageway)
- you and your passengers should leave the vehicle by the nearside doors, away from the traffic
- wait on the embankment near your vehicle, but away from the hard shoulder, in case another vehicle crashes into yours.

DES s15

When you're ready to return to the carriageway, wait for a safe gap in the traffic and then drive along the hard shoulder to gain speed before moving out onto the main carriageway.

HC r276 **DES** s15

If you can't get onto the hard shoulder when you break down,

- switch on your hazard warning lights
- leave your vehicle only when you can get off the carriageway safely.

HC r277 **DES** s15

Meeting the standards

You must be able to

join a motorway or dual carriageway safely and responsibly from the left or the right

allow for other road users joining or leaving the motorway

change lanes safely and responsibly.

You must know and understand

that you mustn't stop on a motorway except in an emergency

that you mustn't

* pick anybody up on a motorway
* set anybody down on a motorway
* walk on a motorway, except in an emergency

the need to look well ahead for other road users joining or leaving the motorway or for queuing traffic

that some stretches of motorway may have

* local, active traffic management (sometimes called managed motorways)
* control systems installed, which will change speed limits and the direction of flow in particular lanes

You must obey the instructions given by these systems.

> Notes

You can use this page to make your own notes or diagrams about the key points you need to remember.

Think about

- At what speed should you be driving when you join the motorway?
- What should you do if you miss the exit that you want to take off the motorway?
- What information do the marker posts give you?
- What should you do if your car breaks down on the motorway?

Your notes

Things to discuss and practise with your instructor

These are just a few examples of what you could discuss and practise with your instructor. Read more about motorway driving to come up with your own ideas.

Discuss with your instructor

- how you should join the motorway and what to look out for as you do so
- the different national speed limits for various vehicles on the motorway, and in which lanes they may travel
- what you should do if you break down on the motorway
- what ATM stands for and its purpose on the motorway.

Practise with your instructor

Until you hold a full driving licence you won't be able to drive on the motorway, so practising your driving there won't be possible. Instead, practise with your instructor

- on a dual carriageway, as some of the techniques are the same as driving on the motorway, eg joining from a slip road, lane discipline and driving at higher speeds
- identifying motorway signs, signals and road markings from *Know Your Traffic Signs* and *The Official Highway Code.*

Mark one answer DES s11, HC r259

When joining a motorway you must always

☐ use the hard shoulder

☐ stop at the end of the acceleration lane

☐ come to a stop before joining the motorway

☐ give way to traffic already on the motorway

You should give way to traffic already on the motorway. Where possible they may move over to let you in but don't force your way into the traffic stream. The traffic may be travelling at high speed so you should match your speed to fit in.

9.2 **Mark one answer** HC r261, p40

What is the national speed limit on motorways for cars and motorcycles?

☐ 30 mph

☐ 50 mph

☐ 60 mph

☐ 70 mph

Travelling at the national speed limit doesn't allow you to hog the right-hand lane. Always use the left-hand lane whenever possible. When leaving a motorway get into the left-hand lane well before your exit. Reduce your speed on the slip road and look out for sharp bends or curves and traffic queuing at roundabouts.

9.3 **Mark one answer** DES s11

The left-hand lane on a three-lane motorway is for use by

☐ any vehicle

☐ large vehicles only

☐ emergency vehicles only

☐ slow vehicles only

On a motorway all traffic should use the left-hand lane unless overtaking. Use the centre or right-hand lanes if you need to overtake. If you're overtaking a number of slower vehicles move back to the left-hand lane when you're safely past. Check your mirrors frequently and don't stay in the middle or right-hand lane if the left-hand lane is free.

9.4 **Mark one answer** DES s11

Which of these IS NOT allowed to travel in the right-hand lane of a three-lane motorway?

☐ A small delivery van

☐ A motorcycle

☐ A vehicle towing a trailer

☐ A motorcycle and sidecar

A vehicle with a trailer is restricted to 60 mph. For this reason it isn't allowed in the right-hand lane as it might hold up the faster-moving traffic that wishes to overtake in that lane.

9.5 | Mark one answer | DES s15, HC r275

You break down on a motorway. You need to call for help. Why may it be better to use an emergency roadside telephone rather than a mobile phone?

☐ It connects you to a local garage

☐ Using a mobile phone will distract other drivers

☐ It allows easy location by the emergency services

☐ Mobile phones do not work on motorways

On a motorway it is best to use a roadside emergency telephone so that the emergency services are able to locate you easily. The nearest telephone is shown by an arrow on marker posts at the edge of the hard shoulder. If you use a mobile, they will need to know your exact location. Before you call, find out the number on the nearest marker post. This number will identify your exact location.

9.6 | Mark one answer | DES s11, HC r276

After a breakdown you need to rejoin the main carriageway of a motorway from the hard shoulder. You should

☐ move out onto the carriageway then build up your speed

☐ move out onto the carriageway using your hazard lights

☐ gain speed on the hard shoulder before moving out onto the carriageway

☐ wait on the hard shoulder until someone flashes their headlights at you

Wait for a safe gap in the traffic before you move out. Indicate your intention and use the hard shoulder to gain speed but don't force your way into the traffic.

9.7 | Mark one answer | DES s11

A crawler lane on a motorway is found

☐ on a steep gradient

☐ before a service area

☐ before a junction

☐ along the hard shoulder

Slow-moving, large vehicles might slow down the progress of other traffic. On a steep gradient this extra lane is provided for these slow-moving vehicles to allow the faster-moving traffic to flow more easily.

What do these motorway signs show?

The exit from a motorway is indicated by countdown markers. These are positioned 90 metres (100 yards) apart, the first being 270 metres (300 yards) from the start of the slip road. Move into the left-hand lane well before you reach the start of the slip road.

☐ They are countdown markers to a bridge

☐ They are distance markers to the next telephone

☐ They are countdown markers to the next exit

☐ They warn of a police control ahead

On a motorway the amber reflective studs can be found between

☐ the hard shoulder and the carriageway

☐ the acceleration lane and the carriageway

☐ the central reservation and the carriageway

☐ each pair of the lanes

On motorways reflective studs are located into the road to help you in the dark and in conditions of poor visibility. Amber-coloured studs are found on the right-hand edge of the main carriageway, next to the central reservation.

What colour are the reflective studs between the lanes on a motorway?

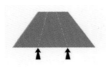

White studs are found between the lanes on motorways. The light from your headlights is reflected back and this is especially useful in bad weather, when visibility is restricted.

☐ Green

☐ Amber

☐ White

☐ Red

9.11
Mark one answer
DES s11, HC r132

What colour are the reflective studs between a motorway and its slip road?

☐ Amber

☐ White

☐ Green

☐ Red

The studs between the carriageway and the hard shoulder are normally red. These change to green where there is a slip road. They will help you identify slip roads when visibility is poor or when it is dark.

9.12
Mark one answer
DES s15, HC r275

You have broken down on a motorway. To find the nearest emergency telephone you should always walk

☐ with the traffic flow

☐ facing oncoming traffic

☐ in the direction shown on the marker posts

☐ in the direction of the nearest exit

Along the hard shoulder there are marker posts at 100-metre intervals. These will direct you to the nearest emergency telephone.

9.13
Mark one answer
DES s15, HC r275

How should you use the emergency telephone on a motorway?

☐ Stay close to the carriageway

☐ Face the oncoming traffic

☐ Keep your back to the traffic

☐ Stand on the hard shoulder

Traffic is passing you at speed. If the draught from a large lorry catches you by surprise it could blow you off balance and even onto the carriageway. By facing the oncoming traffic you can see approaching lorries and so be prepared for their draught. You are also in a position to see other hazards approaching.

9.14
Mark one answer
DES s11, HC r132

You are on a motorway. What colour are the reflective studs on the left of the carriageway?

☐ Green

☐ Red

☐ White

☐ Amber

Red studs are placed between the edge of the carriageway and the hard shoulder. Where slip roads leave or join the motorway the studs are green.

283

On a three-lane motorway which lane should you normally use?

☐ Left

☐ Right

☐ Centre

☐ Either the right or centre

On a three-lane motorway you should travel in the left-hand lane unless you're overtaking. This applies regardless of the speed at which you're travelling.

When going through a contraflow system on a motorway you should

☐ ensure that you do not exceed 30 mph

☐ keep a good distance from the vehicle ahead

☐ switch lanes to keep the traffic flowing

☐ stay close to the vehicle ahead to reduce queues

There's likely to be a speed restriction in force. Keep to this. Don't

• switch lanes

• get too close to traffic in front of you.

Be aware there will be no permanent barrier between you and the oncoming traffic.

You are on a three-lane motorway. There are red reflective studs on your left and white ones to your right. Where are you?

☐ In the right-hand lane

☐ In the middle lane

☐ On the hard shoulder

☐ In the left-hand lane

The colours of the reflective studs on the motorway and their locations are

• red – between the hard shoulder and the carriageway

• white – lane markings

• amber – between the edge of the carriageway and the central reservation

• green – along slip road exits and entrances

• bright green/yellow – roadworks and contraflow systems.

9.18 — Mark one answer — DES s11, HC r288

You are approaching roadworks on a motorway. What should you do?

☐ Speed up to clear the area quickly

☐ Always use the hard shoulder

☐ Obey all speed limits

☐ Stay very close to the vehicle in front

Collisions can often happen at roadworks. Be aware of the speed limits, slow down in good time and keep your distance from the vehicle in front.

9.19 — Mark four answers — HC r253

Which FOUR of these must NOT use motorways?

☐ Learner car drivers

☐ Motorcycles over 50cc

☐ Double-deck buses

☐ Farm tractors

☐ Horse riders

☐ Cyclists

In addition, motorways MUST NOT be used by pedestrians, motorcycles under 50 cc, certain slow-moving vehicles without permission, and invalid carriages weighing less than 254 kg (560 lbs).

9.20 — Mark four answers — HC r253

Which FOUR of these must NOT use motorways?

☐ Learner car drivers

☐ Motorcycles over 50cc

☐ Double-deck buses

☐ Farm tractors

☐ Learner motorcyclists

☐ Cyclists

Learner car drivers and motorcyclists are not allowed on the motorway until they have passed their practical test.

Motorways have rules that you need to know before you venture out for the first time. When you've passed your practical test it's a good idea to have some lessons on motorways. Check with your instructor about this.

9.21 — Mark one answer — DES s11, HC r265

What is the right-hand lane used for on a three-lane motorway?

☐ Emergency vehicles only

☐ Overtaking

☐ Vehicles towing trailers

☐ Coaches only

You should keep to the left and only use the right-hand lane if you're passing slower-moving traffic.

What should you use the hard shoulder of a motorway for?

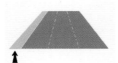

Don't use the hard shoulder for stopping unless it is an emergency. If you want to stop for any other reason go to the next exit or service station.

☐ Stopping in an emergency
☐ Leaving the motorway
☐ Stopping when you are tired
☐ Joining the motorway

You are in the right-hand lane on a motorway. You see these overhead signs. This means

You MUST obey this sign. There might not be any visible signs of a problem ahead. However, there might be queuing traffic or another hazard which you cannot yet see.

☐ move to the left and reduce your speed to 50 mph
☐ there are roadworks 50 metres (55 yards) ahead
☐ use the hard shoulder until you have passed the hazard
☐ leave the motorway at the next exit

You are allowed to stop on a motorway when you

☐ need to walk and get fresh air
☐ wish to pick up hitchhikers
☐ are told to do so by flashing red lights
☐ need to use a mobile telephone

You MUST stop if there are red lights flashing above every lane on the motorway. However, if any of the other lanes do not show flashing red lights or red cross you may move into that lane and continue if it is safe to do so.

9.25 — Mark one answer — DES s11

You are travelling along the left-hand lane of a three-lane motorway. Traffic is joining from a slip road. You should

- ☐ race the other vehicles
- ☐ move to another lane
- ☐ maintain a steady speed
- ☐ switch on your hazard flashers

You should move to another lane if it is safe to do so. This can greatly assist the flow of traffic joining the motorway, especially at peak times.

9.26 — Mark one answer — DES s11, HC r264

A basic rule when on motorways is

- ☐ use the lane that has least traffic
- ☐ keep to the left-hand lane unless overtaking
- ☐ overtake on the side that is clearest
- ☐ try to keep above 50 mph to prevent congestion

You should normally travel in the left-hand lane unless you are overtaking a slower-moving vehicle. When you are past that vehicle move back into the left-hand lane as soon as it's safe to do so. Don't cut across in front of the vehicle that you're overtaking.

9.27 — Mark one answer — DES s11, HC r268

On motorways you should never overtake on the left unless

- ☐ you can see well ahead that the hard shoulder is clear
- ☐ the traffic in the right-hand lane is signalling right
- ☐ you warn drivers behind by signalling left
- ☐ there is a queue of slow-moving traffic to your right that is moving more slowly than you are

Only overtake on the left if traffic is moving slowly in queues and the traffic on your right is moving more slowly than the traffic in your lane.

9.28 — NI EXEMPT — Mark one answer — HC r275, 280

Motorway emergency telephones are usually linked to the police. In some areas they are now linked to

- ☐ the Highways Agency Control Centre
- ☐ the Driver Vehicle Licensing Agency
- ☐ the Driving Standards Agency
- ☐ the local Vehicle Registration Office

In some areas motorway telephones are now linked to a Highways Agency Control Centre, instead of the police. Highways Agency Traffic Officers work in partnership with the police and assist at motorway emergencies and incidents. They are recognised by a high-visibility orange and yellow jacket and high-visibility vehicle with yellow and black chequered markings.

An Emergency Refuge Area is an area

☐ on a motorway for use in cases of emergency or breakdown

☐ for use if you think you will be involved in a road rage incident

☐ on a motorway for a police patrol to park and watch traffic

☐ for construction and road workers to store emergency equipment

Emergency Refuge Areas may be found at the side of the hard shoulder about 500 metres apart. If you break down you should use them rather than the hard shoulder if you are able. When rejoining the motorway you must remember to take extra care especially when the hard shoulder is being used as a running lane within an Active Traffic Management area. Try to match your speed to that of traffic in the lane you are joining.

Highways Agency Traffic Officers

☐ will not be able to assist at a breakdown or emergency

☐ are not able to stop and direct anyone on a motorway

☐ will tow a broken-down vehicle and its passengers home

☐ are able to stop and direct anyone on a motorway

Highways Agency Traffic Officers (HATOs) are able to stop and direct traffic on most motorways and some 'A' class roads. They work in partnership with the police at motorway incidents and provide a highly trained and visible service. Their role is to help keep traffic moving and make your journey as safe and reliable as possible. They are recognised by an orange and yellow jacket and their vehicle has yellow and black markings.

You are on a motorway. A red cross is displayed above the hard shoulder. What does this mean?

Active Traffic Management schemes are being introduced on motorways. Within these areas at certain times the hard shoulder will be used as a running lane. A red cross above the hard shoulder shows that this lane should NOT be used, except for emergencies and breakdowns.

☐ Pull up in this lane to answer your mobile phone

☐ Use this lane as a running lane

☐ This lane can be used if you need a rest

☐ You should not travel in this lane

9.32 NI EXEMPT Mark one answer DES s18, HC r269

You are on a motorway in an Active Traffic Management (ATM) area. A mandatory speed limit is displayed above the hard shoulder. What does this mean?

A mandatory speed limit sign above the hard shoulder shows that it can be used as a running lane between junctions. You must stay within the speed limit. Look out for vehicles that may have broken down and could be blocking the hard shoulder.

☐ You should not travel in this lane

☐ The hard shoulder can be used as a running lane

☐ You can park on the hard shoulder if you feel tired

☐ You can pull up in this lane to answer a mobile phone

9.33 NI EXEMPT Mark one answer DES s18

The aim of an Active Traffic Management scheme on a motorway is to

☐ prevent overtaking

☐ reduce rest stops

☐ prevent tailgating

☐ reduce congestion

Active Traffic Management schemes are intended to reduce congestion and make journey times more reliable. In these areas the hard shoulder may be used as a running lane to ease congestion at peak times or in the event of an incident. It may appear that you could travel faster for a short distance, but keeping traffic flow at a constant speed may improve your journey time.

9.34 NI EXEMPT Mark one answer DES s18, HC r269

You are in an Active Traffic Management area on a motorway. When the Actively Managed mode is operating

☐ speed limits are only advisory

☐ the national speed limit will apply

☐ the speed limit is always 30 mph

☐ all speed limit signals are set

When an Active Traffic Management (ATM) scheme is operating on a motorway you MUST follow the mandatory instructions shown on the gantries above each lane. This includes the hard shoulder.

Why can it be an advantage for traffic speed to stay constant over a longer distance?

☐ You will do more stop-start driving

☐ You will use far more fuel

☐ You will be able to use more direct routes

☐ Your overall journey time will normally improve

When traffic travels at a constant speed over a longer distance, journey times normally improve. You may feel that you could travel faster for short periods but this won't generally improve your overall journey time. Signs will show the maximum speed at which you should travel.

You should not normally travel on the hard shoulder of a motorway. When can you use it?

☐ When taking the next exit

☐ When traffic is stopped

☐ When signs direct you to

☐ When traffic is slow moving

Normally you should only use the hard shoulder for emergencies and breakdowns, and at roadworks when signs direct you to do so. Active Traffic Management (ATM) areas are being introduced to ease traffic congestion. In these areas the hard shoulder may be used as a running lane when speed limit signs are shown directly above.

On a motorway what is used to reduce traffic bunching?

☐ Variable speed limits

☐ Contraflow systems

☐ National speed limits

☐ Lane closures

Congestion can be reduced by keeping traffic at a constant speed. At busy times maximum speed limits are displayed on overhead gantries. These can be varied quickly depending on the amount of traffic. By keeping to a constant speed on busy sections of motorway overall journey times are normally improved.

When should you stop on a motorway?

☐ If you have to read a map

☐ When you are tired and need a rest

☐ If red lights show above every lane

☐ When told to by the police

☐ If your mobile phone rings

☐ When signalled by a Highways Agency Traffic Officer

There are some occasions when you may have to stop on the carriageway of a motorway. These include when being signalled by the police or a Highways Agency Traffic Officer, when flashing red lights show above every lane and in traffic jams.

9.39 | Mark one answer | DES s11, HC r270

When may you stop on a motorway?

☐ If you have to read a map

☐ When you are tired and need a rest

☐ If your mobile phone rings

☐ In an emergency or breakdown

You should not normally stop on a motorway but there may be occasions when you need to do so. If you are unfortunate enough to break down make every effort to pull up on the hard shoulder.

9.40 | NI EXEMPT | Mark one answer | HC r261, p40

You are travelling on a motorway. Unless signs show a lower speed limit you must NOT exceed

☐ 50 mph

☐ 60 mph

☐ 70 mph

☐ 80 mph

The national speed limit for a car or motorcycle on the motorway is 70 mph. Lower speed limits may be in force, for example at roadworks, so look out for the signs. Variable speed limits operate in some areas to control very busy stretches of motorway. The speed limit may change depending on the volume of traffic.

9.41 | Mark one answer | DES s11, HC r270

You are on a motorway. There are red flashing lights above every lane. You must

☐ pull onto the hard shoulder

☐ slow down and watch for further signals

☐ leave at the next exit

☐ stop and wait

Red flashing lights above every lane mean you must not go on any further. You'll also see a red cross illuminated. Stop and wait. Don't

• change lanes

• continue

• pull onto the hard shoulder (unless in an emergency).

You are on a three-lane motorway. A red cross is shown above the hard shoulder and mandatory speed limits above all other lanes. This means

A red cross above the hard shoulder shows it is closed as a running lane and should only be used for emergencies or breakdowns. At busy times within an Active Traffic Management (ATM) area the hard shoulder may be used as a running lane. This will be shown by a mandatory speed limit on the gantry above.

☐ the hard shoulder can be used as a rest area if you feel tired

☐ the hard shoulder is for emergency or breakdown use only

☐ the hard shoulder can be used as a normal running lane

☐ the hard shoulder has a speed limit of 50 mph

You are on a three-lane motorway and see this sign. It means you can use

Mandatory speed limit signs above all lanes including the hard shoulder, show that you are in an Active Traffic Management (ATM) area. In this case you can use the hard shoulder as a running lane. You must stay within the speed limit shown. Look out for any vehicles that may have broken down and be blocking the hard shoulder.

☐ any lane except the hard shoulder

☐ the hard shoulder only

☐ the three right hand lanes only

☐ all the lanes including the hard shoulder

9.44 | **Mark one answer** | DES s11, HC r91

You are travelling on a motorway. You decide you need a rest. You should

☐ stop on the hard shoulder

☐ pull in at the nearest service area

☐ pull up on a slip road

☐ park on the central reservation

If you feel tired stop at the nearest service area. If it's too far away leave the motorway at the next exit and find a safe place to stop. You must not stop on the carriageway or hard shoulder of a motorway except in an emergency, in a traffic queue, when signalled to do so by a police or enforcement officer, or by traffic signals. Plan your journey so that you have regular rest stops.

9.45 | **Mark one answer** | DES s19, HC p40

You are towing a trailer on a motorway. What is your maximum speed limit?

☐ 40 mph

☐ 50 mph

☐ 60 mph

☐ 70 mph

Don't forget that you're towing a trailer. If you're towing a small, light trailer, it won't reduce your vehicle's performance by very much. However, strong winds or buffeting from large vehicles might cause the trailer to snake from side to side. Be aware of your speed and don't exceed the lower limit imposed.

9.46 | **Mark one answer** | DES s11, HC r264

The left-hand lane of a motorway should be used for

☐ breakdowns and emergencies only

☐ overtaking slower traffic in the other lanes

☐ slow vehicles only

☐ normal driving

You should keep to the left-hand lane whenever possible. Only use the other lanes for overtaking or when directed by signals. Using other lanes when the left-hand lane is empty can frustrate drivers behind you.

You are driving on a motorway. You have to slow down quickly due to a hazard. You should

☐ switch on your hazard lights

☐ switch on your headlights

☐ sound your horn

☐ flash your headlights

Using your hazard lights, as well as brake lights, will give following traffic an extra warning of the problem ahead. Only use them for long enough to ensure that your warning has been seen.

You get a puncture on the motorway. You manage to get your vehicle onto the hard shoulder. You should

☐ change the wheel yourself immediately

☐ use the emergency telephone and call for assistance

☐ try to wave down another vehicle for help

☐ only change the wheel if you have a passenger to help you

Due to the danger from passing traffic you should park as far to the left as you can and leave the vehicle by the nearside door.

Do not attempt even simple repairs. Instead walk to an emergency telephone on your side of the road and phone for assistance. While waiting for assistance to arrive wait near your car, keeping well away from the carriageway and hard shoulder.

You are driving on a motorway. By mistake, you go past the exit that you wanted to take. You should

☐ carefully reverse on the hard shoulder

☐ carry on to the next exit

☐ carefully reverse in the left-hand lane

☐ make a U-turn at the next gap in the central reservation

It is against the law to reverse, cross the central reservation or drive against the traffic flow on a motorway. If you have missed your exit ask yourself if your concentration is fading. It could be that you need to take a rest break before completing your journey.

Your vehicle has broken down on a motorway. You are not able to stop on the hard shoulder. What should you do?

☐ Switch on your hazard warning lights

☐ Stop following traffic and ask for help

☐ Attempt to repair your vehicle quickly

☐ Stand behind your vehicle to warn others

If you can't get your vehicle onto the hard shoulder, use your hazard warning lights to warn others. Leave your vehicle only when you can safely get clear of the carriageway. Do not try to repair the vehicle or attempt to place any warning device on the carriageway.

9.51 **Mark one answer** DES s11

Why is it particularly important to carry out a check on your vehicle before making a long motorway journey?

☐ You will have to do more harsh braking on motorways

☐ Motorway service stations do not deal with breakdowns

☐ The road surface will wear down the tyres faster

☐ Continuous high speeds may increase the risk of your vehicle breaking down

Before you start your journey make sure that your vehicle can cope with the demands of high-speed driving. You should check a number of things, the main ones being oil, water and tyres. You also need to plan rest stops if you're going a long way.

9.52 **Mark one answer** DES s11, HC r116

You are driving on a motorway. The car ahead shows its hazard lights for a short time. This tells you that

☐ the driver wants you to overtake

☐ the other car is going to change lanes

☐ traffic ahead is slowing or stopping suddenly

☐ there is a police speed check ahead

If the vehicle in front shows its hazard lights there may be an incident or queuing traffic ahead. As well as keeping a safe distance, look beyond it to help you get an early warning of any hazards and a picture of the situation ahead.

9.53 **Mark one answer** DES s11, HC r272

You are intending to leave the motorway at the next exit. Before you reach the exit you should normally position your vehicle

☐ in the middle lane

☐ in the left-hand lane

☐ on the hard shoulder

☐ in any lane

You'll see the first advance direction sign one mile from the exit. If you're travelling at 60 mph in the right-hand lane you'll only have about 50 seconds before you reach the countdown markers. There will be another sign at the half-mile point. Move into the left-hand lane in good time. Don't cut across traffic at the last moment and don't risk missing your exit.

Mark one answer

As a provisional licence holder you should not drive a car

☐ over 30 mph

☐ at night

☐ on the motorway

☐ with passengers in rear seats

When you've passed your practical test ask your instructor to take you for a lesson on the motorway. You'll need to get used to the speed of traffic and how to deal with multiple lanes. The Pass Plus scheme has been created for new drivers, and includes motorway driving. Ask your ADI for details.

Mark one answer

Your vehicle breaks down on the hard shoulder of a motorway. You decide to use your mobile phone to call for help. You should

☐ stand at the rear of the vehicle while making the call

☐ try to repair the vehicle yourself

☐ get out of the vehicle by the right-hand door

☐ check your location from the marker posts on the left

The emergency services need to know your exact location so they can reach you as quickly as possible. Look for a number on the nearest marker post beside the hard shoulder. Give this number when you call the emergency services as it will help them to locate you. Be ready to describe where you are, for example, by reference to the last junction or service station you passed.

You are on a three-lane motorway towing a trailer. You may use the right-hand lane when

☐ there are lane closures

☐ there is slow moving traffic

☐ you can maintain a high speed

☐ large vehicles are in the left and centre lanes

If you are towing a caravan or trailer you must not use the right-hand lane on a motorway with three or more lanes, except in certain circumstances, such as lane closures.

You are on a motorway. There is a contraflow system ahead. What would you expect to find?

☐ Temporary traffic lights

☐ Lower speed limits

☐ Wider lanes than normal

☐ Speed humps

When approaching a contraflow system reduce speed in good time and obey all speed limits. You may be travelling in a narrower lane than normal with no permanent barrier between you and the oncoming traffic. Be aware that the hard shoulder may be used for traffic and the road ahead could be obstructed by slow-moving or broken down vehicles.

On a motorway you may only stop on the hard shoulder

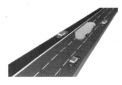

☐ in an emergency

☐ if you feel tired and need to rest

☐ if you miss the exit that you wanted

☐ to pick up a hitchhiker

You should only stop on the hard shoulder in a genuine emergency. DON'T stop on it to have a rest or picnic, pick up hitchhikers, answer a mobile phone or check a map. If you miss your intended exit carry on to the next, never reverse along the hard shoulder.

Section nine Questions

Case study practice – 9 Motorway driving

Beverley is towing a small trailer behind her car and is joining the motorway from a slip road. The motorway is busy with morning traffic.

Further along the motorway, the central reservation barrier is coned off for repair. Lanes have been narrowed for some distance, using cones and temporary reflective studs.

Once past the roadworks, traffic speeds up and the left-hand lane becomes clear.

Beverley then realises she has gone past the exit she needs.

9.1 Who has priority at this motorway/slip road junction?

Mark **one** answer

- [ ] Vehicles already travelling in the left-hand lane
- [ ] Vehicles joining the motorway from the slip road
- [ ] Vehicles travelling along on the hard shoulder
- [ ] Vehicles leaving the motorway via the slip road

`HC` `r259` `DES` `s11`

9.2 What colour would these studs be?

Mark **one** answer

☐ Yellow/blue
☐ Yellow/red
☐ Yellow/green
☐ Yellow/orange

HC r132 **DES** s11

9.3 What lane should Beverley be using after the roadworks?

Mark **one** answer

☐ The middle lane
☐ The right-hand lane
☐ The hard shoulder
☐ The left-hand lane

HC r264 **DES** s11

9.4 What's the national motorway speed limit for Beverley's vehicle and trailer?

Mark **one** answer

☐ 50 mph
☐ 60 mph
☐ 70 mph
☐ 80 mph

HC p40 **DES** s19

9.5 What should Beverley do about leaving the motorway?

Mark **one** answer

☐ Continue on until she reaches the next exit
☐ Reverse back to the exit she's just missed
☐ Go on till she reaches the end of the motorway
☐ Wait on the hard shoulder for traffic officers

HC r272 **DES** s11

Rules of the road

In this section, you'll learn about

- the speed limits that you need to obey
- how to use junctions and lanes safely
- rules about overtaking and reversing
- driving over pedestrian crossings and level crossings
- where you can stop and park safely and legally.

Rules of the road

It's important that everyone knows and follows the rules of the road. Some are legal requirements and some are recommended best practice, but they all help to make the roads safer.

❯ Speed limits

You **MUST NOT** drive faster than the speed limit for the road you're on or your vehicle type. Where no other limit is shown, the national speed limit for cars and motorcycles is

- 60 mph (96 km/h) on a single carriageway road
- 70 mph (112 km/h) on a dual carriageway or motorway.

There are lower speed limits for these vehicles when towing a trailer or caravan

- 50 mph (80 km/h) on a single carriageway road
- 60 mph (96 km/h) on a dual carriageway or motorway.

HC r124, p40

Where there are street lights, there's normally a 30 mph (48 km/h) speed limit for all vehicles unless signs show otherwise.

HC r124, p40

On some roads you may see a sign showing a minimum speed limit. You should travel above the limit shown on the sign unless it's not safe to do so.

HC p107

Speed limits

Type of vehicle	Built-up areas* mph (km/h)	Single carriage-ways mph (km/h)	Dual carriage-ways mph (km/h)	Motorways mph (km/h)
Cars and motorcycles (including car-derived vans up to 2 tonnes maximum laden weight)	30 (48)	60 (96)	70 (112)	70 (112)
Cars towing caravans or trailers (including car-derived vans and motorcycles)	30 (48)	50 (80)	60 (96)	60 (96)
Buses, coaches and minibuses (not exceeding 12 metres in overall length)	30 (48)	50 (80)	60 (96)	70 (112)
Goods vehicles (not exceeding 7.5 tonnes maximum laden weight)	30 (48)	50 (80)	60 (96)	70† (112)
Goods vehicles (exceeding 7.5 tonnes maximum laden weight)	30 (48)	40 (64)	50 (80)	60 (96)

* The 30 mph limit usually applies to all traffic on all roads with street lighting unless signs show otherwise.
† 60 mph (96 km/h) if articulated or towing a trailer.

Be aware that large vehicles may have speed limiters – buses and coaches are restricted to 62 mph and large goods vehicles to 56 mph.

Always drive with care and take account of the road and weather conditions. If you're driving along a street where cars are parked, keep your speed down and beware of

pedestrians (especially children) stepping out from behind parked vehicles

vehicles pulling out

drivers' doors opening.

HC r152 **DES** s10

At roadworks, there may be temporary speed limits to slow traffic down. These are mandatory speed limits and may be enforced by cameras.

HC r288 **KYTS** p90

The Think! road safety website has more advice on speed and speed limits.

❯ http://think.direct.gov.uk/ speed.html

> Lanes and junctions

Some roads have lanes reserved for specific vehicles such as cycles, buses or trams. These are marked by signs and road markings, and should only be used by those vehicles during the lanes' hours of operation, unless signs indicate otherwise.

HC r141

Never drive or park in a cycle lane marked by a solid white line during its hours of operation. Don't drive or park in a cycle lane marked by a broken line unless it's unavoidable.

HC r140–141 **KYTS** p32–36

You should only drive over a footpath when it's necessary in order to reach a property.

HC r145

On a dual carriageway, the right-hand lane is only for turning right or overtaking. The same rule applies to three-lane dual carriageways.

If you want to turn right onto a dual carriageway that has a central reservation that's too narrow to fit the length of your vehicle, wait until the road is clear in both directions before you emerge. If you emerge into the central reservation but your vehicle is too long, it could obstruct traffic coming from your right.

HC r173 **DES** s8

Always be careful at junctions. As you approach a junction, move into the correct position in plenty of time.

When you're turning left, keep well to the left as you approach the junction. In slow-moving traffic, remember to check for cyclists to your left before you turn.

HC r181–183 **DES** s8

If you're on a busy road and you find you're travelling in the wrong direction, or you're in the wrong lane at a busy junction, keep going until you can find somewhere safe, such as a quiet side road, where you can turn around.

HC r200 **DES** s9

A box junction is marked by yellow hatched lines, and should be kept clear. Only enter it if your exit road is clear – otherwise, wait on your side of the junction. You can, however, wait in the box if you want to turn right and are waiting for a gap in the oncoming traffic before you can turn.

HC r174 **DES** s6

If something is blocking your side of the road, such as a parked car, you should give way to oncoming traffic if there isn't room for you both to continue safely.

DES s7

Crossroads

If you're turning right at a crossroads when an oncoming driver is also turning right, it's normally safer to keep the other vehicle to your right and turn behind it. If you have to pass in front of the other vehicle, take extra care as your view may be blocked.

HC r181

At crossroads where there aren't any signs or markings, no-one has priority. Check very carefully in all directions before you drive into the junction.

HC r146 **DES** s8

Roundabouts

Roundabouts are designed to help traffic flow smoothly. Follow signs and road markings as you approach and drive around them. Normally, if you're going straight ahead,

- don't signal as you approach
- signal left just after you pass the exit before the one you want.

HC r185–186 **DES** s8

Some vehicles may not follow the normal rules.

- Cyclists and horse riders may stay in the left-hand lane even if they're turning right.
- Long vehicles may take up a different position to stop the rear of the vehicle hitting the kerb.

HC r187

> Overtaking

Overtaking is dangerous. Ask yourself if you really need to do it, and never overtake if you're in any doubt as to whether it's safe.

HC r163 **DES** s7

You should normally overtake other vehicles on the right, but in a one-way street you can pass slower traffic on the left. Take extra care if you're overtaking on a dual carriageway, as the right-hand lane can also be used by traffic turning right.

HC r137–138 **DES** s7

At night, if a vehicle overtakes you, dip your headlights as soon as it passes you otherwise your lights could dazzle the other driver.

HC r115

> Reversing

Never reverse

- for longer than you have to
- from a side road into a main road.

HC r200–203 **DES** s9

When reversing into a side road, always check road and traffic conditions in all directions. You can undo your seat belt while reversing if it helps you to get a better view. You **MUST** refasten the belt once you've completed the manoeuvre.

If you're not sure whether it's safe, get out and check before you start to reverse. The front of your vehicle swings out as you turn and this may create a hazard for passing traffic.

> Pedestrian crossings

If someone is standing on the pavement waiting to cross at a zebra crossing, stop and let them cross if it's safe to do so.

Pelican crossings are controlled by traffic lights. When the red light changes to flashing amber, wait for any pedestrians to finish crossing before you move off.

On toucan crossings, cyclists are allowed to cycle across at the same time as pedestrians.

HC r195–199 **DES** s7 **KYTS** p124

For more information on pedestrian crossings, see section 6, Vulnerable road users.

> Level crossings

A level crossing is where a railway line crosses the road.

It may have countdown markers to warn you if the crossing is hidden, such as around a bend.

Controlled crossings have traffic light signals with twin flashing red lights, plus a warning alarm for pedestrians.

  Crossings may or may not have barriers.

If this happens ...	you should do this
 The warning lights come on as you're approaching the crossing.	Stop. You **MUST** obey the red lights, by law.
 You're already on the crossing when the warning lights come on or a bell rings.	Keep going and clear the crossing.
 You're waiting at a level crossing and a train has passed but the red lights keep flashing.	You **MUST** wait: there may be another train coming.

HC r293, p109 **DES** s6 **KYTS** p26–29

Some types of level crossing don't have lights. These include crossings with user-operated gates or barriers, and open crossings. Be careful at all level crossings.

HC r295–299 **DES** s7

See the Network Rail guide to using level crossings safely.

⊘ **networkrail.co.uk/level-crossings**

⊘ Stopping and parking

Always think carefully about where you stop and park your car, to make sure it's safe and legal.

At night, the safest place to park your vehicle is in your garage, if you have one. If you're away from home, try to find a secure car park or park in a well-lit area.

HC r239, p131 **DES** s9

If you have to park on a road at night, you **MUST** leave your parking lights on if the speed limit on that road is over 30 mph (48 km/h). You should normally park on the left-hand side of the road so that other road users can see your reflectors, but in a one-way street you can park on either side.

HC r248–250 **DES** s13

You **MUST NOT** stop on a **clearway**. On an urban clearway, you may stop only to drop off and pick up passengers. On a road marked with double white lines (even where one of the lines is broken), you may stop only to drop off and pick up passengers or to load/unload goods.

HC r240 **DES** s6

 Definition

clearway
a stretch of road or street where stopping isn't allowed

Don't park where you would cause a danger or get in the way of other road users, such as

- on or near the brow of a hill
- at a bus stop
- opposite a traffic island
- in front of someone else's drive
- near a school entrance
- opposite or within 10 metres (32 feet) of a junction (in Northern Ireland, within 15 metres or 48 feet of a junction), unless there's an authorised parking space.

HC r242–243

You also need to make sure that you don't cause an obstruction by stopping or parking where there are restrictions shown by signs and yellow lines. In a controlled parking zone, you'll have to pay to park. Make sure you park within marked bays on the days and times shown on the zone entry signs.

HC r238, 245 **DES** s6 **KYTS** p39–50

Controlled ZONE

Mon - Fri
8.30 am - 6.30 pm
Saturday
8.30 am - 1.30 pm

Only park in a disabled parking space if you, or your passenger, are a disabled badge holder. Remember to display the badge when you leave the vehicle.

KYTS p45

By law, you **MUST** stop
- if you're involved in a road traffic incident
- at a red traffic light
- when signalled to do so by a police officer, traffic warden, Vehicle and Operator Services Agency (VOSA) officer, Highways Agency traffic officer or school crossing patrol.

HC r105, 109, 286

Meeting the standards

You must be able to

apply a safe, systematic procedure to safely and responsibly negotiate

- junctions
- roundabouts
- crossings

turn left and right and go ahead safely and responsibly

emerge safely and responsibly into streams of traffic

cross the path of traffic safely when turning right.

You must know and understand

the rules that apply to particular junctions and roundabouts. For example, priority rules

the rules about

- merging into a stream of traffic
- crossing the path of an approaching stream of traffic
- all types of pedestrian crossing
- train and tram crossings

how to work out the speed limit where you can't see speed-limit signs.

> Notes

You can use this page to make your own notes or diagrams about the key points you need to remember.

Think about

- Where might you see a minimum speed limit sign?
- When can you drive in a bus lane?
- What's a box junction? What mustn't you do at one of these junctions?
- When are you allowed to undo your seat belt while driving?
- If you've just driven onto a level crossing and the warning lights start flashing, what should you do?
- How close to a junction are you allowed to park?

Your notes

Things to discuss and practise with your instructor

These are just a few examples of what you could discuss and practise with your instructor. Read more about the rules of the road to come up with your own ideas.

Discuss with your instructor

- what the 'national speed limit applies' sign looks like. What does this mean in mph on different roads and for different vehicles?
- what the speed limit will usually be if there are street lights along the road
- what the different lanes are used for on
  - a two-lane dual carriageway
  - a three-lane dual carriageway
  - a motorway.

Practise with your instructor

- roundabouts with several lanes on approach
- driving in areas with changing speed limits
- entering, exiting and overtaking on busy dual carriageways.

10.1

Mark one answer

HC p106, KYTS p20

What is the meaning of this sign?

This sign doesn't tell you the speed limit in figures. You should know the speed limit for the type of road that you're on. Study your copy of The Highway Code.

- ☐ Local speed limit applies
- ☐ No waiting on the carriageway
- ☐ National speed limit applies
- ☐ No entry to vehicular traffic

10.2

Mark one answer

HC p40

What is the national speed limit for cars and motorcycles on a dual carriageway?

- ☐ 30 mph
- ☐ 50 mph
- ☐ 60 mph
- ☐ 70 mph

Ensure that you know the speed limit for the road that you're on. The speed limit on a dual carriageway or motorway is 70 mph for cars and motorcycles, unless there are signs to indicate otherwise. The speed limits for different types of vehicle are listed in The Highway Code.

10.3

Mark one answer

HC r124

There are no speed limit signs on the road. How is a 30 mph limit indicated?

- ☐ By hazard warning lines
- ☐ By street lighting
- ☐ By pedestrian islands
- ☐ By double or single yellow lines

There is usually a 30 mph speed limit where there are street lights unless there are signs showing another limit.

10.4

Mark one answer

HC r124

Where you see street lights but no speed limit signs the limit is usually

- ☐ 30 mph
- ☐ 40 mph
- ☐ 50 mph
- ☐ 60 mph

The presence of street lights generally shows that there is a 30 mph speed limit, unless signs tell you otherwise.

10.5 Mark one answer KYTS p21

What does this sign mean?

A red slash through this sign indicates that the restriction has ended. In this case the restriction was a minimum speed limit of 30 mph.

☐ Minimum speed 30 mph

☐ End of maximum speed

☐ End of minimum speed

☐ Maximum speed 30 mph

10.6 Mark one answer DES s7, HC r163

There is a tractor ahead of you. You wish to overtake but you are NOT sure if it is safe to do so. You should

☐ follow another overtaking vehicle through

☐ sound your horn to the slow vehicle to pull over

☐ speed through but flash your lights to oncoming traffic

☐ not overtake if you are in doubt

Never overtake if you're not sure whether it's safe. Can you see far enough down the road to ensure that you can complete the manoeuvre safely? If the answer is no, DON'T GO.

10.7 Mark three answers HC r187

Which three of the following are most likely to take an unusual course at roundabouts?

☐ Horse riders

☐ Milk floats

☐ Delivery vans

☐ Long vehicles

☐ Estate cars

☐ Cyclists

Long vehicles might have to take a slightly different position when approaching the roundabout or going around it. This is to stop the rear of the vehicle cutting in and mounting the kerb.

Horse riders and cyclists might stay in the left-hand lane although they are turning right. Be aware of this and allow them room.

On a clearway you must not stop

☐ at any time

☐ when it is busy

☐ in the rush hour

☐ during daylight hours

Clearways are in place so that traffic can flow without the obstruction of parked vehicles. Just one parked vehicle will cause an obstruction for all other traffic. You MUST NOT stop where a clearway is in force, not even to pick up or set down passengers.

What is the meaning of this sign?

☐ No entry

☐ Waiting restrictions

☐ National speed limit

☐ School crossing patrol

This sign indicates that there are waiting restrictions. It is normally accompanied by details of when restrictions are in force.

Details of most signs which are in common use are shown in The Highway Code and a more comprehensive selection is available in Know Your Traffic Signs.

You can park on the right-hand side of a road at night

☐ in a one-way street

☐ with your sidelights on

☐ more than 10 metres (32 feet) from a junction

☐ under a lamppost

Red rear reflectors show up when headlights shine on them. These are useful when you are parked at night but will only reflect if you park in the same direction as the traffic flow. Normally you should park on the left, but if you're in a one-way street you may also park on the right-hand side.

10.11 | Mark one answer | DES s11, HC r137–138

On a three-lane dual carriageway the right-hand lane can be used for

- ☐ overtaking only, never turning right
- ☐ overtaking or turning right
- ☐ fast-moving traffic only
- ☐ turning right only, never overtaking

You should normally use the left-hand lane on any dual carriageway unless you are overtaking or turning right.

When overtaking on a dual carriageway, look for vehicles ahead that are turning right. They're likely to be slowing or stopped. You need to see them in good time so that you can take appropriate action.

10.12 | Mark one answer | DES s5, 9

You are approaching a busy junction. There are several lanes with road markings. At the last moment you realise that you are in the wrong lane. You should

- ☐ continue in that lane
- ☐ force your way across
- ☐ stop until the area has cleared
- ☐ use clear arm signals to cut across

There are times where road markings can be obscured by queuing traffic, or you might be unsure which lane you need to be in.

If you realise that you're in the wrong lane, don't cut across lanes or bully other drivers to let you in. Follow the lane you're in and find somewhere safe to turn around if you need to.

10.13 | Mark one answer | DES s7, HC r138

Where may you overtake on a one-way street?

- ☐ Only on the left-hand side
- ☐ Overtaking is not allowed
- ☐ Only on the right-hand side
- ☐ Either on the right or the left

You can overtake other traffic on either side when travelling in a one-way street. Make full use of your mirrors and ensure that it's clear all around before you attempt to overtake. Look for signs and road markings and use the most suitable lane for your destination.

When going straight ahead at a roundabout you should

☐ indicate left before leaving the roundabout

☐ not indicate at any time

☐ indicate right when approaching the roundabout

☐ indicate left when approaching the roundabout

When you want to go straight on at a roundabout, don't signal as you approach it, but indicate left just after you pass the exit before the one you wish to take.

Which vehicle might have to use a different course to normal at roundabouts?

☐ Sports car

☐ Van

☐ Estate car

☐ Long vehicle

A long vehicle may have to straddle lanes either on or approaching a roundabout so that the rear wheels don't cut in over the kerb.

If you're following a long vehicle, stay well back and give it plenty of room.

You may only enter a box junction when

Yellow box junctions are marked on the road to prevent the road becoming blocked. Don't enter one unless your exit road is clear. You may only wait in the yellow box if your exit road is clear but oncoming traffic is preventing you from completing the turn.

☐ there are less than two vehicles in front of you

☐ the traffic lights show green

☐ your exit road is clear

☐ you need to turn left

10.17 | Mark one answer | DES s6, HC r174

You may wait in a yellow box junction when

The purpose of this road marking is to keep the junction clear of queuing traffic. You may only wait in the marked area when you're turning right and your exit lane is clear but you can't complete the turn because of oncoming traffic.

- ☐ oncoming traffic is preventing you from turning right
- ☐ you are in a queue of traffic turning left
- ☐ you are in a queue of traffic to go ahead
- ☐ you are on a roundabout

10.18 | Mark three answers | HC r105–109

You MUST stop when signalled to do so by which THREE of these?

- ☐ A police officer
- ☐ A pedestrian
- ☐ A school crossing patrol
- ☐ A bus driver
- ☐ A red traffic light

Looking well ahead and 'reading' the road will help you to anticipate hazards. This will enable you to stop safely at traffic lights or if ordered to do so by an authorised person.

10.19 | Mark one answer | DES s7, HC r195

Someone is waiting to cross at a zebra crossing. They are standing on the pavement. You should normally

- ☐ go on quickly before they step onto the crossing
- ☐ stop before you reach the zigzag lines and let them cross
- ☐ stop, let them cross, wait patiently
- ☐ ignore them as they are still on the pavement

By standing on the pavement, the pedestrian is showing an intention to cross. If you are looking well down the road you will give yourself enough time to slow down and stop safely. Don't forget to check your mirrors before slowing down.

Mark two answers

Who can use a toucan crossing?

☐ Trains

☐ Cyclists

☐ Buses

☐ Pedestrians

☐ Trams

Toucan crossings are similar to pelican crossings but there is no flashing amber phase. Cyclists share the crossing with pedestrians and are allowed to cycle across when the green cycle symbol is shown.

Mark one answer

At a pelican crossing, what does a flashing amber light mean?

☐ You must not move off until the lights stop flashing

☐ You must give way to pedestrians still on the crossing

☐ You can move off, even if pedestrians are still on the crossing

☐ You must stop because the lights are about to change to red

If there is no-one on the crossing when the amber light is flashing, you may proceed over the crossing. You don't need to wait for the green light to show.

Mark one answer

When can you park on the left opposite these road markings?

☐ If the line nearest to you is broken

☐ When there are no yellow lines

☐ To pick up or set down passengers

☐ During daylight hours only

You MUST NOT park or stop on a road marked with double white lines (even where one of the lines is broken) except to pick up or set down passengers.

You are intending to turn right at a crossroads. An oncoming driver is also turning right. It will normally be safer to

☐ keep the other vehicle to your RIGHT and turn behind it (offside to offside)

☐ keep the other vehicle to your LEFT and turn in front of it (nearside to nearside)

☐ carry on and turn at the next junction instead

☐ hold back and wait for the other driver to turn first

At some junctions the layout may make it difficult to turn offside to offside. If this is the case, be prepared to pass nearside to nearside, but take extra care as your view ahead will be obscured by the vehicle turning in front of you.

You are going along a street with parked vehicles on the left-hand side. For which THREE reasons should you keep your speed down?

☐ So that oncoming traffic can see you more clearly

☐ You may set off car alarms

☐ Vehicles may be pulling out

☐ Drivers' doors may open

☐ Children may run out from between the vehicles

Travel slowly and carefully where there are parked vehicles in a built-up area. Beware of

- vehicles pulling out, especially bicycles and other motorcycles
- pedestrians, especially children, who may run out from between cars
- drivers opening their doors.

You meet an obstruction on your side of the road. You should

☐ carry on, you have priority

☐ give way to oncoming traffic

☐ wave oncoming vehicles through

☐ accelerate to get past first

Take care if you have to pass a parked vehicle on your side of the road. Give way to oncoming traffic if there isn't enough room for you both to continue safely.

10.26 **Mark two answers** HC r137

You are on a two-lane dual carriageway. For which TWO of the following would you use the right-hand lane?

☐ Turning right

☐ Normal progress

☐ Staying at the minimum allowed speed

☐ Constant high speed

☐ Overtaking slower traffic

☐ Mending punctures

Normally you should travel in the left-hand lane and only use the right-hand lane for overtaking or turning right. Move back into the left lane as soon as it's safe but don't cut in across the path of the vehicle you've just passed.

10.27 **Mark one answer** DES s8, HC r146

Who has priority at an unmarked crossroads?

☐ The larger vehicle

☐ No one has priority

☐ The faster vehicle

☐ The smaller vehicle

Practise good observation in all directions before you emerge or make a turn. Proceed only when you're sure it's safe to do so.

10.28 **NI EXEMPT** **Mark one answer** HC r243

What is the nearest you may park to a junction?

☐ 10 metres (32 feet)

☐ 12 metres (39 feet)

☐ 15 metres (49 feet)

☐ 20 metres (66 feet)

Don't park within 10 metres (32 feet) of a junction (unless in an authorised parking place). This is to allow drivers emerging from, or turning into, the junction a clear view of the road they are joining. It also allows them to see hazards such as pedestrians or cyclists at the junction.

10.29 **NI EXEMPT** **Mark three answers** HC r243

In which THREE places must you NOT park?

☐ Near the brow of a hill

☐ At or near a bus stop

☐ Where there is no pavement

☐ Within 10 metres (32 feet) of a junction

☐ On a 40 mph road

Other traffic will have to pull out to pass you. They may have to use the other side of the road, and if you park near the brow of a hill, they may not be able to see oncoming traffic. It's important not to park at or near a bus stop as this could inconvenience passengers, and may put them at risk as they get on or off the bus. Parking near a junction could restrict the view for emerging vehicles.

10.30 — Mark one answer — DES s6, HC r293, KYTS p27

You are waiting at a level crossing. A train has passed but the lights keep flashing. You must

☐ carry on waiting
☐ phone the signal operator
☐ edge over the stop line and look for trains
☐ park and investigate

If the lights at a level crossing continue to flash after a train has passed, you should still wait as there might be another train coming. Time seems to pass slowly when you're held up in a queue. Be patient and wait until the lights stop flashing.

10.31 — Mark one answer — HC p107

What does this sign tell you?

The blue and red circular sign on its own means that waiting restrictions are in force. This sign shows that you are leaving the controlled zone and waiting restrictions no longer apply.

☐ That it is a no-through road
☐ End of traffic calming zone
☐ Free parking zone ends
☐ No waiting zone ends

10.32 — Mark one answer — HC r288, KYTS p139

You are entering an area of roadworks. There is a temporary speed limit displayed. You should

☐ not exceed the speed limit
☐ obey the limit only during rush hour
☐ ignore the displayed limit
☐ obey the limit except at night

Where there are extra hazards such as roadworks, it's often necessary to slow traffic down by imposing a temporary speed limit. These speed limits aren't advisory, they must be obeyed.

10.33 — Mark one answer — HC r115

You are travelling on a well-lit road at night in a built-up area. By using dipped headlights you will be able to

☐ see further along the road
☐ go at a much faster speed
☐ switch to main beam quickly
☐ be easily seen by others

You may be difficult to see when you're travelling at night, even on a well lit road. If you use dipped headlights rather than sidelights other road users will see you more easily.

The dual carriageway you are turning right onto has a very narrow central reservation. What should you do?

☐ Proceed to the central reservation and wait

☐ Wait until the road is clear in both directions

☐ Stop in the first lane so that other vehicles give way

☐ Emerge slightly to show your intentions

When the central reservation is narrow you should treat a dual carriageway as one road. Wait until the road is clear in both directions before emerging to turn right. If you try to treat it as two separate roads and wait in the middle, you are likely to cause an obstruction and possibly a collision.

What is the national speed limit on a single carriageway road for cars and motorcycles?

☐ 30 mph

☐ 50 mph

☐ 60 mph

☐ 70 mph

Exceeding the speed limit is dangerous and can result in you receiving penalty points on your licence. It isn't worth it. You should know the speed limit for the road that you're on by observing the road signs. Different speed limits apply if you are towing a trailer.

You park at night on a road with a 40 mph speed limit. You should park

☐ facing the traffic

☐ with parking lights on

☐ with dipped headlights on

☐ near a street light

You MUST use parking lights when parking at night on a road or lay-by with a speed limit greater than 30 mph. You MUST also park in the direction of the traffic flow and not close to a junction.

10.37 · Mark one answer · KYTS p27

You will see these red and white markers when approaching

☐ the end of a motorway

☐ a concealed level crossing

☐ a concealed speed limit sign

☐ the end of a dual carriageway

If there is a bend just before the level crossing you may not be able to see the level crossing barriers or waiting traffic. These signs give you an early warning that you may find these hazards just around the bend.

10.38 · NI EXEMPT · Mark one answer · DES s18, HC r108

You are travelling on a motorway. You MUST stop when signalled to do so by which of these?

☐ Flashing amber lights above your lane

☐ A Highways Agency Traffic Officer

☐ Pedestrians on the hard shoulder

☐ A driver who has broken down

You will find Highways Agency Traffic Officers on many of Britain's motorways. They work in partnership with the police, helping to keep traffic moving and to make your journey as safe as possible. It is an offence not to comply with the directions given by a Traffic Officer.

10.39 · Mark one answer · DES s8, HC r186

You are going straight ahead at a roundabout. How should you signal?

☐ Signal right on the approach and then left to leave the roundabout

☐ Signal left after you leave the roundabout and enter the new road

☐ Signal right on the approach to the roundabout and keep the signal on

☐ Signal left just after you pass the exit before the one you will take

To go straight ahead at a roundabout you should normally approach in the left-hand lane. You will not normally need to signal, but look out for the road markings. At some roundabouts the left lane on approach is marked as 'left turn only', so make sure you use the correct lane to go ahead. Signal before you leave as other road users need to know your intentions.

Mark one answer

You may drive over a footpath

☐ to overtake slow-moving traffic

☐ when the pavement is very wide

☐ if no pedestrians are near

☐ to get into a property

It is against the law to drive on or over a footpath, except to gain access to a property. If you need to cross a pavement, watch for pedestrians in both directions.

Mark one answer

A single carriageway road has this sign. What is the maximum permitted speed for a car towing a trailer?

☐ 30 mph

☐ 40 mph

☐ 50 mph

☐ 60 mph

When towing trailers, speed limits are also lower on dual carriageways and motorways. These speed limits apply to vehicles pulling all sorts of trailers including caravans, horse boxes etc.

Mark one answer

You are towing a small caravan on a dual carriageway. You must not exceed

☐ 50 mph

☐ 40 mph

☐ 70 mph

☐ 60 mph

The speed limit is reduced for vehicles towing caravans and trailers, to lessen the risk of the outfit becoming unstable. Due to the increased weight and size of the vehicle and caravan combination, you should plan well ahead. Be extra-careful in windy weather, as strong winds could cause a caravan or large trailer to snake from side to side.

You want to park and you see this sign. On the days and times shown you should

☐ park in a bay and not pay

☐ park on yellow lines and pay

☐ park on yellow lines and not pay

☐ park in a bay and pay

Parking restrictions apply in a variety of places and situations. Make sure you know the rules and understand where and when restrictions apply. Controlled parking areas will be indicated by signs and road markings. Parking in the wrong place could cause an obstruction and danger to other traffic. It can also result in a fine.

You are driving along a road that has a cycle lane. The lane is marked by a solid white line. This means that during its period of operation

☐ the lane may be used for parking your car

☐ you may drive in that lane at any time

☐ the lane may be used when necessary

☐ you must not drive in that lane

Leave the lane free for cyclists. At other times, when the lane is not in operation, you should still be aware that there may be cyclists about. Give them room and don't pass too closely.

While driving, you intend to turn left into a minor road. On the approach you should

☐ keep just left of the middle of the road

☐ keep in the middle of the road

☐ swing out wide just before turning

☐ keep well to the left of the road

Don't swing out into the centre of the road in order to make the turn. This could endanger oncoming traffic and may cause other road users to misunderstand your intentions.

Mark one answer

You are waiting at a level crossing. The red warning lights continue to flash after a train has passed by. What should you do?

At a level crossing flashing red lights mean you must stop. If the train passes but the lights keep flashing, wait. There may be another train coming.

☐ Get out and investigate

☐ Telephone the signal operator

☐ Continue to wait

☐ Drive across carefully

Mark one answer

You are driving over a level crossing. The warning lights come on and a bell rings. What should you do?

Keep going, don't stop on the crossing. If the amber warning lights come on as you're approaching the crossing, you MUST stop unless it is unsafe to do so. Red flashing lights together with an audible signal mean you MUST stop.

☐ Get everyone out of the vehicle immediately

☐ Stop and reverse back to clear the crossing

☐ Keep going and clear the crossing

☐ Stop immediately and use your hazard warning lights

Mark one answer

You are on a busy main road and find that you are travelling in the wrong direction. What should you do?

Don't turn round in a busy street or reverse from a side road into a main road. Find a quiet side road and choose a place where you won't obstruct an entrance or exit. Look out for pedestrians and cyclists as well as other traffic.

☐ Turn into a side road on the right and reverse into the main road

☐ Make a U-turn in the main road

☐ Make a 'three-point' turn in the main road

☐ Turn round in a side road

10.49   Mark one answer   DES s9

You may remove your seat belt when carrying out a manoeuvre that involves

☐ reversing

☐ a hill start

☐ an emergency stop

☐ driving slowly

Don't forget to put your seat belt back on when you've finished reversing.

10.50   Mark one answer   DES s9, HC r203

You must not reverse

☐ for longer than necessary

☐ for more than a car's length

☐ into a side road

☐ in a built-up area

You may decide to turn your vehicle around by reversing into an opening or side road. When you reverse, always look behind and all around and watch for pedestrians. Don't reverse from a side road into a main road. You MUST NOT reverse further than is necessary.

10.51   Mark one answer   DES s9

When you are NOT sure that it is safe to reverse your vehicle you should

☐ use your horn

☐ rev your engine

☐ get out and check

☐ reverse slowly

If you can't see all around your vehicle get out and have a look. You could also ask someone reliable outside the vehicle to guide you. A small child could easily be hidden directly behind you. Don't take risks.

10.52   Mark one answer   DES s9, HC r201

When may you reverse from a side road into a main road?

☐ Only if both roads are clear of traffic

☐ Not at any time

☐ At any time

☐ Only if the main road is clear of traffic

Don't reverse into a main road from a side road. The main road is likely to be busy and the traffic on it moving quickly. Cut down the risks by reversing into a quiet side road.

10.53   Mark one answer   DES s6, HC r174

You want to turn right at a box junction. There is oncoming traffic. You should

☐ wait in the box junction if your exit is clear

☐ wait before the junction until it is clear of all traffic

☐ drive on, you cannot turn right at a box junction

☐ drive slowly into the box junction when signalled by oncoming traffic

You can move into the box junction to wait as long as your exit is clear. The oncoming traffic will stop when the traffic lights change, allowing you to proceed.

10.54   Mark one answer   DES s9

You are reversing your vehicle into a side road. When would the greatest hazard to passing traffic occur?

☐ After you've completed the manoeuvre

☐ Just before you actually begin to manoeuvre

☐ After you've entered the side road

☐ When the front of your vehicle swings out

Always check road and traffic conditions in all directions before reversing into a side road. Keep a good look-out throughout the manoeuvre. Act on what you see and wait if necessary.

10.55   Mark one answer   DES s9

Where is the safest place to park your vehicle at night?

☐ In a garage

☐ On a busy road

☐ In a quiet car park

☐ Near a red route

If you have a garage, use it. Your vehicle is less likely to be a victim of car crime if it's in a garage. Also in winter the windows will be free from ice and snow.

10.56   Mark one answer   HC p107, KYTS p55

You are driving on an urban clearway. You may stop only to

☐ set down and pick up passengers

☐ use a mobile telephone

☐ ask for directions

☐ load or unload goods

Urban clearways may be in built-up areas and their times of operation will be clearly signed. You should stop only for as long as is reasonable to pick up or set down passengers. You should ensure that you are not causing an obstruction for other traffic.

10.57 Mark one answer   HC r241, KYTS p47

You are looking for somewhere to park your vehicle. The area is full EXCEPT for spaces marked 'disabled use'. You can

☐ use these spaces when elsewhere is full

☐ park if you stay with your vehicle

☐ use these spaces, disabled or not

☐ not park there unless permitted

It is illegal to park in a parking space reserved for disabled users.

These spaces are provided for people with limited mobility, who may need extra space to get in and out of their vehicle.

10.58 Mark one answer   DES s10, HC r155

You are on a road that is only wide enough for one vehicle. There is a car coming towards you. What should you do?

☐ Pull into a passing place on your right

☐ Force the other driver to reverse

☐ Pull into a passing place if your vehicle is wider

☐ Pull into a passing place on your left

Pull into the nearest passing place on the left if you meet another vehicle in a narrow road. If the nearest passing place is on the right, wait opposite it.

10.59 Mark one answer   DES s13

You are driving at night with full beam headlights on. A vehicle is overtaking you. You should dip your lights

☐ some time after the vehicle has passed you

☐ before the vehicle starts to pass you

☐ only if the other driver dips their headlights

☐ as soon as the vehicle passes you

On full beam your lights could dazzle the driver in front. Make sure that your light beam falls short of the vehicle in front.

10.60 Mark one answer   KYTS p32

When may you drive a motor car in this bus lane?

```
┌─────────────────┐
│  ▐■local■▌       │
│  ⬤▦ taxi         │
│ ┌─────────┐      │
│ │ Mon-Fri │      │
│ │ 7-10am  │      │
│ │4.00-6.30pm│    │
│ └─────────┘      │
└─────────────────┘
```

☐ Outside its hours of operation

☐ To get to the front of a traffic queue

☐ You may not use it at any time

☐ To overtake slow-moving traffic

Some bus lanes only operate during peak hours and other vehicles may use them outside these hours. Make sure you check the sign for the hours of operation before driving in a bus lane.

10.61 — Mark one answer — DES s5

Signals are normally given by direction indicators and

☐ brake lights
☐ side lights
☐ fog lights
☐ interior lights

Your brake lights will give an indication to traffic behind that you're slowing down. Good anticipation will allow you time to check your mirrors before slowing.

10.62 — Mark one answer — DES s9, HC r200

You are parked in a busy high street. What is the safest way to turn your vehicle around so you can go the opposite way?

☐ Find a quiet side road to turn round in
☐ Drive into a side road and reverse into the main road
☐ Get someone to stop the traffic
☐ Do a U-turn

Make sure you carry out the manoeuvre without causing a hazard to other vehicles. Choose a place to turn which is safe and convenient for you and for other road users.

10.63 — Mark one answer — DES s20

To help keep your vehicle secure at night, where should you park?

☐ Near a police station
☐ In a quiet road
☐ On a red route
☐ In a well-lit area

Whenever possible park in an area which will be well lit at night.

10.64 — Mark one answer — DES s11, HC r288–289

You are in the right-hand lane of a dual carriageway. You see signs showing that the right-hand lane is closed 800 yards ahead. You should

GET IN LANE
↑ ↑ ┬
800 yards

☐ keep in that lane until you reach the queue
☐ move to the left immediately
☐ wait and see which lane is moving faster
☐ move to the left in good time

Keep a look-out for traffic signs. If you're directed to change lanes, do so in good time. Don't

• push your way into traffic in another lane
• leave changing lanes until the last moment.

10.65 — Mark two answers — HC r140

You are driving on a road that has a cycle lane. The lane is marked by a broken white line. This means that

☐ you should not drive in the lane unless it is unavoidable

☐ you should not park in the lane unless it is unavoidable

☐ cyclists can travel in both directions in that lane

☐ the lane must be used by motorcyclists in heavy traffic

Where signs or road markings show lanes are for cyclists only, leave them free. Do not drive or park in a cycle lane unless it is unavoidable.

10.66 — Mark one answer — DES s9, HC r241

What MUST you have to park in a disabled space?

☐ A Blue Badge

☐ A wheelchair

☐ An advanced driver certificate

☐ An adapted vehicle

Don't park in a space reserved for disabled people unless you or your passenger are a disabled badge holder. The badge must be displayed in your vehicle in the bottom left-hand corner of the windscreen.

10.67 — Mark three answers — HC r105–109, 286

On which THREE occasions MUST you stop your vehicle?

☐ When in an incident where damage or injury is caused

☐ At a red traffic light

☐ When signalled to do so by a police or traffic officer

☐ At a junction with double broken white lines

☐ At a pelican crossing when the amber light is flashing and no pedestrians are crossing

Situations when you MUST stop include the following. When signalled to do so by a police or traffic officer, traffic warden, school crossing patrol or red traffic light. You must also stop if you are involved in an incident which causes damage or injury to any other person, vehicle, animal or property.

Case study practice – 10 Rules of the road

> It's early evening and street lamps are lit.
>
> Anita is driving home at 30 mph, although there are no speed limit signs. The road is a single carriageway and Anita is alone in her vehicle.
>
> Sleet is falling steadily and it's cold. Ahead, a vehicle is spreading salt on the road.
>
> In town there are high-occupancy vehicle lanes which Anita doesn't use.
>
> Her home is level with a zebra crossing but she parks beyond its markings further down the road.

10.1 How has Anita identified a 30 mph requirement?
Mark **one** answer

☐ There are many retail outlets still open in the town
☐ There are regularly spaced street lights in the area
☐ There are yellow lines painted on the road surface
☐ There are plenty of pedestrians and cyclists around

HC r124, p40

10.2 What would the normal centre white line markings be on this road?
Mark **one** answer

☐ Short dashes with short spaces
☐ Long dashes with short spaces
☐ Short dashes with long spaces
☐ Long dashes with long spaces

HC r127, p114

10.3 What colour flashing beacon would the salting vehicle have?

Mark **one** answer

☐ White
☐ Green
☐ Red
☐ Amber

HC r225

10.4 Why would Anita not use this type of lane on her journey?

Mark **one** answer

☐ It's for vehicles of all types, but only at certain times
☐ It's for vehicles that have two or more occupants
☐ It's for vehicles of as many types and sizes as possible
☐ It's for vehicles that have flashing amber beacons

HC p112 **DES** s6 **KYTS** p140–141

10.5 What does The Highway Code tell Anita about parking?

Mark **one** answer

☐ You **SHOULD NOT** park on pedestrian crossings
☐ You **MUST NOT** park on pedestrian crossings
☐ You **MAY NOT** park on pedestrian crossings
☐ You **WILL NOT** park on pedestrian crossings

HC r240 **DES** s7

Section eleven

Road and traffic signs

In this section, you'll learn about

- what the shapes of road sign can tell you
- what road markings mean
- the sequence and meaning of traffic lights
- motorway warning lights
- the signals used by other drivers and by police officers.

Road and traffic signs

Road and traffic signs give important information to keep you safe on the road, so it's essential that you know what they mean and what you need to do when you see them.

> Signs

The shape and colour of a road sign tell you about its meaning.

Circular signs give orders.

Blue circles give an instruction or show which sort of road user can use a route, eg cyclists, pedestrians, trams.

Red rings or circles tell you what you mustn't do.

Triangular signs give warnings.

Rectangular signs give information.

Signs with a brown background give tourist information.

KYTS p9, 84, 100–104

The exception to the shape rule is the 'stop' sign: this is octagonal so that it stands out and can be understood even if it's partly covered, eg by snow.

HC r109 **DES** s6 **KYTS** p9

Maximum speed limits are shown inside red circles: you **MUST NOT** go faster than the speed shown. Where no speed limit is shown, the national speed limits (given on page 302) apply. Speed limit signs may be combined with other signs, such as those indicating a traffic-calmed area.

HC p106 **KYTS** p20

It's impossible to mention all the signs here. *Know Your Traffic Signs* shows all the signs you're likely to see and *The Official Highway Code* contains important advice, information on current laws in Great Britain, and best practice in road safety. It's important that you get to know these to make sure that you don't break the law.

Test your knowledge of signs using the activity on the Safe Driving for Life website.

> **safedrivingforlife.info/signsquiz**

> Road markings

Markings on the road give information, orders or warnings. As a general rule, the more paint there is, the more important the message.

HC r127–131 **DES** s8 **KYTS** p62–64

There are three types of road markings.

Along the middle of the road

Short broken white lines mark the centre of the road.

Longer broken white lines show that a hazard is ahead: only overtake if the road ahead is clear.

You **MUST NOT** cross or straddle double white lines with a solid white line on your side of the road unless

- you're turning into a junction or an entrance
- you need to pass a stationary vehicle
- you need to overtake a cyclist, horse or road maintenance vehicle if they're moving at 10 mph or less.

White diagonal stripes or chevrons separate lanes of traffic or protect traffic turning right.

Sometimes red tarmac is used within a block of white lines or diagonals. This highlights the area that separates traffic flowing in opposite directions.

HC p114 DES s6 KYTS p62–64

Along the side of the road

A white line shows the edge of the carriageway.

Yellow lines show waiting and stopping restrictions.

Zigzag lines (white at pedestrian crossings, yellow outside schools) mean no stopping or parking at any time.

HC p115, 116 DES s6 KYTS p39–44, 56, 65, 122

Lines on or across the road

Broken lines across the road mean 'give way'. At a roundabout, give way to traffic from the right.

A single solid line means 'stop'.

Various markings on the road, for example 'give way' triangles, road hump markings and rumble strips, warn of a hazard.

HC p114–116 **KYTS** p62–75

As with signs, you should look at *Know Your Traffic Signs* and *The Official Highway Code* to learn more about road markings.

You may see reflective studs on motorways and other roads. These are especially useful at night and when visibility is poor, as they help to make the lanes and edges of the road easier to see. Different coloured studs are used on motorways to help drivers identify which lane they're using. See section 9, Motorway driving, for more details.

HC r132

> Traffic lights and warning lights

Traffic lights work in a sequence.

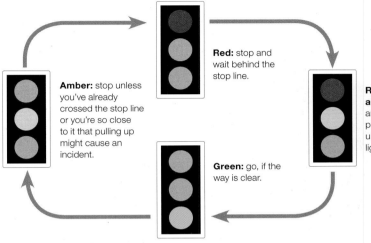

Red: stop and wait behind the stop line.

Amber: stop unless you've already crossed the stop line or you're so close to it that pulling up might cause an incident.

Red and amber: stop and wait; don't pass or start until the green light shows.

Green: go, if the way is clear.

HC p102 **DES** s6 **KYTS** p119–120

On some traffic lights there's a green filter arrow. This means you can go in the direction of the arrow, even if the main light isn't showing green.

If a set of traffic lights is out of order, drive very carefully: nobody has priority. There may be a sign telling you that the lights aren't working.

DES s6

Red flashing lights are used at level crossings and other locations, such as lifting bridges and outside some fire stations. You **MUST** stop when these show.

HC r293, p102 **KYTS** p13, 26–29, 120

At roadworks, traffic can be controlled by

- a police officer
- traffic lights
- a 'stop/go' board.

HC r288 **KYTS** p136

On motorways, signals on the overhead gantries or at the roadside may also have flashing lights.

Amber warns you of a hazard (eg lane closures, to leave at the next exit, fog) or a temporary maximum speed advised for the conditions.

Red above your lane tells you that the lane is closed beyond this point, and you should move into another lane.

Red above all the lanes, on the central reservation or on the roadside tells you to stop. You **MUST NOT** go beyond that point in any lane.

`HC` r255–258, p102 `KYTS` p89–91

⊳ Signals given by drivers and the police

Road users normally signal where they're intending to turn by using their indicators. Make sure that your indicators are cancelled after you've turned, to avoid confusing other road users. Be aware that another driver may have left their indicator on by mistake.

If you're emerging from a junction and a driver coming along the main road from the right is close to you and indicating left, wait until the vehicle starts to turn before you emerge.

`HC` r103–104 `DES` s5

You may need to use an arm signal to strengthen or clarify the message given by your indicators, such as when you're

- signalling to turn right in busy traffic
- slowing down to give way at a zebra crossing.

If you're slowing down and stopping just after a junction, wait to signal until you're passing the junction, or just after it.

You can use the horn to warn others that you're there. You **MUST NOT** use it between 11.30 pm and 7.00 am when driving in a built-up area, except when another road user puts you in danger. You **MUST NOT** use your horn when stationary unless another vehicle is likely to cause a danger.

The only reason you should flash your headlights is to warn other road users that you're there.

HC r110–112 **DES** s5

If you're driving on a motorway or unrestricted dual carriageway, you can briefly use your hazard warning lights to warn drivers behind you that there's an obstruction ahead.

HC r116 **DES** s3, 11

Police or traffic officers may signal to you if they're directing traffic. Make sure that you know all the official arm signals in case you need to use or react to them.

HC p103–105

A police or Highways Agency traffic officer following you in a patrol vehicle may flash their headlights, indicate left and point to the left to direct you to stop. Pull up on the left as soon as it's safe to do so.

HC r106

Remember, you **MUST** obey any signals given by police or traffic officers, traffic wardens and signs used by school crossing patrols.

HC r105–108, p104–105

⊜ Road lanes

Contraflow lanes are lanes that flow in the opposite direction to most of the traffic. Bus and cycle contraflow lanes may be found in one-way streets. They'll be signed and marked on the road. Don't try to drive against the flow of traffic in these lanes.

HC r140–141, 143 **DES** s6

You may also see contraflow lanes at roadworks. When you see the signs

- reduce your speed and comply with any temporary speed limits
- choose an appropriate lane in good time
- keep the correct distance from the vehicle in front.

DES s11 **KYTS** p128–133

The centre and right-hand lanes of a three-lane motorway are overtaking lanes. Always move back to a lane on your left after overtaking, to allow other vehicles to overtake. On a free-flowing motorway or dual carriageway, you mustn't overtake other vehicles on their left.

HC r264, 268 **DES** s11

Meeting the standards

You must be able to

respond correctly to all

- permanent traffic signals, signs and road markings
- temporary traffic signals, signs and road markings.

You must know and understand

the meaning of all mandatory traffic signs and how to respond to them

the meaning of all warning signs and how to respond to them

the meaning of all road markings and how to respond to them.

Notes

You can use this page to make your own notes or diagrams about the key points you need to remember.

Think about

- When are you allowed to cross double white lines along the centre of the road?
- What must you never do on zigzag lines?
- What shape is the 'stop' sign?
- What should you do at an amber traffic light?
- When might you need to use arm signals?

Your notes

Things to discuss and practise with your instructor

These are just a few examples of what you could discuss and practise with your instructor. Read more about road and traffic signs to come up with your own ideas.

Discuss with your instructor

- which is the only octagonal road sign and why it's unique
- what these shapes of sign tell you
  - round
  - triangular
  - rectangular
- what different patterns of road markings mean, eg double white lines, yellow boxes, etc.

Practise with your instructor

- identifying signs from *The Official Highway Code* and *Know Your Traffic Signs*
- driving through a busy town centre and identifying all the warning signs that you see
- driving to a level crossing and identifying the signs and signals that you find there.

Mark one answer

You MUST obey signs giving orders. These signs are mostly in

- ☐ green rectangles
- ☐ red triangles
- ☐ blue rectangles
- ☐ red circles

There are three basic types of traffic sign, those that warn, inform or give orders. Generally, triangular signs warn, rectangular ones give information or directions, and circular signs usually give orders. An exception is the eight-sided 'STOP' sign.

Mark one answer

Traffic signs giving orders are generally which shape?

☐ ⟩ ☐ ▭

☐ △ ☐ ◯

Road signs in the shape of a circle give orders. Those with a red circle are mostly prohibitive. The 'stop' sign is octagonal to give it greater prominence. Signs giving orders MUST always be obeyed.

Mark one answer

What does this sign mean?

- ☐ Maximum speed limit with traffic calming
- ☐ Minimum speed limit with traffic calming
- ☐ '20 cars only' parking zone
- ☐ Only 20 cars allowed at any one time

If you're in places where there are likely to be pedestrians such as outside schools, near parks, residential areas and shopping areas, you should be extra-cautious and keep your speed down.

Many local authorities have taken measures to slow traffic down by creating traffic calming measures such as speed humps. They are there for a reason; slow down.

11.4 | Mark one answer | DES s6, HC p106, KYTS p17

Which sign means no motor vehicles are allowed?

☐

☐

☐

You would generally see this sign at the approach to a pedestrian-only zone.

11.5 | Mark one answer | DES s6, HC p106, KYTS p20

What does this sign mean?

Where you see this sign the 20 mph restriction ends. Check all around for possible hazards and only increase your speed if it's safe to do so.

☐ New speed limit 20 mph

☐ No vehicles over 30 tonnes

☐ Minimum speed limit 30 mph

☐ End of 20 mph zone

11.6 | Mark one answer | DES s6, HC p106, KYTS p17

What does this sign mean?

'No entry' signs are used in places such as one-way streets to prevent vehicles driving against the traffic. To ignore one would be dangerous, both for yourself and other road users, as well as being against the law.

☐ No parking

☐ No road markings

☐ No through road

☐ No entry

What does this sign mean?

The 'no right turn' sign may be used to warn road users that there is a 'no entry' prohibition on a road to the right ahead.

☐ Bend to the right
☐ Road on the right closed
☐ No traffic from the right
☐ No right turn

What does this sign mean?

Avoid blocking tram routes. Trams are fixed on their route and can't manoeuvre around other vehicles and pedestrians. Modern trams travel quickly and are quiet so you might not hear them approaching.

☐ Route for trams only
☐ Route for buses only
☐ Parking for buses only
☐ Parking for trams only

Which type of vehicle does this sign apply to?

The triangular shapes above and below the dimensions indicate a height restriction that applies to the road ahead.

☐ Wide vehicles
☐ Long vehicles
☐ High vehicles
☐ Heavy vehicles

11.10 | **Mark one answer** | DES s6, HC p106, KYTS p17

Which sign means NO motor vehicles allowed?

This sign is used to enable pedestrians to walk free from traffic. It's often found in shopping areas.

11.11 | **Mark one answer** | DES s6, HC p106, KYTS p18

What does this sign mean?

Road signs that prohibit overtaking are placed in locations where passing the vehicle in front is dangerous. If you see this sign don't attempt to overtake. The sign is there for a reason and you must obey it.

- ☐ You have priority
- ☐ No motor vehicles
- ☐ Two-way traffic
- ☐ No overtaking

11.12 | **Mark one answer** | DES s6, HC p107, KYTS p54

What does this sign mean?

There will be a plate or additional sign to tell you when the restrictions apply.

- ☐ Waiting restrictions apply
- ☐ Waiting permitted
- ☐ National speed limit applies
- ☐ Clearway (no stopping)

What does this sign mean?

Even though you have left the restricted area, make sure that you park where you won't endanger other road users or cause an obstruction.

- ☐ End of restricted speed area
- ☐ End of restricted parking area
- ☐ End of clearway
- ☐ End of cycle route

Which sign means 'no stopping'?

Stopping where this clearway restriction applies is likely to cause congestion. Allow the traffic to flow by obeying the signs.

What does this sign mean?

If you intend to stop and rest, this sign allows you time to reduce speed and pull over safely.

- ☐ Distance to parking place ahead
- ☐ Distance to public telephone ahead
- ☐ Distance to public house ahead
- ☐ Distance to passing place ahead

11.16 | **Mark one answer** | **DES s6, KYTS p50**

What does this sign mean?

In order to keep roads free from parked cars, there are some areas where you're allowed to park on the verge. Only do this where you see the sign. Parking on verges or footways anywhere else could lead to a fine.

☐ Vehicles may not park on the verge or footway

☐ Vehicles may park on the left-hand side of the road only

☐ Vehicles may park fully on the verge or footway

☐ Vehicles may park on the right-hand side of the road only

11.17 | **Mark one answer** | **DES s6, HC p106, KYTS p18**

What does this traffic sign mean?

Priority signs are normally shown where the road is narrow and there isn't enough room for two vehicles to pass. These can be at narrow bridges, road works and where there's a width restriction.

Make sure that you know who has priority, don't force your way through. Show courtesy and consideration to other road users.

☐ No overtaking allowed

☐ Give priority to oncoming traffic

☐ Two way traffic

☐ One-way traffic only

What is the meaning of this traffic sign?

Don't force your way through. Show courtesy and consideration to other road users. Although you have priority, make sure oncoming traffic is going to give way before you continue.

☐ End of two-way road

☐ Give priority to vehicles coming towards you

☐ You have priority over vehicles coming towards you

☐ Bus lane ahead

What shape is a STOP sign at a junction?

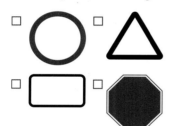

To make it easy to recognise, the 'stop' sign is the only sign of this shape. You must stop and take effective observation before proceeding.

At a junction you see this sign partly covered by snow. What does it mean?

The STOP sign is the only road sign that is octagonal. This is so that it can be recognised and obeyed even if it is obscured, for example by snow.

☐ Cross roads

☐ Give way

☐ Stop

☐ Turn right

11.21 | Mark one answer | DES s6, HC p107, KYTS p21

What does this sign mean?

This sign is shown where slow-moving vehicles would impede the flow of traffic, for example in tunnels. However, if you need to slow down or even stop to avoid an incident or potential collision, you should do so.

☐ Service area 30 miles ahead

☐ Maximum speed 30 mph

☐ Minimum speed 30 mph

☐ Lay-by 30 miles ahead

11.22 | Mark one answer | DES s6, HC p107, KYTS p19

What does this sign mean?

These signs are often seen in one-way streets that have more than one lane. When you see this sign, use the route that's the most convenient and doesn't require a late change of direction.

☐ Give way to oncoming vehicles

☐ Approaching traffic passes you on both sides

☐ Turn off at the next available junction

☐ Pass either side to get to the same destination

11.23 | Mark one answer | DES s6, HC p107, KYTS p30

What does this sign mean?

Take extra care when you encounter trams. Look out for road markings and signs that alert you to them. Modern trams are very quiet and you may not hear them approaching.

☐ Route for trams

☐ Give way to trams

☐ Route for buses

☐ Give way to buses

What does a circular traffic sign with a blue background do?

Signs with blue circles give a positive instruction. These are often found in urban areas and include signs for mini-roundabouts and directional arrows.

☐ Give warning of a motorway ahead

☐ Give directions to a car park

☐ Give motorway information

☐ Give an instruction

Where would you see a contraflow bus and cycle lane?

☐ On a dual carriageway

☐ On a roundabout

☐ On an urban motorway

☐ On a one-way street

In a contraflow lane the traffic permitted to use it travels in the opposite direction to traffic in the other lanes on the road.

What does this sign mean?

There will also be markings on the road surface to indicate the bus lane. You must not use this lane for parking or overtaking.

☐ Bus station on the right

☐ Contraflow bus lane

☐ With-flow bus lane

☐ Give way to buses

11.27

Mark one answer

DES s6, KYTS p84

What does a sign with a brown background show?

Signs with a brown background give directions to places of interest. They will often be seen on a motorway directing you along the easiest route to the attraction.

- ☐ Tourist directions
- ☐ Primary roads
- ☐ Motorway routes
- ☐ Minor routes

11.28

Mark one answer

DES s6, KYTS p100

This sign means

These signs indicate places of interest and are designed to guide you by the easiest route. They are particularly useful if you are unfamiliar with the area.

- ☐ tourist attraction
- ☐ beware of trains
- ☐ level crossing
- ☐ beware of trams

11.29

Mark one answer

DES s6, HC p108, KYTS p10

What are triangular signs for?

This type of sign will warn you of hazards ahead.

Make sure you look at each sign that you pass on the road, so that you do not miss any vital instructions or information.

- ☐ To give warnings
- ☐ To give information
- ☐ To give orders
- ☐ To give directions

Mark one answer

DES s6, HC p108, KYTS p10

What does this sign mean?

This type of sign will warn you of hazards ahead. Make sure you look at each sign and road markings that you pass, so that you do not miss any vital instructions or information. This particular sign shows there is a T-junction with priority over vehicles from the right.

☐ Turn left ahead

☐ T-junction

☐ No through road

☐ Give way

Mark one answer

DES s6, HC p109, KYTS p13

What does this sign mean?

It will take up to ten times longer to stop when it's icy. Where there is a risk of icy conditions you need to be aware of this and take extra care. If you think the road may be icy, don't brake or steer harshly as your tyres could lose their grip on the road.

☐ Multi-exit roundabout

☐ Risk of ice

☐ Six roads converge

☐ Place of historical interest

Mark one answer

DES s6, HC p108, KYTS p10

What does this sign mean?

The priority through the junction is shown by the broader line. You need to be aware of the hazard posed by traffic crossing or pulling out onto a major road.

☐ Crossroads

☐ Level crossing with gate

☐ Level crossing without gate

☐ Ahead only

Mark one answer

What does this sign mean?

As you approach a roundabout look well ahead and check all signs. Decide which exit you wish to take and move into the correct position as you approach the roundabout, signalling as required.

☐ Ring road
☐ Mini-roundabout
☐ No vehicles
☐ Roundabout

Mark four answers

Which FOUR of these would be indicated by a triangular road sign?

Warning signs are there to make you aware of potential hazards on the road ahead. Act on the signs so you are prepared and can take whatever action is necessary.

☐ Road narrows
☐ Ahead only
☐ Low bridge
☐ Minimum speed
☐ Children crossing
☐ T-junction

Section eleven Questions

What does this sign mean?

Where there's a cycle route ahead, a sign will show a bicycle in a red warning triangle. Watch out for children on bicycles and cyclists rejoining the main road.

- ☐ Cyclists must dismount
- ☐ Cycles are not allowed
- ☐ Cycle route ahead
- ☐ Cycle in single file

Which sign means that pedestrians may be walking along the road?

☐   ☐

When you pass pedestrians in the road, leave plenty of room. You might have to use the right-hand side of the road, so look well ahead, as well as in your mirrors, before pulling out. Take great care if there is a bend in the road obscuring your view ahead.

☐   ☐

Which of these signs means there is a double bend ahead?

☐   ☐

Triangular signs give you a warning of hazards ahead. They are there to give you time to prepare for the hazard, for example by adjusting your speed.

☐   ☐

11.38

Mark one answer

DES s6, KYTS p30

What does this sign mean?

Obey the 'give way' signs. Trams are unable to steer around you if you misjudge when it is safe to enter the junction.

☐ Wait at the barriers

☐ Wait at the crossroads

☐ Give way to trams

☐ Give way to farm vehicles

11.39

Mark one answer

DES s6, HC p109, KYTS p72

What does this sign mean?

These have been put in place to slow the traffic down. They're usually found in residential areas. Slow down to an appropriate speed.

☐ Hump bridge

☐ Humps in the road

☐ Entrance to tunnel

☐ Soft verges

11.40

Mark one answer

DES s6, HC p108, KYTS p11

Which of these signs means the end of a dual carriageway?

If you're overtaking make sure you move back safely into the left-hand lane before you reach the end of the dual carriageway.

☐ ☐

☐ ☐

Mark one answer

What does this sign mean?

Don't leave moving into the left-hand lane until the last moment.˙ Plan ahead and don't rely on other traffic letting you in.

☐ End of dual carriageway

☐ Tall bridge

☐ Road narrows

☐ End of narrow bridge

Mark one answer

What does this sign mean?

A warning sign with a picture of a windsock will indicate there may be strong crosswinds. This sign is often found on exposed roads.

☐ Crosswinds

☐ Road noise

☐ Airport

☐ Adverse camber

Mark one answer

What does this traffic sign mean?

This sign is there to alert you to the likelihood of danger ahead. It may be accompanied by a plate indicating the type of hazard. Be ready to reduce your speed and take avoiding action.

☐ Slippery road ahead

☐ Tyres liable to punctures ahead

☐ Danger ahead

☐ Service area ahead

11.44 Mark one answer DES s6, HC p108, KYTS p26

What does this sign mean?

Some crossings have gates but no attendant or signals. You should stop, look both ways, listen and make sure that there is no train approaching. If there is a telephone, contact the signal operator to make sure that it's safe to cross.

☐ Level crossing with gate or barrier

☐ Gated road ahead

☐ Level crossing without gate or barrier

☐ Cattle grid ahead

11.45 Mark one answer DES s6, HC p108, KYTS p30

What does this sign mean?

This sign warns you to beware of trams. If you don't usually drive in a town where there are trams, remember to look out for them at junctions and look for tram rails, signs and signals.

☐ No trams ahead

☐ Oncoming trams

☐ Trams crossing ahead

☐ Trams only

11.46 Mark one answer DES s6, HC p108, KYTS p12

What does this sign mean?

This sign will give you an early warning that the road ahead will slope downhill. Prepare to alter your speed and gear. Looking at the sign from left to right will show you whether the road slopes uphill or downhill.

☐ Adverse camber

☐ Steep hill downwards

☐ Uneven road

☐ Steep hill upwards

Mark one answer

What does this sign mean?

This sign is found where a shallow stream crosses the road. Heavy rainfall could increase the flow of water. If the water looks too deep or the stream has spread over a large distance, stop and find another route.

☐ Uneven road surface

☐ Bridge over the road

☐ Road ahead ends

☐ Water across the road

Mark one answer

What does this sign mean?

If you intend to take a left turn, this sign shows you that you can't get through to another route using the left-turn junction ahead.

☐ Turn left for parking area

☐ No through road on the left

☐ No entry for traffic turning left

☐ Turn left for ferry terminal

Mark one answer

What does this sign mean?

You will not be able to find a through route to another road. Use this road only for access.

☐ T-junction

☐ No through road

☐ Telephone box ahead

☐ Toilet ahead

11.50 | Mark one answer | DES s6, HC p111

Which is the sign for a ring road?

☐   ☐

☐   ☐

Ring roads are designed to relieve congestion in towns and city centres.

11.51 | Mark one answer | DES s6, HC p113, KYTS p129

What does this sign mean?

☐ The right-hand lane ahead is narrow

☐ Right-hand lane for buses only

☐ Right-hand lane for turning right

☐ The right-hand lane is closed

Yellow and black temporary signs may be used to inform you of roadworks or lane restrictions. Look well ahead. If you have to change lanes, do so in good time.

11.52 | Mark one answer | DES s6, HC p113, KYTS p130

What does this sign mean?

☐ Change to the left lane

☐ Leave at the next exit

☐ Contraflow system

☐ One-way street

If you use the right-hand lane in a contraflow system, you'll be travelling with no permanent barrier between you and the oncoming traffic. Observe speed limits and keep a good distance from the vehicle ahead.

Mark one answer

What does this sign mean?

Where there's a long, steep, uphill gradient on a motorway, a crawler lane may be provided. This helps the traffic to flow by diverting the slower heavy vehicles into a dedicated lane on the left.

☐ Leave motorway at next exit

☐ Lane for heavy and slow vehicles

☐ All lorries use the hard shoulder

☐ Rest area for lorries

Mark one answer

A red traffic light means

Make sure you learn and understand the sequence of traffic lights. Whatever light appears you will then know what light is going to appear next and be able to take the appropriate action. For example if amber is showing on its own you'll know that red will appear next, giving you ample time to slow and stop safely.

☐ you should stop unless turning left

☐ stop, if you are able to brake safely

☐ you must stop and wait behind the stop line

☐ proceed with caution

Mark one answer

At traffic lights, amber on its own means

When amber is showing on its own red will appear next. The amber light means STOP, unless you have already crossed the stop line or you are so close to it that pulling up might cause a collision.

☐ prepare to go

☐ go if the way is clear

☐ go if no pedestrians are crossing

☐ stop at the stop line

You are at a junction controlled by traffic lights. When should you NOT proceed at green?

As you approach the lights look into the road you wish to take. Only proceed if your exit road is clear. If the road is blocked hold back, even if you have to wait for the next green signal.

☐ When pedestrians are waiting to cross

☐ When your exit from the junction is blocked

☐ When you think the lights may be about to change

☐ When you intend to turn right

You are in the left-hand lane at traffic lights. You are waiting to turn left. At which of these traffic lights must you NOT move on?

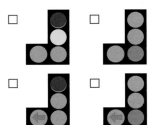

At some junctions there may be a separate signal for different lanes. These are called 'filter' lights. They're designed to help traffic flow at major junctions. Make sure that you're in the correct lane and proceed if the way is clear and the green light shows for your lane.

Section eleven Questions

What does this sign mean?

Where traffic lights are out of order you might see this sign. Proceed with caution as nobody has priority at the junction.

☐ Traffic lights out of order

☐ Amber signal out of order

☐ Temporary traffic lights ahead

☐ New traffic lights ahead

These flashing red lights mean STOP. In which THREE of the following places could you find them?

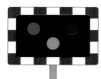

You must always stop when the red lights are flashing, whether or not the way seems to be clear.

☐ Pelican crossings

☐ Lifting bridges

☐ Zebra crossings

☐ Level crossings

☐ Motorway exits

☐ Fire stations

What do these zigzag lines at pedestrian crossings mean?

The approach to, and exit from, a pedestrian crossing is marked with zigzag lines. You must not park on them or overtake the leading vehicle when approaching the crossing. Parking here would block the view for pedestrians and the approaching traffic.

- [ ] No parking at any time
- [ ] Parking allowed only for a short time
- [ ] Slow down to 20 mph
- [ ] Sounding horns is not allowed

When may you cross a double solid white line in the middle of the road?

You may cross the solid white line to pass a stationary vehicle, pedal cycle, horse or road maintenance vehicle if they are travelling at 10 mph or less. You may also cross the solid line to enter into a side road or access a property.

- [ ] To pass traffic that is queuing back at a junction
- [ ] To pass a car signalling to turn left ahead
- [ ] To pass a road maintenance vehicle travelling at 10 mph or less
- [ ] To pass a vehicle that is towing a trailer

What does this road marking mean?

Road markings will warn you of a hazard ahead. A single, broken line along the centre of the road, with long markings and short gaps, is a hazard warning line. Don't cross it unless you can see that the road is clear well ahead.

- [ ] Do not cross the line
- [ ] No stopping allowed
- [ ] You are approaching a hazard
- [ ] No overtaking allowed

Section eleven Questions

Where would you see this road marking?

Due to the dark colour of the road, changes in level aren't easily seen. White triangles painted on the road surface give you an indication of where there are road humps.

☐ At traffic lights

☐ On road humps

☐ Near a level crossing

☐ At a box junction

Which is a hazard warning line?

☐   ☐

☐   ☐

You need to know the difference between the normal centre line and a hazard warning line. If there is a hazard ahead, the markings are longer and the gaps shorter. This gives you advanced warning of an unspecified hazard ahead.

At this junction there is a stop sign with a solid white line on the road surface. Why is there a stop sign here?

If your view is restricted at a road junction you must stop. There may also be a 'stop' sign. Don't emerge until you're sure there's no traffic approaching.

IF YOU DON'T KNOW, DON'T GO.

☐ Speed on the major road is de-restricted

☐ It is a busy junction

☐ Visibility along the major road is restricted

☐ There are hazard warning lines in the centre of the road .

11.66 Mark one answer DES s6, HC p114, KYTS p68

You see this line across the road at the entrance to a roundabout. What does it mean?

Slow down as you approach the roundabout and check for traffic from the right. If you need to stop and give way, stay behind the broken line until it is safe to emerge onto the roundabout.

☐ Give way to traffic from the right

☐ Traffic from the left has right of way

☐ You have right of way

☐ Stop at the line

11.67 Mark one answer DES s6, HC r106

How will a police officer in a patrol vehicle normally get you to stop?

☐ Flash the headlights, indicate left and point to the left

☐ Wait until you stop, then approach you

☐ Use the siren, overtake, cut in front and stop

☐ Pull alongside you, use the siren and wave you to stop

You must obey signals given by the police. If a police officer in a patrol vehicle wants you to pull over they will indicate this without causing danger to you or other traffic.

11.68 Mark one answer DES s6, HC p104

You approach a junction. The traffic lights are not working. A police officer gives this signal. You should

If a police officer or traffic warden is directing traffic you must obey them. They will use the arm signals shown in The Highway Code. Learn what these mean and act accordingly.

☐ turn left only

☐ turn right only

☐ stop level with the officer's arm

☐ stop at the stop line

The driver of the car in front is giving this arm signal. What does it mean?

There might be an occasion where another driver uses an arm signal. This may be because the vehicle's indicators are obscured by other traffic. In order for such signals to be effective all drivers should know the meaning of them. Be aware that the 'left turn' signal might look similar to the 'slowing down' signal.

☐ The driver is slowing down

☐ The driver intends to turn right

☐ The driver wishes to overtake

☐ The driver intends to turn left

Where would you see these road markings?

When driving on a motorway or slip road, you must not enter into an area marked with chevrons and bordered by a solid white line for any reason, except in an emergency.

☐ At a level crossing

☐ On a motorway slip road

☐ At a pedestrian crossing

☐ On a single-track road

What does this motorway sign mean?

On the motorway, signs sometimes show temporary warnings due to traffic or weather conditions. They may be used to indicate

☐ Change to the lane on your left

☐ Leave the motorway at the next exit

☐ Change to the opposite carriageway

☐ Pull up on the hard shoulder

- lane closures
- temporary speed limits
- weather warnings.

11.72 | Mark one answer | DES s6, HC

What does this motorway sign mean?

☐ Temporary minimum speed 50 mph

☐ No services for 50 miles

☐ Obstruction 50 metres (164 feet) ahead

☐ Temporary maximum speed 50 mph

Look out for signs a lane or on the cent These will give you information or warning the road ahead. Due to the high speed of motorway traffic these signs may light up some distance from any hazard. Don't ignore the signs just because the road looks clear to you.

11.73 | Mark one answer | DES s6, HC p102, KYTS p90

What does this sign mean?

☐ Through traffic to use left lane

☐ Right-hand lane T-junction only

☐ Right-hand lane closed ahead

☐ 11 tonne weight limit

You should move into the lanes as directed by the sign. Here the right-hand lane is closed and the left-hand and centre lanes are available. Merging in turn is recommended when it's safe and traffic is going slowly, for example at road works or a road traffic incident. When vehicles are travelling at speed this is not advisable and you should move into the appropriate lane in good time.

11.74 | Mark one answer | DES s6, HC p110, KYTS p79

What does '25' mean on this motorway sign?

☐ The distance to the nearest town

☐ The route number of the road

☐ The number of the next junction

☐ The speed limit on the slip road

Before you set out on your journey use a road map to plan your route. When you see advance warning of your junction, make sure you get into the correct lane in plenty of time. Last-minute harsh braking and cutting across lanes at speed is extremely hazardous.

Mark one answer DES s6

The right-hand lane of a three-lane motorway is

☐ for lorries only

☐ an overtaking lane

☐ the right-turn lane

☐ an acceleration lane

You should stay in the left-hand lane of a motorway unless overtaking. The right-hand lane of a motorway is an overtaking lane and not a 'fast lane'.

After overtaking, move back to the left when it is safe to do so.

11.76 **Mark one answer** DES s6, HC r132, KYTS p71

Where can you find reflective amber studs on a motorway?

☐ Separating the slip road from the motorway

☐ On the left-hand edge of the road

☐ On the right-hand edge of the road

☐ Separating the lanes

At night or in poor visibility reflective studs on the road help you to judge your position on the carriageway.

11.77 **Mark one answer** DES s6, HC r132, KYTS p71

Where on a motorway would you find green reflective studs?

☐ Separating driving lanes

☐ Between the hard shoulder and the carriageway

☐ At slip road entrances and exits

☐ Between the carriageway and the central reservation

Knowing the colours of the reflective studs on the road will help you judge your position, especially at night, in foggy conditions or when visibility is poor.

11.78 **Mark one answer** DES s6, HC p102, KYTS p90

You are travelling along a motorway. You see this sign. You should

You'll see this sign if the motorway is closed ahead. Pull into the nearside lane as soon as it is safe to do so. Don't leave it to the last moment.

☐ leave the motorway at the next exit

☐ turn left immediately

☐ change lane

☐ move onto the hard shoulder

11.79

Mark one answer

DES s6, HC p112, KYTS p89

What does this sign mean?

When you leave the motorway make sure that you check your speedometer. You may be going faster than you realise. Slow down and look out for speed limit signs.

- ☐ No motor vehicles
- ☐ End of motorway
- ☐ No through road
- ☐ End of bus lane

11.80

Mark one answer

DES s6, HC p106, KYTS p20

Which of these signs means that the national speed limit applies?

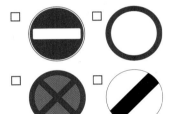

You should know the speed limit for the road on which you are travelling and the vehicle that you are driving. The different speed limits are shown in The Highway Code.

11.81

Mark one answer

DES s6, HC p40

What is the maximum speed on a single carriageway road?

- ☐ 50 mph
- ☐ 60 mph
- ☐ 40 mph
- ☐ 70 mph

If you're travelling on a dual carriageway that becomes a single carriageway road, reduce your speed gradually so that you aren't exceeding the limit as you enter. There might not be a sign to remind you of the limit, so make sure you know what the speed limits are for different types of roads and vehicles.

What does this sign mean?

Temporary restrictions on motorways are shown on signs which have flashing amber lights. At the end of the restriction you will see this sign without any flashing lights.

☐ End of motorway
☐ End of restriction
☐ Lane ends ahead
☐ Free recovery ends

This sign is advising you to

When a diversion route has been put in place, drivers are advised to follow a symbol which may be a triangle, square, circle or diamond shape on a yellow background.

☐ follow the route diversion
☐ follow the signs to the picnic area
☐ give way to pedestrians
☐ give way to cyclists

Why would this temporary speed limit sign be shown?

In the interests of road safety, temporary speed limits are imposed at all major road works. Signs like this, giving advanced warning of the speed limit, are normally placed about three quarters of a mile ahead of where the speed limit comes into force.

☐ To warn of the end of the motorway
☐ To warn you of a low bridge
☐ To warn you of a junction ahead
☐ To warn of road works ahead

11.85 | **Mark one answer** | DES s6, HC p113, KYTS p138

This traffic sign means there is

The sign gives you an early warning of a speed restriction. If you are travelling at a higher speed, slow down in good time. You could come across queuing traffic due to roadworks or a temporary obstruction.

☐ a compulsory maximum speed limit

☐ an advisory maximum speed limit

☐ a compulsory minimum speed limit

☐ an advised separation distance

11.86 | **Mark one answer** | DES s6, HC p108, KYTS p139

You see this sign at a crossroads. You should

When traffic lights are out of order treat the junction as an unmarked crossroad. Be very careful as no one has priority and be prepared to stop.

☐ maintain the same speed

☐ carry on with great care

☐ find another route

☐ telephone the police

11.87 | **Mark one answer** | DES s6, HC r103, p103

You are signalling to turn right in busy traffic. How would you confirm your intention safely?

☐ Sound the horn

☐ Give an arm signal

☐ Flash your headlights

☐ Position over the centre line

In some situations you may feel your indicators cannot be seen by other road users. If you think you need to make your intention more clearly seen, give the arm signal shown in The Highway Code.

Mark one answer

What does this sign mean?

You must comply with all traffic signs and be especially aware of those signs which apply specifically to the type of vehicle you are using.

☐ Motorcycles only

☐ No cars

☐ Cars only

☐ No motorcycles

Mark one answer

You are on a motorway. You see this sign on a lorry that has stopped in the right-hand lane. You should

Sometimes work is carried out on the motorway without closing the lanes. When this happens, signs are mounted on the back of lorries to warn other road users of roadworks ahead.

☐ move into the right-hand lane

☐ stop behind the flashing lights

☐ pass the lorry on the left

☐ leave the motorway at the next exit

Mark one answer

You are on a motorway. Red flashing lights appear above your lane only. What should you do?

☐ Continue in that lane and look for further information

☐ Move into another lane in good time

☐ Pull onto the hard shoulder

☐ Stop and wait for an instruction to proceed

Flashing red lights above your lane show that your lane is closed. You should move into another lane as soon as you can do so safely.

11.91

Mark one answer

DES s6, HC r112

When may you sound the horn?

☐ To give you right of way

☐ To attract a friend's attention

☐ To warn others of your presence

☐ To make slower drivers move over

Never sound the horn aggressively. You MUST NOT sound it when driving in a built-up area between 11.30 pm and 7.00 am or when you are stationary, an exception to this is when another road user poses a danger. Do not scare animals by sounding your horn.

11.92

Mark one answer

DES s6, HC r112

You must not use your horn when you are stationary

☐ unless a moving vehicle may cause you danger

☐ at any time whatsoever

☐ unless it is used only briefly

☐ except for signalling that you have just arrived

When stationary only sound your horn if you think there is a risk of danger from another road user. Don't use it just to attract someone's attention. This causes unnecessary noise and could be misleading.

11.93

Mark one answer

DES s6, HC p107, KYTS p55

What does this sign mean?

URBAN CLEARWAY
Monday to Friday

am	pm
8.00 - 9.30	4.30 - 6.30

Urban clearways are provided to keep traffic flowing at busy times. You may stop only briefly to set down or pick up passengers. Times of operation will vary from place to place so always check the signs.

☐ You can park on the days and times shown

☐ No parking on the days and times shown

☐ No parking at all from Monday to Friday

☐ End of the urban clearway restrictions

Mark one answer DES s6, HC p109, KYTS p12

What does this sign mean?

You should be careful in these locations as the road surface is likely to be wet and slippery. There may be a steep drop to the water, and there may not be a barrier along the edge of the road.

☐ Quayside or river bank

☐ Steep hill downwards

☐ Uneven road surface

☐ Road liable to flooding

Mark one answer DES s6, HC r127, p114, KYTS p62

A white line like this along the centre of the road is a

The centre of the road is usually marked by a broken white line, with lines that are shorter than the gaps. When the lines become longer than the gaps this is a hazard warning line. Look well ahead for these, especially when you are planning to overtake or turn off.

☐ bus lane marking

☐ hazard warning

☐ give way marking

☐ lane marking

What is the reason for the yellow criss-cross lines painted on the road here?

☐ To mark out an area for trams only

☐ To prevent queuing traffic from blocking the junction on the left

☐ To mark the entrance lane to a car park

☐ To warn you of the tram lines crossing the road

Yellow 'box junctions' like this are often used where it's busy. Their purpose is to keep the junction clear for crossing traffic. Don't enter the painted area unless your exit is clear. The exception to this is when you are turning right and are only prevented from doing so by oncoming traffic or by other vehicles waiting to turn right.

What is the reason for the area marked in red and white along the centre of this road?

☐ It is to separate traffic flowing in opposite directions

☐ It marks an area to be used by overtaking motorcyclists

☐ It is a temporary marking to warn of the roadworks

☐ It is separating the two sides of the dual carriageway

Areas of 'hatched markings' such as these are to separate traffic streams which could be a danger to each other. They are often seen on bends or where the road becomes narrow. If the area is bordered by a solid white line, you must not enter it except in an emergency.

Mark one answer

Other drivers may sometimes flash their headlights at you. In which situation are they allowed to do this?

☐ To warn of a radar speed trap ahead

☐ To show that they are giving way to you

☐ To warn you of their presence

☐ To let you know there is a fault with your vehicle

If other drivers flash their headlights this isn't a signal to show priority. The flashing of headlights has the same meaning as sounding the horn, it's a warning of their presence.

Mark one answer

In some narrow residential streets you may find a speed limit of

☐ 20 mph

☐ 25 mph

☐ 35 mph

☐ 40 mph

In some built-up areas, you may find the speed limit reduced to 20 mph. Driving at a slower speed will help give you the time and space to see and deal safely with hazards such as pedestrians and parked cars.

Mark one answer

At a junction you see this signal. It means

The white light shows that trams must stop, but the green light shows that other vehicles may go if the way is clear. You may not live in an area where there are trams but you should still learn the signs. You never know when you may go to a town with trams.

☐ cars must stop

☐ trams must stop

☐ both trams and cars must stop

☐ both trams and cars can continue

11.101

Mark one answer

DES s6, KYTS p69

Where would you find these road markings?

These markings show the direction in which the traffic should go at a mini-roundabout.

☐ At a railway crossing

☐ At a junction

☐ On a motorway

☐ On a pedestrian crossing

11.102

Mark one answer

DES s6, HC r106

There is a police car following you. The police officer flashes the headlights and points to the left. What should you do?

You must pull up on the left as soon as it's safe to do so and switch off your engine.

☐ Turn left at the next junction

☐ Pull up on the left

☐ Stop immediately

☐ Move over to the left

11.103

Mark one answer

DES s6, HC p102, KYTS p119

You see this amber traffic light ahead. Which light or lights, will come on next?

At junctions controlled by traffic lights you must stop behind the white line until the lights change to green. Red and amber lights showing together also mean stop.

You may proceed when the light is green unless your exit road is blocked or pedestrians are crossing in front of you.

If you're approaching traffic lights that are visible from a distance and the light has been green for some time they are likely to change. Be ready to slow down and stop.

☐ Red alone

☐ Red and amber together

☐ Green and amber together

☐ Green alone

You see this signal overhead on the motorway. What does it mean?

☐ Leave the motorway at the next exit

☐ All vehicles use the hard shoulder

☐ Sharp bend to the left ahead

☐ Stop, all lanes ahead closed

You will see this sign if there has been an incident ahead and the motorway is closed. You MUST obey the sign. Make sure that you prepare to leave as soon as you see the warning sign.

Don't pull over at the last moment or cut across other traffic.

What MUST you do when you see this sign?

STOP signs are situated at junctions where visibility is restricted or there is heavy traffic. They MUST be obeyed. You MUST stop.

Take good all-round observation before moving off.

☐ Stop, only if traffic is approaching

☐ Stop, even if the road is clear

☐ Stop, only if children are waiting to cross

☐ Stop, only if a red light is showing

Which shape is used for a 'give way' sign?

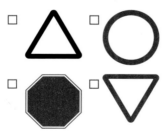

Other warning signs are the same shape and colour, but the 'give way' sign triangle points downwards. When you see this sign you MUST give way to traffic on the road which you are about to enter.

11.107 | **Mark one answer** | DES s6, HC p107, KYTS p19

What does this sign mean?

When you see this sign, look out for any direction signs and judge whether you need to signal your intentions. Do this in good time so that other road users approaching the roundabout know what you're planning to do.

☐ Buses turning
☐ Ring road
☐ Mini-roundabout
☐ Keep right

11.108 | **Mark one answer** | DES s6, HC p108, KYTS p11

What does this sign mean?

Be prepared for traffic approaching from junctions on either side of you. Try to avoid unnecessary changing of lanes just before the junction.

☐ Two-way traffic straight ahead
☐ Two-way traffic crosses a one-way road
☐ Two-way traffic over a bridge
☐ Two-way traffic crosses a two-way road

11.109 | **Mark one answer** | DES s6, HC p108, KYTS p11

What does this sign mean?

This sign may be at the end of a dual carriageway or a one-way street. It is there to warn you of oncoming traffic.

☐ Two-way traffic ahead across a one-way road
☐ Traffic approaching you has priority
☐ Two-way traffic straight ahead
☐ Motorway contraflow system ahead

Mark one answer

What does this sign mean?

☐ Hump bridge
☐ Traffic calming hump
☐ Low bridge
☐ Uneven road

You will need to slow down. At hump bridges your view ahead will be restricted and the road will often be narrow on the bridge. If the bridge is very steep or your view is restricted sound your horn to warn others of your approach. Going too fast over the bridge is highly dangerous to other road users and could even cause your wheels to leave the road, with a resulting loss of control.

Mark one answer

What does this sign mean?

☐ Direction to park-and-ride car park
☐ No parking for buses or coaches
☐ Directions to bus and coach park
☐ Parking area for cars and coaches

To ease the congestion in town centres, some cities and towns provide park-and-ride schemes. These allow you to park in a designated area and ride by bus into the centre.

Park-and-ride schemes are usually cheaper and easier than car parking in the town centre.

Mark one answer

You are approaching traffic lights. Red and amber are showing. This means

☐ pass the lights if the road is clear
☐ there is a fault with the lights – take care
☐ wait for the green light before you cross the stop line
☐ the lights are about to change to red

Be aware that other traffic might still be clearing the junction. Make sure the way is clear before continuing.

11.113 | Mark one answer | DES s6, HC p116, KYTS p69

This marking appears on the road just before a

- ☐ 'no entry' sign
- ☐ 'give way' sign
- ☐ 'stop' sign
- ☐ 'no through road' sign

Where you see this road marking you should give way to traffic on the main road. It might not be used at junctions where there is relatively little traffic. However, if there is a double broken line across the junction the 'give way' rules still apply.

11.114 | Mark one answer | DES s6, HC r293, p102

At a railway level crossing the red light signal continues to flash after a train has gone by. What should you do?

- ☐ Phone the signal operator
- ☐ Alert drivers behind you
- ☐ Wait
- ☐ Proceed with caution

You MUST always obey red flashing stop lights. If a train passes but the lights continue to flash, another train will be passing soon. Cross only when the lights go off and the barriers open.

11.115 | Mark one answer | DES s6, KYTS p116

You are in a tunnel and you see this sign. What does it mean?

- ☐ Direction to emergency pedestrian exit
- ☐ Beware of pedestrians, no footpath ahead
- ☐ No access for pedestrians
- ☐ Beware of pedestrians crossing ahead

If you have to leave your vehicle in a tunnel and leave by an emergency exit, do so as quickly as you can. Follow the signs directing you to the nearest exit point. If there are several people using the exit, don't panic but try to leave in a calm and orderly manner.

Mark one answer

Which of these signs shows that you are entering a one-way system?

☐   ☐

☐   ☐

If the road has two lanes you can use either lane and overtake on either side. Use the lane that's more convenient for your destination unless signs or road markings indicate otherwise.

Mark one answer

What does this sign mean?

☐ With-flow bus and cycle lane

☐ Contraflow bus and cycle lane

☐ No buses and cycles allowed

☐ No waiting for buses and cycles

Buses and cycles can travel in this lane. In this case they will flow in the same direction as other traffic. If it's busy they may be passing you on the left, so watch out for them. Times on the sign will show its hours of operation. No times shown, or no sign at all, means it's 24 hours. In some areas other vehicles, such as taxis and motorcycles, are allowed to use bus lanes. The sign will show these.

Mark one answer

What does this sign mean?

Look well ahead and be ready to stop for any pedestrians crossing, or about to cross, the road. Also check the pavements for anyone who looks like they might step or run into the road.

☐ School crossing patrol

☐ No pedestrians allowed

☐ Pedestrian zone – no vehicles

☐ Zebra crossing ahead

Mark one answer

DES s6, HC r103, p103

Which arm signal tells you that the car you are following is going to pull up?

There may be occasions when drivers need to give an arm signal to confirm an indicator. This could include in bright sunshine, at a complex road layout, when stopping at a pedestrian crossing or when turning right just after passing a parked vehicle. You should understand what each arm signal means. If you give arm signals, make them clear, correct and decisive.

11.120

Mark one answer

DES s6, HC p107, KYTS p19

Which of these signs means turn left ahead?

Blue circles tell you what you must do and this sign gives a clear instruction to turn left ahead. You should be looking out for signs at all times and know what they mean.

11.121

Mark one answer

DES s6, HC p102, KYTS p119

You are approaching a red traffic light. What will the signal show next?

If you know which light is going to show next you can plan your approach accordingly. This can help prevent excessive braking or hesitation at the junction.

☐ Red and amber
☐ Green alone
☐ Amber alone
☐ Green and amber

Mark one answer

DES s6, HC p108, KYTS p12

What does this sign mean?

When approaching a tunnel switch on your dipped headlights. Be aware that your eyes might need to adjust to the sudden darkness. You may need to reduce your speed.

☐ Low bridge ahead

☐ Tunnel ahead

☐ Ancient monument ahead

☐ Traffic danger spot ahead

Mark one answer

DES s6, HC r103, p103

You are approaching a zebra crossing where pedestrians are waiting. Which arm signal might you give?

☐   ☐

A 'slowing down' signal will indicate your intentions to oncoming and following vehicles. Be aware that pedestrians might start to cross as soon as they see this signal.

☐   ☐

Mark one answer

DES s6, HC p114, KYTS p65

The white line along the side of the road

A continuous white line is used on many roads to indicate the edge of the carriageway. This can be useful when visibility is restricted. The line is discontinued at junctions, lay-bys and entrances and exits from private drives.

☐ shows the edge of the carriageway

☐ shows the approach to a hazard

☐ means no parking

☐ means no overtaking

11.125

Mark one answer

DES s6, KYTS p63

You see this white arrow on the road ahead. It means

- ☐ entrance on the left
- ☐ all vehicles turn left
- ☐ keep left of the hatched markings
- ☐ road bending to the left

Don't attempt to overtake here, as there might be unseen hazards over the brow of the hill. Keep to the left.

11.126

Mark one answer

DES s6, HC r103, p103

How should you give an arm signal to turn left?

☐   ☐

☐   ☐

There may be occasions where other road users are unable to see your indicator, such as in bright sunlight or at a busy, complicated junction. In these cases a hand signal will help others to understand your intentions.

You are waiting at a T-junction. A vehicle is coming from the right with the left signal flashing. What should you do?

Other road users may give misleading signals. When you're waiting at a junction don't emerge until you're sure of their intentions.

☐ Move out and accelerate hard

☐ Wait until the vehicle starts to turn in

☐ Pull out before the vehicle reaches the junction

☐ Move out slowly

When may you use hazard warning lights when driving?

☐ Instead of sounding the horn in a built-up area between 11.30 pm and 7 am

☐ On a motorway or unrestricted dual carriageway, to warn of a hazard ahead

☐ On rural routes, after a warning sign of animals

☐ On the approach to toucan crossings where cyclists are waiting to cross

When there's queuing traffic ahead and you have to slow down or even stop, showing your hazard warning lights will alert following traffic to the hazard. Don't forget to switch them off as the queue forms behind you.

You should NOT normally stop on these markings near schools

At schools you should not stop on yellow zigzag lines for any length of time, not even to set down or pick up children or other passengers.

☐ except when picking up children

☐ under any circumstances

☐ unless there is nowhere else available

☐ except to set down children

11.130   Mark one answer   DES s6, HC r103

Why should you make sure that your indicators are cancelled after turning?

☐ To avoid flattening the battery

☐ To avoid misleading other road users

☐ To avoid dazzling other road users

☐ To avoid damage to the indicator relay

Leaving your indicators on could confuse other road users and may even lead to a crash. Be aware that if you haven't taken a sharp turn your indicators may not self-cancel and you will need to turn them off manually.

11.131   Mark one answer   DES s6, HC r103

You are driving in busy traffic. You want to pull up on the left just after a junction on the left. When should you signal?

☐ As you are passing or just after the junction

☐ Just before you reach the junction

☐ Well before you reach the junction

☐ It would be better not to signal at all

You need to signal to let other drivers know your intentions. However, if you indicate too early they may think you are turning left into the junction. Correct timing of the signal is very important to avoid misleading others.

Case study practice – 11
Road and traffic signs

Ajay is driving through an area where there are many pedestrians.

There's a turning ahead with a red-bordered round sign, showing a car with a motorcycle above it.

Outside town, the single carriageway road has a double unbroken white centre line.

Ajay sees several signs with brown backgrounds.

He approaches a traffic light signal which is showing green. The signal changes just before Ajay reaches it.

11.1 What's meant by the round sign described above?
Mark **one** answer

☐   No large vehicles
☐   No motor vehicles
☐   No through road
☐   No vehicle parking

HC p106

11.2 What does this centre line road marking tell Ajay?

Mark one answer

- [ ] No speeding
- [ ] No reversing
- [ ] No parking
- [ ] No overtaking

HC r129, p114 **KYTS** p64

11.3 What's the national speed limit for cars on this type of road?

Mark one answer

- [ ] 40 mph
- [ ] 50 mph
- [ ] 60 mph
- [ ] 70 mph

HC p40

11.4 What details would Ajay find on the brown signs?

Mark one answer

- [ ] Tourist information
- [ ] Safety information
- [ ] Cyclist information
- [ ] Weather information

DES s6 **KYTS** p101–104

11.5 As the traffic lights change, what colour signal would Ajay see next?

Mark one answer

- [ ] A red light on its own
- [ ] Red and amber together
- [ ] An amber light on its own
- [ ] Green and amber together

HC p102 **DES** s6

Section twelve

Essential documents

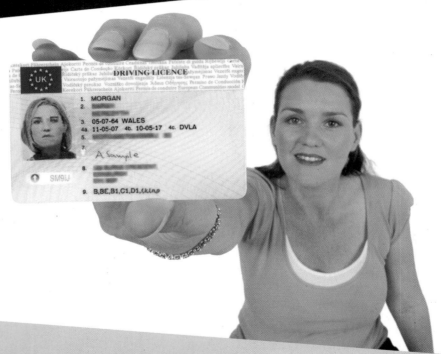

In this section, you'll learn about

- the documents you need when owning and keeping a car
- the driving licence
- buying insurance
- the MOT test.

Essential documents

Before you can legally drive on a public road, you **MUST**

- ensure a valid tax disc is displayed on the vehicle you're driving
- hold a valid driving licence
- have valid insurance cover
- ensure the vehicle you're driving has a valid MOT certificate if it's more than three years old (four in Northern Ireland).

You won't be able to tax your vehicle unless you have

- a valid MOT certificate if your vehicle is more than three years old (four in Northern Ireland)
- appropriate, current insurance cover.

HC p122 **DES** s2

> Registering and owning a car

The vehicle registration certificate (V5C) contains details of

- the vehicle, including make, model, engine size and year of registration
- the registered keeper.

If you're the registered keeper, you **MUST** tell the Driver and Vehicle Licensing Agency (DVLA), or the Driver and Vehicle Agency (DVA) in Northern Ireland, when you change

- your vehicle
- your name
- your permanent address.

If you buy a second-hand vehicle, tell the DVLA/DVA immediately that the keeper of the vehicle has changed.

Find out more about the V5C at this website.

❯ **www.gov.uk**

Vehicles used on public roads **MUST** have a valid tax disc clearly displayed. This shows that the vehicle excise duty (road tax) has been paid.

`HC` `p122` `DES` `s2`

If you're not going to use your vehicle on public roads, you won't have to pay road tax as long as you tell the DVLA/DVA in advance. This is called a Statutory Off-Road Notification (SORN) declaration and lasts for 12 months.

`DES` `s2`

❯ Your driving licence

Before driving on a public road, a learner **MUST** have a valid provisional driving licence.

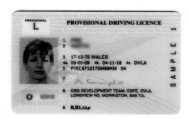

You **MUST** tell the licensing authority if

- your health is likely to affect your driving
- your eyesight doesn't meet the required standard.

`HC` `r90` `DES` `s1`

Eyesight: to be able to drive you **MUST** be able to read in good daylight, with glasses or contact lenses if you wear them, a vehicle number plate from 20 metres (about 66 feet) – which is about five car lengths.

If you want to practise driving before you pass your test, you **MUST** be accompanied by someone who's at least 21 years old and has held (and still holds) a full licence for the category of vehicle you're driving, for three years.

HC **p123** **DES** **s2**

For two years after you pass your first practical test (car or motorcycle), there's a probation period. This means that if you get six or more penalty points within this two year probation period, you'll lose your licence. You'll then have to

- reapply for a provisional licence
- pass your theory and practical tests again.

Any points on your provisional licence will be transferred to your new licence when you pass your test.

HC **p127, 134**

Insurance

You **MUST** have at least third-party insurance cover before driving on public roads. This covers

- injury to another person
- damage to someone else's property
- damage to other vehicles.

Driving without insurance is a criminal offence and can lead to a maximum fine of £5000, and possibly disqualification.

HC **p121–122** **DES** **s2**

Certificate of Motor Insurance		
Registration mark of vehicle	ANY 1234	Certificate number 000123496
Name of Policyholder	Mr A N Other	
Effective date of the commencement of insurance for the purposes of the relevant law	01/07/12 (Noon)	Date of expiry of insurance 01/07/13 (Noon)

You'll need to show your insurance certificate when you're taxing your vehicle or if a police officer asks you for it. Your insurer may give you a temporary cover note until you receive your insurance certificate.

Remember, if your vehicle is unused or off the road it **MUST** have either a SORN declaration or valid insurance. If you have neither, and ignore any subsequent reminders sent to you as the registered keeper, you risk

- a fixed-penalty fine of £100
- court prosecution and a fine of up to £1000
- having the vehicle clamped, seized and destroyed.

DES s2

If a police officer asks to see your documents and you don't have them with you, you can produce them at a police station within seven days.
HC p122 **DES** s16

The cost of your insurance is generally lower if you're over 25 years old. Your insurance policy may have an excess of, for example, £100. This means you'll have to pay the first £100 of any claim.

Before you drive anyone else's vehicle, make sure it's insured for you to drive.
HC p121–122 **DES** s2

⊘ MOT test

The MOT test makes sure your vehicle meets road safety and environmental standards. Cars **MUST** first have an MOT test when they're three years old (four in Northern Ireland). MOT certificates are valid for one year.

HC p121 **DES** s2

Trailers and caravans don't need an MOT, but they do need to be kept in good order.

HC p121

The only time when you can drive your car without an MOT certificate is when you're driving to or from an appointment at an MOT centre or to have MOT repairs carried out.

If your vehicle needs an MOT certificate and you don't have one,

- you won't be able to renew your road tax
- you could be prosecuted
- your insurance may be invalid.

HC p121 **DES** s2

 For more information about MOT tests, see this website.

❯ www.gov.uk

Meeting the standards

You must be able to

make sure that your driving licence is valid for the category of vehicle that you're driving

make sure that the vehicle is registered and a valid tax disc is correctly displayed

make sure that you have valid insurance for your use of the vehicle

make sure that the vehicle has a current MOT certificate (if necessary).

You must know and understand

that you must have a valid driving licence for the vehicle you drive. You must also comply with any restrictions on your licence

that the vehicle must be registered with DVLA/DVA

that you must tell DVLA/DVA if you

- change your name
- change your address
- have or develop a medical condition that will affect your ability to drive

that the vehicle you drive must have a valid MOT certificate, if it's more than three years old.

> Notes

You can use this page to make your own notes or diagrams about the key points you need to remember.

Think about

- What documents do you need when taxing your vehicle?
- You must tell DVLA/DVA when certain details change: what are they?
- What's a SORN?
- What's the minimum level of insurance you must have before driving on public roads?
- What does an MOT test cover?

Your notes

Things to discuss and practise with your instructor

These are just a few examples of what you could discuss with your instructor. Read more about essential documents to come up with your own ideas.

Discuss with your instructor

- what will happen if you accumulate six or more penalty points on your licence within two years of passing your test
- what the letters 'SORN' stand for and what this means to the keeper of a vehicle
- what you **MUST** have to use a vehicle legally on the road, eg a valid driving licence.

Practise with your instructor

It's difficult to practise your knowledge and understanding of documents. Just remember that the safer and more responsibly you drive, the less likely you are to

- cause high wear and tear to your car
- accumulate penalty points
- be involved in an incident and damage your car.

Meaning that

- your car will be more likely to be roadworthy and pass its MOT test
- you'll be able to find cheaper car insurance
- you won't lose your licence, under the New Driver's Act and beyond.

An MOT certificate is normally valid for

☐ three years after the date it was issued

☐ 10,000 miles

☐ one year after the date it was issued

☐ 30,000 miles

Make a note of the date that your MOT certificate expires. Some garages remind you that your vehicle is due an MOT but not all do. You may take your vehicle for MOT up to one month in advance and have the certificate post dated.

A cover note is a document issued before you receive your

☐ driving licence

☐ insurance certificate

☐ registration document

☐ MOT certificate

Sometimes an insurance company will issue a temporary insurance certificate called a cover note. It gives you the same insurance cover as your certificate, but lasts for a limited period, usually one month.

You have just passed your practical test. You do not hold a full licence in another category. Within two years you get six penalty points on your licence. What will you have to do?

☐ Retake only your theory test

☐ Retake your theory and practical tests

☐ Retake only your practical test

☐ Reapply for your full licence immediately

☐ Reapply for your provisional licence

If you accumulate six or more penalty points within two years of gaining your first full licence it will be revoked. The six or more points include any gained due to offences you committed before passing your test. If this happens you may only drive as a learner until you pass both the theory and practical tests again.

How long will a Statutory Off Road Notification (SORN) last for?

☐ 12 months

☐ 24 months

☐ 3 years

☐ 10 years

A SORN declaration allows you to keep a vehicle off road and untaxed for 12 months. If you want to keep your vehicle off road beyond that you must send a further SORN form to DVLA, or DVA in Northern Ireland. If the vehicle is sold SORN will end and the new owner becomes responsible immediately.

12.5 — NI EXEMPT — Mark one answer — DES s2, HC p122

What is a Statutory Off Road Notification (SORN) declaration?

☐ A notification to tell VOSA that a vehicle does not have a current MOT

☐ Information kept by the police about the owner of the vehicle

☐ A notification to tell DVLA that a vehicle is not being used on the road

☐ Information held by insurance companies to check the vehicle is insured

If you want to keep a vehicle off the public road you must declare SORN. It is an offence not to do so. You then won't have to pay road tax. If you don't renew the SORN declaration or re-license the vehicle, you will incur a penalty.

12.6 — Mark one answer — DES s2, HC p126

What is the maximum specified fine for driving without insurance?

☐ £50

☐ £500

☐ £1,000

☐ £5,000

It is a serious offence to drive without insurance. As well as a heavy fine you may be disqualified or incur penalty points.

12.7 — Mark one answer — DES s2, HC p122

Who is legally responsible for ensuring that a Vehicle Registration Certificate (V5C) is updated?

☐ The registered vehicle keeper

☐ The vehicle manufacturer

☐ Your insurance company

☐ The licensing authority

It is your legal responsibility to keep the details of your Vehicle Registration Certificate (V5C) up to date. You should tell the licensing authority of any changes. These include your name, address, or vehicle details. If you don't do this you may have problems when you sell your vehicle.

12.8 — Mark one answer — DES s2, HC p122

For which of these MUST you show your insurance certificate?

☐ When making a SORN declaration

☐ When buying or selling a vehicle

☐ When a police officer asks you for it

☐ When having an MOT inspection

You MUST be able to produce your valid insurance certificate when requested by a police officer. If you can't do this immediately you may be asked to take it to a police station. Other documents you may be asked to produce are your driving licence and MOT certificate.

Which THREE of these do you need before you can use a vehicle on the road legally?

☐ A valid driving licence

☐ A valid tax disc clearly displayed

☐ Proof of your identity

☐ Proper insurance cover

☐ Breakdown cover

☐ A vehicle handbook

Using a vehicle on the road illegally carries a heavy fine and can lead to penalty points on your licence. Things you MUST have include a valid driving licence, a current valid tax disc, and proper insurance cover.

When you apply to renew your Vehicle Excise Duty (tax disc) you must have

☐ valid insurance

☐ the old tax disc

☐ the handbook

☐ a valid driving licence

Tax discs can be renewed at post offices, vehicle registration offices, online or by post. When applying make sure you have all the relevant valid documents, including MOT where applicable.

A police officer asks to see your documents. You do not have them with you. You may be asked to take them to a police station within

☐ 5 days

☐ 7 days

☐ 14 days

☐ 21 days

You don't have to carry the documents for your vehicle around with you. If a police officer asks to see them and you don't have them with you, you may be asked to produce them at a police station within seven days.

To drive on the road learners MUST

☐ have NO penalty points on their licence

☐ have taken professional instruction

☐ have a signed, valid provisional licence

☐ apply for a driving test within 12 months

Before you drive on the road you MUST have a valid provisional licence, for the category of vehicle that you're driving. It must show your signature, it isn't valid without it.

12.13

Mark one answer

DES s2

Before driving anyone else's motor vehicle you should make sure that

☐ the vehicle owner has third party insurance cover

☐ your own vehicle has insurance cover

☐ the vehicle is insured for your use

☐ the owner has left the insurance documents in the vehicle

Driving a vehicle without insurance cover is illegal. If you cause injury to anyone or damage to property, it could be very expensive and you could also be subject to a criminal prosecution. You can arrange insurance cover with an insurance company, a broker and some motor manufacturers or dealers.

12.14

Mark one answer

DES s2, HC p121

Your car needs an MOT certificate. If you drive without one this could invalidate your

☐ vehicle service record

☐ insurance

☐ road tax disc

☐ vehicle registration document

If your vehicle requires an MOT certificate, it's illegal to drive it without one. The only exceptions are that you may drive to a pre-arranged MOT test appointment, or to a garage for repairs required for the test. As well as being illegal, the vehicle may also be unsafe for use on the road and could endanger you, any passengers and other road users.

12.15

Mark one answer

DES s2, HC p121–122

A newly qualified driver must

☐ display green 'L' plates

☐ not exceed 40 mph for 12 months

☐ be accompanied on a motorway

☐ have valid motor insurance

It is your responsibility to make sure you are properly insured for the vehicle you are driving.

12.16

Mark three answers

DES s2, HC p121

You have third party insurance. What does this cover?

☐ Damage to your own vehicle

☐ Damage to your vehicle by fire

☐ Injury to another person

☐ Damage to someone's property

☐ Damage to other vehicles

☐ Injury to yourself

Third party insurance doesn't cover damage to your own vehicle or injury to yourself. If you have a crash and your vehicle is damaged you might have to carry out the repairs at your own expense.

Vehicle excise duty is often called 'Road Tax' or 'The Tax Disc'. You must

☐ keep it with your registration document

☐ display it clearly on your vehicle

☐ keep it concealed safely in your vehicle

☐ carry it on you at all times

The tax disc should be displayed at the bottom of the windscreen on the nearside (left-hand side). This allows it to be easily seen from the kerbside. It must be current, and you can't transfer the disc from vehicle to vehicle.

Which THREE pieces of information are found on a vehicle registration document?

☐ Registered keeper

☐ Make of the vehicle

☐ Service history details

☐ Date of the MOT

☐ Type of insurance cover

☐ Engine size

Every vehicle used on the road has a registration certificate. This is issued by the Driver and Vehicle Licensing Agency (DVLA) or Driver and Vehicle Agency (DVA) in Northern Ireland. The document shows vehicle details including date of first registration, registration number, previous keeper, registered keeper, make of vehicle, engine size and chassis number, year of manufacture and colour.

You have a duty to contact the licensing authority when

☐ you go abroad on holiday

☐ you change your vehicle

☐ you change your name

☐ your job status is changed

☐ your permanent address changes

☐ your job involves travelling abroad

The licensing authority need to keep their records up to date. They send out a reminder when your road tax is due and need your current address to send this to you. Every vehicle in the country is registered, so it's possible to trace its history.

12.20 Mark three answers DES s1, HC r90

You must notify the licensing authority when

☐ your health affects your driving

☐ your eyesight does not meet a set standard

☐ you intend lending your vehicle

☐ your vehicle requires an MOT certificate

☐ you change your vehicle

The Driver and Vehicle Licensing Agency (DVLA) hold the records of all vehicles and drivers in Great Britain (DVA in Northern Ireland). They need to know of any change in circumstances so that they can keep their records up to date. Your health might affect your ability to drive safely. Don't risk endangering your own safety or that of other road users.

12.21 NI EXEMPT Mark one answer DES s1, 11

The cost of your insurance may reduce if you

☐ are under 25 years old

☐ do not wear glasses

☐ pass the driving test first time

☐ take the Pass Plus scheme

The cost of insurance varies with your age and how long you have been driving. Usually, the younger you are the more expensive it is, especially if you are under 25 years of age.

The Pass Plus scheme provides additional training to newly qualified drivers. Pass Plus is recognised by many insurance companies and taking this extra training could give you reduced insurance premiums, as well as improving your skills and experience.

12.22 Mark two answers DES s2, HC p123

To supervise a learner driver you must

☐ have held a full licence for at least 3 years

☐ be at least 21 years old

☐ be an approved driving instructor

☐ hold an advanced driving certificate

Don't just take someone's word that they are qualified to supervise you. The person who sits alongside you while you are learning should be a responsible adult and an experienced driver.

When is it legal to drive a car over three years old without an MOT certificate?

☐ Up to seven days after the old certificate has run out

☐ When driving to an MOT centre to arrange an appointment

☐ Just after buying a second-hand car with no MOT

☐ When driving to an appointment at an MOT centre

Any car over three years old MUST have a valid MOT certificate before it can be used on the road. Exceptionally, you may drive to a pre-arranged test appointment or to a garage for repairs required for the test. However you should check this with your insurance company. Driving an unroadworthy vehicle may invalidate your insurance.

Motor cars must first have an MOT test certificate when they are

☐ one year old

☐ three years old

☐ five years old

☐ seven years old

The vehicle you drive MUST be roadworthy and in good condition. If it's over three years old it MUST have a valid MOT test certificate. The MOT test ensures that a vehicle meets minimum legal standards in terms of safety, components and environmental impact at the time it is tested.

The Pass Plus scheme has been created for new drivers. What is its main purpose?

☐ To allow you to drive faster

☐ To allow you to carry passengers

☐ To improve your basic skills

☐ To let you drive on motorways

New drivers are far more vulnerable on the road and more likely to be involved in incidents and collisions. The Pass Plus scheme has been designed to improve new drivers' basic skills and help widen their driving experience.

12.26 Mark two answers DES s2, HC p121

Your vehicle is insured third party only. This covers

☐ damage to your vehicle

☐ damage to other vehicles

☐ injury to yourself

☐ injury to others

☐ all damage and injury

This type of insurance cover is usually cheaper than comprehensive. However, it does not cover any damage to your own vehicle or property. It only covers damage and injury to others.

12.27 Mark one answer DES s2, HC p121

What is the legal minimum insurance cover you must have to drive on public roads?

☐ Third party, fire and theft

☐ Comprehensive

☐ Third party only

☐ Personal injury cover

The minimum insurance required by law is third party cover. This covers others involved in a collision but not damage to your vehicle. Basic third party insurance won't cover theft or fire damage. Check with your insurance company for advice on the best cover for you and make sure that you read the policy carefully.

12.28 Mark one answer DES s2

You claim on your insurance to have your car repaired. Your policy has an excess of £100. What does this mean?

☐ The insurance company will pay the first £100 of any claim

☐ You will be paid £100 if you do not claim within one year

☐ Your vehicle is insured for a value of £100 if it is stolen

☐ You will have to pay the first £100 of the cost of repair to your car

Having an excess on your policy will help to keep down the premium, but if you make a claim you will have to pay the excess yourself, in this case £100.

The Pass Plus scheme is designed to

☐ give you a discount on your MOT

☐ improve your basic driving skills

☐ increase your mechanical knowledge

☐ allow you to drive anyone else's vehicle

After passing your practical driving test you can take further training. This is known as the Pass Plus scheme. It is designed to improve your basic driving skills and involves a series of modules including night time and motorway driving. The sort of things you may not have covered whilst learning.

The Pass Plus scheme is aimed at all newly qualified drivers. It enables them to

☐ widen their driving experience

☐ supervise a learner driver

☐ increase their insurance premiums

☐ avoid mechanical breakdowns

The Pass Plus scheme was created by DSA for newly qualified drivers. It aims to widen their driving experience and improve basic skills. After passing the practical driving test additional professional training can be taken with an Approved Driving Instructor (ADI). Some insurance companies also offer discounts to holders of a Pass Plus certificate.

> Case study practice – 12
Essential documents

Monique has just bought her first car, a good second-hand vehicle. It has passed its MOT, but the tax disc expires in five days.

Monique arranges and pays for the highest level of insurance cover available and receives the usual form of temporary cover note for use until her full certificate arrives.

Taking her documents, she then goes to the local post office to purchase a new tax disc.

12.1 What's meant when a vehicle passes its MOT?
Mark **one** answer

☐ That the vehicle meets the required minimum legal standards
☐ That the vehicle's engine capacity is suitable for your needs
☐ That the vehicle is a good bargain and the seats recline properly
☐ That the vehicle registration document is properly filled out

DES s2

12.2 When would Monique need to contact DVLA?
Mark **one** answer

☐ If she changes her employment status
☐ If she changes her name and address
☐ If she chooses to go abroad for a holiday
☐ If she's told to do so by a traffic officer

HC p122 **DES** s2

12.3 What's the highest level of insurance cover available?

Mark **one** answer

☐ Complimentary

☐ Comprehensive

☐ Complicated

☐ Compromising

HC p122 **DES** s2

12.4 How long will Monique's temporary cover note be valid for?

Mark **one** answer

☐ One week

☐ Three weeks

☐ One month

☐ Three months

DES s2

12.5 When renewing a tax disc at a post office, what two documents MUST Monique show?

Mark **one** answer

☐ Birth certificate and insurance certificate

☐ Driving licence and MOT certificate

☐ Insurance certificate and MOT certificate

☐ Insurance certificate and driving licence

DES s2

Section thirteen

Incidents, accidents and emergencies

In this section, you'll learn about

- what to do if your car breaks down
- how to drive safely in a tunnel, and what to do if you have an emergency
- what to do if you're the first to arrive at an incident
- first aid and how to help casualties at an incident
- reporting an incident to the police.

Incidents, accidents and emergencies

If you're involved in an incident on the road, such as your car breaking down or arriving first at the scene of a crash, knowing what to do can prevent a more serious situation from developing.

> It's useful to carry a first aid kit, a warning triangle and a fire extinguisher in your car for use in an emergency. This equipment could help to prevent or lessen an injury. You may be able to tackle a small fire if you have a fire extinguisher, but don't take any risks.

> Breakdowns

Knowing what to do if your car breaks down will help keep you and your passengers safe, and avoid creating problems for other road users, such as traffic jams.

If a warning light shows on the instrument panel of your vehicle, you may have a problem that affects the safety of the vehicle. If necessary, stop as soon as you can do so safely and check the problem.

HC p128 **DES** s15

If your tyre bursts or you get a puncture while you're driving,

- hold the steering wheel firmly
- pull up slowly or roll to a stop at the side of the road.

> If you smell petrol while you're driving, stop and investigate as soon as you can do so safely. Don't ignore it.

If an emergency happens while you're on a motorway, try to get onto the hard shoulder and call for help from an emergency telephone. Marker posts show you the way to the nearest phone. The police or Highways Agency will answer and ask you

- the number on the phone, which will tell the services where you are
- details of yourself and your vehicle
- whether you belong to a motoring organisation.

HC r270, 275 **DES** s15

Driver location signs can help you give the emergency services precise information about where you are. See this link for more details.

● **direct.gov.uk/prod_consum_dg/ groups/dg_digitalassets/@dg/@ en/documents/digitalasset/ dg_185820.pdf**

A person who has a disability that affects their mobility may display a 'help' pennant if they can't reach an emergency phone.

HC r278

If you break down on a level crossing,

- get everyone out of the vehicle and clear of the crossing
- call the signal operator from the phone provided
- only move your vehicle if the operator tells you to do so.

If you're waiting at a level crossing and the red light signal continues to flash after a train has gone by, you **MUST** wait, as another train may be coming.

HC r293, 299 **DES** s6 **KYTS** p27

 Watch the Think! 'Van of Elvises' video to find out what to do if you break down on a motorway.

❯ **youtube.com/thinkuk**

❯ Warning others of a breakdown or incident

Use your hazard warning lights

- if you need to suddenly slow down or stop on a motorway or high-speed road because of an incident or hazard ahead; as soon as the traffic behind you has reacted to your hazard lights, you should turn them off
- when your vehicle has broken down and is temporarily obstructing traffic.

HC r116, 274

If you have a warning triangle, place it at least 45 metres (147 feet) behind your vehicle. This will warn other road users that you've broken down. Never place a warning triangle on a motorway: there's too much danger from passing traffic.

HC r274 **DES** s15, 16

 If you're driving on a motorway and you see something fall from another vehicle, or if anything falls from your own vehicle, stop at the next emergency telephone and report the hazard to the police. Don't try to retrieve it yourself.

> Safety in tunnels

You need to take extra care when driving in a tunnel because

- when you enter the tunnel, visibility is suddenly reduced
- the confined space can make incidents difficult to deal with.

Before driving through a tunnel, remove your sunglasses if you're wearing them and switch on dipped headlights. It's particularly important to keep a safe distance from the vehicle in front when driving in a tunnel, even if it's congested.

DES s7

Look out for signs that warn of accidents or congestion. Signs may also display a radio frequency that you should tune your radio to.

If your vehicle is involved in an incident or breaks down in a tunnel,

- switch off the engine
- put your hazard warning lights on
- go and call for help immediately from the nearest emergency telephone point.

If your vehicle catches fire while you're driving through a tunnel, drive it out of the tunnel if you can do so without causing further danger. If this isn't possible then you should

- stop
- switch on your hazard warning lights
- try to put out the fire – but only if it's a small fire
- call for help at the nearest emergency point.

DES s16

If your engine catches fire while you're driving, pull up as quickly and safely as possible. Get yourself and any passengers out and away from the vehicle. Then call the fire brigade. Don't open the bonnet, as this will make the fire worse.

❯ Stopping at an incident

If you're the first to arrive at the scene of an incident or crash, stop and warn other traffic. Switch on your hazard warning lights. Don't put yourself at risk.

- Make sure that the emergency services are called as soon as possible.
- Ensure that the engines of any vehicles at the scene are switched off.
- Move uninjured people away from the scene.

HC r283 **DES** s16

A vehicle carrying dangerous goods will display an orange label or a hazard warning plate on the back. If a vehicle carrying something hazardous is involved in an incident, report what the label says when you call the emergency services. The different plates are shown in *The Official Highway Code*.

HC p117 **DES** s16

❯ Helping others and giving first aid

Even if you don't know any first aid, you can help any injured people by

- keeping them warm and comfortable
- keeping them calm by talking to them reassuringly
- making sure they're not left alone.

HC p131–132 **DES** s16

Don't move an injured person if the area is safe. Only move them if they're in obvious danger, and then with extreme care. If a motorcyclist is involved, never remove their helmet unless it's essential in order to keep them alive, because removing the helmet could cause more serious injury. Always get medical help and never offer a casualty any food or drink, or a cigarette to calm them down.

HC p131–133 **DES** s16

There are three vital priorities

1. ensure a clear airway
2. check for breathing
3. try to stop any heavy bleeding.

If someone is unconscious, follow the **DR ABC** code.

Danger

Check for danger, such as approaching traffic, before you move towards the casualty.

Response

Ask the casualty questions and gently shake the shoulders to check for a response.

Airway

Check the airway is clear.

Breathing

Check for breathing for up to 10 seconds.

Compressions

Using two hands in the centre of the chest, press down 4–5 cm at a rate of 100 per minute. Use one hand, gently for a small child (two fingers for an infant).

If the casualty isn't breathing, consider giving mouth-to-mouth resuscitation.

Check and, if necessary, clear their mouth and airway.

Gently tilt their head back as far as possible.

Pinch their nostrils together.

Place your mouth over theirs. Give two breaths, each lasting one second.

Continue with cycles of 30 chest compressions and two breaths until medical help arrives.

Only stop when they can breathe without help. If the casualty is a small child, breathe very gently. Once the casualty is breathing normally, place them in the recovery position and check the airway to make sure it's clear. Keep checking them, and don't leave them alone.

If they're bleeding, apply firm pressure to the wound. If the casualty is bleeding from a limb, raise it as long as it isn't broken. This will help reduce the bleeding.

People at the scene may be suffering from shock: signs include a rapid pulse, sweating and pale grey skin.

To help someone suffering from shock,

- reassure them constantly
- keep them warm
- make them as comfortable as you can
- avoid moving them unless it's necessary
- make sure they're not left alone.

If someone is suffering from burns,

- douse the burns thoroughly with cool non-toxic liquid for at least 10 minutes
- don't remove anything sticking to the burn.

❯ Reporting an incident

You **MUST** stop if you're involved in an incident. It's an offence not to stop and call the police if any other person is injured. If there's damage to another vehicle, property or animal, report it to the owner. If you don't do this at the time, you **MUST** report the incident to the police within 24 hours (immediately in Northern Ireland).

HC r286 **DES** s16

If another vehicle is involved, find out

- who owns the vehicle
- the make and registration number of the vehicle
- the other driver's name, address and telephone number and details of their insurance.

Following an incident (or at any other time), the police may ask you for

- your insurance certificate
- the MOT certificate for the vehicle you're driving
- your driving licence.

HC r286, p122

Meeting the standards

At the scene of an incident, you must be able to

stop and park your vehicle in a safe place, if necessary

make sure that warning is given to other road users

give help to others if you can

where possible, record information about what you saw or the scene that you found. It may be helpful to take photographs and draw sketch plans.

You must know and understand

how to keep control of the vehicle, where possible, if it breaks down

how and when to use a warning triangle or hazard warning lights

what the law says about stopping if you're involved in an incident that causes damage or injury to

- any other person
- another vehicle
- an animal
- someone's property

This includes what to do about

- stopping
- providing your details
- giving statements
- producing documents

how to contact the emergency services and how important it is to give them accurate information.

Notes

You can use this page to make your own notes or diagrams about the key points you need to remember.

Think about

- What should you do if your car breaks down on the motorway?
- How can you warn other road users if you've broken down on the road?
- If you're the first person to arrive at the scene of a crash, what should you do?
- If a motorcyclist is involved in the crash, should you remove their helmet?
- What does DR ABC stand for?
- If you're involved in an incident with another vehicle, what must you do?

Your notes

Things to discuss and practise with your instructor

These are just a few examples of what you could discuss and practise with your instructor. Read more about incidents, accidents and emergencies to come up with your own ideas.

Discuss with your instructor

- what it means if you see a driver displaying a 'help' pennant
- when you may and may not use your hazard warning lights
- what you should do if you arrive at the scene of a crash and find
  - someone bleeding badly with nothing embedded in their wound
  - someone with a burn
  - someone who isn't breathing normally
  - an injured motorcyclist wearing a helmet.

Practise with your instructor

Hopefully, you won't have the opportunity to practise what to do in the event of an incident or emergency during your driving lesson. Instead, practise with your instructor

- learning the rules relating to
  - breakdowns on all roads, including motorways
  - obstructions
  - incidents, eg warning signs and flashing lights
  - passing and being involved in a crash
  - incidents involving dangerous goods
  - which documents you'll need to produce if you're involved in a crash
  - incidents in tunnels.

13.1
Mark one answer
DES s15, HC r278

You see a car on the hard shoulder of a motorway with a HELP pennant displayed. This means the driver is most likely to be

☐ a disabled person

☐ first aid trained

☐ a foreign visitor

☐ a rescue patrol person

If a disabled driver's vehicle breaks down and they are unable to walk to an emergency phone, they are advised to stay in their car and switch on the hazard warning lights. They may also display a 'Help' pennant in their vehicle.

13.2
Mark two answers
DES s3, 11, 15, 16, HC r116, 274

For which TWO should you use hazard warning lights?

☐ When you slow down quickly on a motorway because of a hazard ahead

☐ When you have broken down

☐ When you wish to stop on double yellow lines

☐ When you need to park on the pavement

Hazard warning lights are fitted to all modern cars and some motorcycles. They should only be used to warn other road users of a hazard ahead.

13.3
Mark one answer
DES s3, 11, 15, 16, HC r116

When are you allowed to use hazard warning lights?

☐ When stopped and temporarily obstructing traffic

☐ When travelling during darkness without headlights

☐ When parked for shopping on double yellow lines

☐ When travelling slowly because you are lost

You must not use hazard warning lights when moving, except when slowing suddenly on a motorway or unrestricted dual carriageway to warn the traffic behind.

Never use hazard warning lights to excuse dangerous or illegal parking.

13.4 Mark one answer DES s7, HC r126

You are going through a congested tunnel and have to stop. What should you do?

☐ Pull up very close to the vehicle in front to save space

☐ Ignore any message signs as they are never up to date

☐ Keep a safe distance from the vehicle in front

☐ Make a U-turn and find another route

It's important to keep a safe distance from the vehicle in front at all times. This still applies in congested tunnels even if you are moving very slowly or have stopped. If the vehicle in front breaks down you may need room to manoeuvre past it.

13.5 Mark one answer DES s11, HC r275

On the motorway, the hard shoulder should be used

☐ to answer a mobile phone

☐ when an emergency arises

☐ for a short rest when tired

☐ to check a road atlas

Pull onto the hard shoulder and use the emergency telephone to report your problem. This lets the emergency services know your exact location so they can send help. Never cross the carriageway to use the telephone on the other side.

13.6 Mark one answer DES s16, HC p133

You arrive at the scene of a crash. Someone is bleeding badly from an arm wound. There is nothing embedded in it. What should you do?

☐ Apply pressure over the wound and keep the arm down

☐ Dab the wound

☐ Get them a drink

☐ Apply pressure over the wound and raise the arm

If possible, lay the casualty down. Check for anything that may be in the wound. Apply firm pressure to the wound using clean material, without pressing on anything which might be in it. Raising the arm above the level of the heart will also help to stem the flow of blood.

13.7 Mark one answer DES s16, HC p132

You are at an incident where a casualty is unconscious. Their breathing should be checked. This should be done for at least

☐ 2 seconds

☐ 10 seconds

☐ 1 minute

☐ 2 minutes

Once the airway is open, check breathing. Listen and feel for breath. Do this by placing your cheek over their mouth and nose, and look to see if the chest rises. This should be done for up to 10 seconds.

Following a collision someone has suffered a burn. The burn needs to be cooled. What is the shortest time it should be cooled for?

☐ 5 minutes

☐ 10 minutes

☐ 15 minutes

☐ 20 minutes

Check the casualty for shock and if possible try to cool the burn for at least ten minutes. Use a clean, cold non-toxic liquid preferably water.

A casualty is not breathing normally. Chest compressions should be given. At what rate?

☐ 50 per minute

☐ 100 per minute

☐ 200 per minute

☐ 250 per minute

If a casualty is not breathing normally chest compressions may be needed to maintain circulation. Place two hands on the centre of the chest and press down about 4–5 centimetres, at the rate of 100 per minute.

A person has been injured. They may be suffering from shock. What are the warning signs to look for?

☐ Flushed complexion

☐ Warm dry skin

☐ Slow pulse

☐ Pale grey skin

The effects of shock may not be immediately obvious. Warning signs are rapid pulse, sweating, pale grey skin and rapid shallow breathing.

An injured person has been placed in the recovery position. They are unconscious but breathing normally. What else should be done?

☐ Press firmly between the shoulders

☐ Place their arms by their side

☐ Give them a hot sweet drink

☐ Check the airway is clear

After a casualty has been placed in the recovery position, their airway should be checked to make sure it's clear. Don't leave them alone until medical help arrives. Where possible do NOT move a casualty unless there's further danger.

13.12

Mark one answer

DES s16

An injured motorcyclist is lying unconscious in the road. You should always

☐ remove the safety helmet

☐ seek medical assistance

☐ move the person off the road

☐ remove the leather jacket

If someone has been injured, the sooner proper medical attention is given the better. Send someone to phone for help or go yourself. An injured person should only be moved if they're in further danger. An injured motorcyclist's helmet should NOT be removed unless it is essential.

13.13

Mark one answer

DES s11, HC r280

You are on a motorway. A large box falls onto the road from a lorry. The lorry does not stop. You should

☐ go to the next emergency telephone and report the hazard

☐ catch up with the lorry and try to get the driver's attention

☐ stop close to the box until the police arrive

☐ pull over to the hard shoulder, then remove the box

Lorry drivers can be unaware of objects falling from their vehicles. If you see something fall onto a motorway look to see if the driver pulls over. If they don't stop, do not attempt to retrieve it yourself. Pull on to the hard shoulder near an emergency telephone and report the hazard. You will be connected to the police or a Highways Agency control centre.

13.14

Mark one answer

DES s7

You are going through a long tunnel. What will warn you of congestion or an incident ahead?

☐ Hazard warning lines

☐ Other drivers flashing their lights

☐ Variable message signs

☐ Areas marked with hatch markings

Follow the instructions given by the signs or by tunnel officials.

In congested tunnels a minor incident can soon turn into a major one with serious or even fatal results.

13.15

Mark one answer

DES s16, HC p132

An adult casualty is not breathing. To maintain circulation, compressions should be given. What is the correct depth to press?

☐ 1 to 2 centimetres

☐ 4 to 5 centimetres

☐ 10 to 15 centimetres

☐ 15 to 20 centimetres

An adult casualty is not breathing normally. To maintain circulation place two hands on the centre of the chest. Then press down 4 to 5 centimetres at a rate of 100 times per minute.

13.16

Mark two answers

DES s16, HC p131

You are the first to arrive at the scene of a crash. Which TWO of these should you do?

☐ Leave as soon as another motorist arrives

☐ Make sure engines are switched off

☐ Drag all casualties away from the vehicles

☐ Call the emergency services promptly

At a crash scene you can help in practical ways, even if you aren't trained in first aid. Make sure you do not put yourself or anyone else in danger. The safest way to warn other traffic is by switching on your hazard warning lights.

13.17

Mark three answers

DES s16, HC p131

You are the first person to arrive at an incident where people are badly injured. Which THREE should you do?

☐ Switch on your own hazard warning lights

☐ Make sure that someone telephones for an ambulance

☐ Try and get people who are injured to drink something

☐ Move the people who are injured clear of their vehicles

☐ Get people who are not injured clear of the scene

If you're the first to arrive at a crash scene the first concerns are the risk of further collision and fire. Ensuring that vehicle engines are switched off will reduce the risk of fire. Use hazard warning lights so that other traffic knows there's a need for caution. Make sure the emergency services are contacted, don't assume this has already been done.

13.18

Mark one answer

DES s16, HC p131–132

You arrive at the scene of a motorcycle crash. The rider is injured. When should the helmet be removed?

☐ Only when it is essential

☐ Always straight away

☐ Only when the motorcyclist asks

☐ Always, unless they are in shock

DO NOT remove a motorcyclist's helmet unless it is essential. Remember they may be suffering from shock. Don't give them anything to eat or drink but do reassure them confidently.

13.19

Mark one answer

DES s16, HC p132

You arrive at an incident. A motorcyclist is unconscious. Your FIRST priority is the casualty's

☐ breathing

☐ bleeding

☐ broken bones

☐ bruising

At the scene of an incident always be aware of danger from further collisions or fire. The first priority when dealing with an unconscious person is to ensure they can breathe. This may involve clearing their airway if you can see an obstruction or if they're having difficulty breathing.

13.20   Mark three answers   DES s16, HC p132

At an incident a casualty is unconscious. Which THREE of these should you check urgently?

☐ Circulation

☐ Airway

☐ Shock

☐ Breathing

☐ Broken bones

Remember DR ABC. An unconscious casualty may have difficulty breathing. Check that their airway is clear by tilting the head back gently and unblock it if necessary. Then make sure they are breathing. If there is bleeding, stem the flow by placing clean material over any wounds but without pressing on any objects in the wound. Compressions may need to be given to maintain circulation.

13.21   Mark three answers   DES s16, HC p132

At an incident someone is unconscious. Your THREE main priorities should be to

☐ sweep up the broken glass

☐ take the names of witnesses

☐ count the number of vehicles involved

☐ check the airway is clear

☐ make sure they are breathing

☐ stop any heavy bleeding

Remember this procedure by saying DR ABC. This stands for Danger, Response, Airway, Breathing, Compressions.

13.22   Mark three answers   DES s16, HC p131–132

You have stopped at an incident to give help. Which THREE things should you do?

☐ Keep injured people warm and comfortable

☐ Keep injured people calm by talking to them reassuringly

☐ Keep injured people on the move by walking them around

☐ Give injured people a warm drink

☐ Make sure that injured people are not left alone

There are a number of things you can do to help, even without expert training. Be aware of further danger and fire, make sure the area is safe. People may be in shock. Don't give them anything to eat or drink. Keep them warm and comfortable and reassure them. Don't move injured people unless there is a risk of further danger.

There has been a collision. A driver is suffering from shock. What TWO of these should you do?

☐ Give them a drink

☐ Reassure them

☐ Not leave them alone

☐ Offer them a cigarette

☐ Ask who caused the incident

Be aware they could have an injury that is not immediately obvious. Ensure the emergency services are called. Reassure and stay with them until the experts arrive.

You arrive at the scene of a motorcycle crash. No other vehicle is involved. The rider is unconscious and lying in the middle of the road. The FIRST thing you should do is

☐ move the rider out of the road

☐ warn other traffic

☐ clear the road of debris

☐ give the rider reassurance

The motorcyclist is in an extremely vulnerable position, exposed to further danger from traffic. Approaching vehicles need advance warning in order to slow down and safely take avoiding action or stop. Don't put yourself or anyone else at risk. Use the hazard warning lights on your vehicle to alert other road users to the danger.

At an incident a small child is not breathing. To restore normal breathing you should breathe into their mouth

☐ sharply

☐ gently

☐ heavily

☐ rapidly

If a young child has stopped breathing, first check that the airway is clear. Then give compressions to the chest using one hand (two fingers for an infant) and begin mouth-to-mouth resuscitation. Breathe very gently and continue the procedure until they can breathe without help.

13.26   Mark three answers   DES s16, HC p132

At an incident a casualty is not breathing. To start the process to restore normal breathing you should

☐ tilt their head forward

☐ clear the airway

☐ turn them on their side

☐ tilt their head back gently

☐ pinch the nostrils together

☐ put their arms across their chest

It's important to ensure that the airways are clear before you start mouth-to-mouth resuscitation. Gently tilt their head back and use your finger to check for and remove any obvious obstruction in the mouth.

13.27   Mark one answer   DES s16, HC p133

You arrive at an incident where someone is suffering from severe burns. You should

☐ apply lotions to the injury

☐ burst any blisters

☐ remove anything stuck to the burns

☐ douse the burns with clean cool non-toxic liquid

Use a liquid that is clean, cold and non-toxic, preferably water. Its coolness will help take the heat out of the burn and relieve the pain. Keep the wound doused for at least ten minutes. If blisters appear don't attempt to burst them as this could lead to infection.

13.28   Mark two answers   DES s16, HC p133

You arrive at an incident. A pedestrian has a severe bleeding leg wound. It is not broken and there is nothing in the wound. What TWO of these should you do?

☐ Dab the wound to stop bleeding

☐ Keep both legs flat on the ground

☐ Apply firm pressure to the wound

☐ Raise the leg to lessen bleeding

☐ Fetch them a warm drink

First check for anything that may be in the wound such as glass. If there's nothing in it apply a pad of clean cloth or bandage. Raising the leg will lessen the flow of blood. Don't tie anything tightly round the leg. This will restrict circulation and can result in long-term injury.

13.29   Mark one answer   DES s16, HC p131–132

At an incident a casualty is unconscious but still breathing. You should only move them if

☐ an ambulance is on its way

☐ bystanders advise you to

☐ there is further danger

☐ bystanders will help you to

Do not move a casualty unless there is further danger, for example, from other traffic or fire. They may have unseen or internal injuries. Moving them unnecessarily could cause further injury. Do NOT remove a motorcyclist's helmet unless it's essential.

At an incident it is important to look after any casualties. When the area is safe, you should

☐ get them out of the vehicle

☐ give them a drink

☐ give them something to eat

☐ keep them in the vehicle

When the area is safe and there's no danger from other traffic or fire it's better not to move casualties. Moving them may cause further injury.

A tanker is involved in a collision. Which sign shows that it is carrying dangerous goods?

☐   ☐

☐   ☐ ⚠

There will be an orange label on the side and rear of the tanker. Look at this carefully and report what it says when you phone the emergency services. Details of hazard warning plates are given in The Highway Code.

You are involved in a collision. Because of this which THREE of these documents may the police ask you to produce?

☐ Vehicle registration document

☐ Driving licence

☐ Theory test certificate

☐ Insurance certificate

☐ MOT test certificate

☐ Vehicle service record

You MUST stop if you have been involved in a collision which results in injury or damage. The police may ask to see your documents at the time or later at a police station.

13.33 — Mark one answer — DES s16, HC p131

After a collision someone is unconscious in their vehicle. When should you call the emergency services?

- [ ] Only as a last resort
- [ ] As soon as possible
- [ ] After you have woken them up
- [ ] After checking for broken bones

It is important to make sure that emergency services arrive on the scene as soon as possible. When a person is unconscious, they could have serious injuries that are not immediately obvious.

13.34 — Mark one answer — DES s16, HC p133

A casualty has an injured arm. They can move it freely but it is bleeding. Why should you get them to keep it in a raised position?

- [ ] Because it will ease the pain
- [ ] It will help them to be seen more easily
- [ ] To stop them touching other people
- [ ] It will help to reduce the blood flow

If a casualty is bleeding heavily, raise the limb to a higher position. This will help to reduce the blood flow. Before raising the limb you should make sure that it is not broken.

13.35 — Mark two answers — DES s16, HC p132

At an incident a casualty has stopped breathing. You should

- [ ] remove anything that is blocking the mouth
- [ ] keep the head tilted forwards as far as possible
- [ ] raise the legs to help with circulation
- [ ] try to give the casualty something to drink
- [ ] tilt the head back gently to clear the airway

Unblocking the airway and gently tilting the head back will help the casualty to breathe. They will then be in the correct position if mouth-to-mouth resuscitation is required. Don't move a casualty unless there's further danger.

13.36 — Mark four answers — DES s16, HC p132

You are at the scene of an incident. Someone is suffering from shock. You should

- [ ] reassure them constantly
- [ ] offer them a cigarette
- [ ] keep them warm
- [ ] avoid moving them if possible
- [ ] avoid leaving them alone
- [ ] give them a warm drink

The signs of shock may not be immediately obvious. Prompt treatment can help to minimise the effects. Lay the casualty down, loosen tight clothing, call an ambulance and check their breathing and pulse.

Mark one answer **DES s16, HC p131–132**

There has been a collision. A motorcyclist is lying injured and unconscious. Unless it's essential, why should you usually NOT attempt to remove their helmet?

☐ Because they may not want you to

☐ This could result in more serious injury

☐ They will get too cold if you do this

☐ Because you could scratch the helmet

When someone is injured, any movement which is not absolutely necessary should be avoided since it could make injuries worse. Unless it is essential, it's generally safer to leave a motorcyclist's helmet in place.

13.38 Mark one answer **DES s15, HC r274**

You have broken down on a two-way road. You have a warning triangle. You should place the warning triangle at least how far from your vehicle?

☐ 5 metres (16 feet)

☐ 25 metres (82 feet)

☐ 45 metres (147 feet)

☐ 100 metres (328 feet)

Advance warning triangles fold flat and don't take up much room. Use it to warn other road users if your vehicle has broken down or there's been an incident. Place it at least 45 metres (147 feet) behind your vehicle or incident on the same side of the road or verge. Place it further back if the scene is hidden by, for example, a bend, hill or dip in the road. Don't use them on motorways.

13.39 Mark three answers **DES s6, HC r299, KYTS p27**

You break down on a level crossing. The lights have not yet begun to flash. Which THREE things should you do?

☐ Telephone the signal operator

☐ Leave your vehicle and get everyone clear

☐ Walk down the track and signal the next train

☐ Move the vehicle if a signal operator tells you to

☐ Tell drivers behind what has happened

If your vehicle breaks down on a level crossing, your first priority is to get everyone out of the vehicle and clear of the crossing. Then use the railway telephone, if there is one, to tell the signal operator. If you have time before the train arrives, move the vehicle clear of the crossing, but only do this if alarm signals are not on.

13.40   Mark two answers   DES s15, HC p129

Your tyre bursts while you are driving. Which TWO things should you do?

☐ Pull on the handbrake

☐ Brake as quickly as possible

☐ Pull up slowly at the side of the road

☐ Hold the steering wheel firmly to keep control

☐ Continue on at a normal speed

A tyre bursting can lead to a loss of control, especially if you're travelling at high speed. Using the correct procedure should help you to stop the vehicle safely.

13.41   Mark one answer   DES s15, HC r275, p129

Your vehicle has a puncture on a motorway. What should you do?

☐ Drive slowly to the next service area to get assistance

☐ Pull up on the hard shoulder. Change the wheel as quickly as possible

☐ Pull up on the hard shoulder. Use the emergency phone to get assistance

☐ Switch on your hazard lights. Stop in your lane

Pull up on the hard shoulder and make your way to the nearest emergency telephone to call for assistance.

Do not attempt to repair your vehicle while it is on the hard shoulder because of the risk posed by traffic passing at high speeds.

13.42   Mark one answer   DES s6, HC r299

You have stalled in the middle of a level crossing and cannot restart the engine. The warning bell starts to ring. You should

☐ get out and clear of the crossing

☐ run down the track to warn the signal operator

☐ carry on trying to restart the engine

☐ push the vehicle clear of the crossing

Try to stay calm, especially if you have passengers on board. If you can't restart your engine before the warning bells ring, leave the vehicle and get yourself and any passengers well clear of the crossing.

You are on a motorway. When can you use hazard warning lights?

☐ When a vehicle is following too closely

☐ When you slow down quickly because of danger ahead

☐ When you are towing another vehicle

☐ When driving on the hard shoulder

☐ When you have broken down on the hard shoulder

Hazard warning lights will warn the traffic travelling behind you that there is a hazard ahead.

You have broken down on a motorway. When you use the emergency telephone you will be asked

☐ for the number on the telephone that you are using

☐ for your driving licence details

☐ for the name of your vehicle insurance company

☐ for details of yourself and your vehicle

☐ whether you belong to a motoring organisation

Have these details ready before you use the emergency telephone and be sure to give the correct information. For your own safety always face the traffic when you speak on a roadside telephone.

Before driving through a tunnel what should you do?

☐ Switch your radio off

☐ Remove any sunglasses

☐ Close your sunroof

☐ Switch on windscreen wipers

If you are wearing sunglasses you should remove them before driving into a tunnel. If you don't, your vision will be restricted, even in tunnels that appear to be well-lit.

13.46   Mark one answer   DES s7

You are driving through a tunnel and the traffic is flowing normally. What should you do?

☐ Use parking lights

☐ Use front spot lights

☐ Use dipped headlights

☐ Use rear fog lights

Before entering a tunnel you should switch on your dipped headlights, as this will allow you to see and be seen. In many tunnels it is a legal requirement.

Don't wear sunglasses while driving in a tunnel. You may wish to tune your radio into a local channel.

13.47   Mark two answers   DES s16, HC p130

What TWO safeguards could you take against fire risk to your vehicle?

☐ Keep water levels above maximum

☐ Carry a fire extinguisher

☐ Avoid driving with a full tank of petrol

☐ Use unleaded petrol

☐ Check out any strong smell of petrol

☐ Use low octane fuel

The fuel in your vehicle can be a dangerous fire hazard. Never

- use a naked flame near the vehicle if you can smell fuel
- smoke when refuelling your vehicle.

13.48   Mark one answer   DES s11, HC r279–280

You are on the motorway. Luggage falls from your vehicle. What should you do?

☐ Stop at the next emergency telephone and contact the police

☐ Stop on the motorway and put on hazard lights while you pick it up

☐ Walk back up the motorway to pick it up

☐ Pull up on the hard shoulder and wave traffic down

If any object falls onto the motorway carriageway from your vehicle pull over onto the hard shoulder near an emergency telephone and phone for assistance. You will be connected to the police or a Highways Agency control centre. Don't stop on the carriageway or attempt to retrieve anything.

Mark one answer

While driving, a warning light on your vehicle's instrument panel comes on. You should

☐ continue if the engine sounds all right

☐ hope that it is just a temporary electrical fault

☐ deal with the problem when there is more time

☐ check out the problem quickly and safely

Make sure you know what the different warning lights mean. An illuminated warning light could mean that your car is unsafe to drive. Don't take risks. If you aren't sure about the problem get a qualified mechanic to check it.

Mark one answer

Your vehicle breaks down in a tunnel. What should you do?

☐ Stay in your vehicle and wait for the police

☐ Stand in the lane behind your vehicle to warn others

☐ Stand in front of your vehicle to warn oncoming drivers

☐ Switch on hazard lights then go and call for help immediately

A broken-down vehicle in a tunnel can cause serious congestion and danger to other road users. If your vehicle breaks down, get help without delay. Switch on your hazard warning lights, then go to an emergency telephone point to call for help.

Mark one answer

Your vehicle catches fire while driving through a tunnel. It is still driveable. What should you do?

☐ Leave it where it is with the engine running

☐ Pull up, then walk to an emergency telephone point

☐ Park it away from the carriageway

☐ Drive it out of the tunnel if you can do so

If it's possible, and you can do so without causing further danger, it may be safer to drive a vehicle which is on fire out of a tunnel. The greatest danger in a tunnel fire is smoke and suffocation.

13.52   Mark two answers   DES s16

You are in a tunnel. Your vehicle is on fire and you CANNOT drive it. What should you do?

☐ Stay in the vehicle and close the windows

☐ Switch on hazard warning lights

☐ Leave the engine running

☐ Try and put out the fire

☐ Switch off all of your lights

☐ Wait for other people to phone for help

It's usually better to drive a burning vehicle out of a tunnel. If you can't do this pull over and stop at an emergency point if possible. Switch off the engine, use hazard warning lights, and leave the vehicle immediately. Call for help from the nearest emergency point. If you have an extinguisher it may help to put out a small fire but do NOT try to tackle a large one.

13.53   Mark one answer   DES s7

When approaching a tunnel it is good advice to

☐ put on your sunglasses and use the sun visor

☐ check your tyre pressures

☐ change down to a lower gear

☐ make sure your radio is tuned to the frequency shown

On the approach to tunnels a sign will usually show a local radio channel. It should give a warning of any incidents or congestion in the tunnel ahead. Many radios can be set to automatically pick up traffic announcements and local frequencies. If you have to tune the radio manually don't be distracted while doing so. Incidents in tunnels can lead to serious casualties. The greatest hazard is fire. Getting an advance warning of problems could save your life and others.

13.54   Mark one answer   DES s6, HC r299, KYTS p27

Your vehicle has broken down on an automatic railway level crossing. What should you do FIRST?

☐ Get everyone out of the vehicle and clear of the crossing

☐ Telephone your vehicle recovery service to move it

☐ Walk along the track to give warning to any approaching trains

☐ Try to push the vehicle clear of the crossing as soon as possible

Firstly get yourself and anyone else well away from the crossing. If there's a railway phone use that to get instructions from the signal operator. Then if there's time move the vehicle clear of the crossing.

443

13.55 — Mark three answers — DES s16, 21

Which THREE of these items should you carry for use in the event of a collision?

- ☐ Road map
- ☐ Can of petrol
- ☐ Jump leads
- ☐ Fire extinguisher
- ☐ First aid kit
- ☐ Warning triangle

Used correctly, these items can provide invaluable help in the event of a collision or breakdown. They could even save a life.

13.56 — Mark one answer — DES s16, HC r286

You have a collision whilst your car is moving. What is the FIRST thing you must do?

- ☐ Stop only if someone waves at you
- ☐ Call the emergency services
- ☐ Stop at the scene of the incident
- ☐ Call your insurance company

If you are in a collision that causes damage or injury to any other person, vehicle, animal or property, by law you MUST STOP. Give your name, the vehicle owner's name and address, and the vehicle's registration number to anyone who has reasonable grounds for requiring them.

13.57 — Mark four answers — DES s16, HC r286

You are in collision with another moving vehicle. Someone is injured and your vehicle is damaged. Which FOUR of the following should you find out?

- ☐ Whether the driver owns the other vehicle involved
- ☐ The other driver's name, address and telephone number
- ☐ The make and registration number of the other vehicle
- ☐ The occupation of the other driver
- ☐ The details of the other driver's vehicle insurance
- ☐ Whether the other driver is licensed to drive

Try to keep calm and don't rush. Ensure that you have all the details before you leave the scene. If possible take pictures and note the positions of all the vehicles involved.

You lose control of your car and damage a garden wall. No one is around. What must you do?

☐ Report the incident to the police within 24 hours

☐ Go back to tell the house owner the next day

☐ Report the incident to your insurance company when you get home

☐ Find someone in the area to tell them about it immediately

If the property owner is not available at the time, you MUST inform the police of the incident. This should be done as soon as possible, and within 24 hours.

> Case study practice – 13
Incidents, accidents and emergencies

Marco witnesses a road traffic incident involving three vehicles. He stops his vehicle, quickly places a warning triangle on the road, then telephones the emergency services.

He checks on the people involved. Two people are slightly injured and another is in shock. Marco stays with them until the emergency services arrive.

While paramedics check the three casualties, Marco explains the situation to the police and offers his own contact details. The officers then speak to the casualties.

13.1 How else could Marco have used his own vehicle to warn other traffic?

Mark **one** answer

☐ By parking it in the middle of the road
☐ By switching on hazard warning lights
☐ By leaving headlights on main beam
☐ By constantly sounding the horn

HC r283 **DES** s16

13.2 Apart from casualty information, what details would Marco also need to give to the emergency services?

Mark **one** answer

- ☐ Location of the incident
- ☐ Time and date of his call
- ☐ Driving licence details
- ☐ Insurance information

HC r283 **DES** s16

13.3 How should Marco deal with someone suffering from shock?

Mark **one** answer

- ☐ Find out their full name then leave them alone
- ☐ Offer them a cigarette and get them a hot drink
- ☐ Offer some water then sit them down somewhere
- ☐ Stay with them and reassure them confidently

HC p132 **DES** s16

13.4 Why would Marco provide his own details?

Mark **one** answer

- ☐ He might be required to supply a witness statement
- ☐ He wanted to get his triangular warning sign back later
- ☐ He needed the police to keep him informed of progress
- ☐ He was interested in becoming involved in emergency work

DES s16

13.5 Which documents would police officers normally ask to see, from the people involved in the incident?

Mark **one** answer

- ☐ Vehicle registration certificate and MOT certificate
- ☐ Driving licence and insurance certificate
- ☐ Insurance certificate and birth certificate
- ☐ MOT certificate and driving licence

HC r286–287 **DES** s16

> Section fourteen
Vehicle loading

In this section, you'll learn about

- ⊃ how to carry loads safely in your car
- ⊃ carrying passengers and animals safely
- ⊃ towing a caravan or trailer
- ⊃ the effect of carrying a load on your vehicle's fuel consumption.

Vehicle loading

Loading your vehicle carefully will help to ensure that you can travel safely, whether your load is passengers, animals, a caravan or simply rubbish for the tip.

❯ Keeping your car stable

As a driver, you need to make sure that your vehicle isn't overloaded. Overloading can seriously affect the vehicle's handling, especially the steering and braking.

HC **r98** **DES** **s2**

When you're carrying or towing a heavy load, you may need to make adjustments to your vehicle, such as

- increasing the air pressure in the tyres
- adjusting the aim of the headlights.

You should load your vehicle carefully to avoid upsetting the vehicle's stability.

- Distribute the weight evenly.
- Make sure that the load is fastened so that it can't move when you're cornering or braking.
- Ensure loads don't obstruct your view when you're driving, or stick out where they could be dangerous for other road users.

Carrying a load on a roof rack

- will increase wind resistance
- may make your vehicle less stable.

As the load is exposed to the weather, you may need to cover it to protect it from rain. Specially designed roof boxes are available, which cut down the wind resistance and keep loads secure and dry.

DES **s2**

449

You should inflate your tyres to a higher pressure than normal

- when you're carrying a heavy load
- if you're driving for a long distance on a dual carriageway or motorway at the speed limit for these roads.

Your vehicle handbook should tell you the correct pressure for different circumstances.

DES s14

❯ Passengers

All passengers **MUST** wear seat belts if they're fitted. As a driver, you're responsible for ensuring all children (under 14 years) wear a suitable restraint in your vehicle. The type of restraint varies with the age of the child but it **MUST** be suitable for the child's weight and size.

Baby carrier

Child seat

Booster seat

See section 3, Safety and your vehicle, for more information.

 Watch the Think! 'Thing of beauty' video to find out more about child seats.

❯ **youtube.com/thinkuk**

Never allow a passenger to travel in a caravan while it's being towed.

`DES` `s19`

❯ Animals

Animals should be restrained to ensure that they don't interfere with the driver or block the driver's view.

Dogs may travel in a special cage or behind a dog guard, and may be strapped in using a harness for added security. Other animals should travel in cages or in pet carriers that can be secured with a seat belt.

❯ Towing

If you're planning to tow a caravan, it'll help the handling of your vehicle if you have a stabiliser fitted to your towbar. This will particularly help when you're driving in crosswinds.

If your caravan or trailer has a braking system, you can also fit a breakaway cable as an extra safety device. This will pull on the brakes of a braked trailer or caravan if it becomes detached from the towing vehicle while being towed.

`DES` `s19`

If a trailer or caravan starts to swerve or snake as you're driving along,

- ease off the accelerator
- reduce your speed gradually to regain control.

 The maximum weight that can be put on your vehicle's towbar (called the 'noseweight') can normally be found in your vehicle handbook.

DES s19

 Find out more about towing a caravan or trailer at this website.

❯ **www.gov.uk**

There's a lower national speed limit for all vehicles towing trailers.

On a dual carriageway or motorway 	Maximum speed 60 mph (96 km/h) A vehicle towing a trailer on a motorway that has more than two lanes **MUST NOT** be driven in the right-hand lane.
On a single carriageway 	Maximum speed 50 mph (80 km/h)

HC r98, p40 **DES** s19

Saving fuel

Carrying a load will increase your vehicle's fuel consumption because of the extra weight. Carrying a load on a roof rack will increase the fuel consumption even more because of the wind resistance and drag created by the load.

When you've finished using a roof rack or box, remove it from the vehicle. Even when it's empty, it will increase the fuel consumption because of the drag it creates.

Meeting the standards

You must be able to

make sure that passengers are seated legally, correctly and securely

make sure that loads are secure and distributed correctly, depending on the vehicle

allow for the effect that any extra load may have on how the vehicle handles.

You must know and understand

what the law says about the fitting and use of seat belts

what the vehicle handbook says about safely loading the vehicle

how to adjust the vehicle to allow for extra weight. For example, you may need to put more air in the tyres

how to change your driving to allow for extra weight. You may also need to think about how weight in different places can affect your driving. For example

- in the boot
- in a roof box
- on the back seat
- in a trailer.

Notes

You can use this page to make your own notes or diagrams about the key points you need to remember.

Think about

- What sorts of load might you carry in your vehicle that could affect its stability?
- When might you need to increase the tyre pressures?
- Are you likely to carry animals in your car? If so, what sort of carrier or restraint do you need?
- If you wanted to tow a trailer or caravan, what preparation would you need to do on your car?

Your notes

Things to discuss and practise with your instructor

These are just a few examples of what you could discuss and practise with your instructor. Read more about vehicle loading to come up with your own ideas.

Discuss with your instructor

- the effects that carrying a heavy load, such as a roof rack, might have on your car and your driving
- the motorway regulations for vehicles towing trailers
- the safety checks you should carry out before starting a journey towing a caravan.

Practise with your instructor

- driving with passengers in the car. Ask your instructor whether they would mind if you took along some friends for part of the lesson, so you can get used to
  - how the car handles differently with more weight in the back
  - how the presence of passengers can distract you.

14.1

Mark two answers

DES s19, HC r98, p40

You are towing a small trailer on a busy three-lane motorway. All the lanes are open. You must

☐ not exceed 60 mph

☐ not overtake

☐ have a stabiliser fitted

☐ use only the left and centre lanes

You should be aware of the motorway regulations for vehicles towing trailers. These state that a vehicle towing a trailer must not

• use the right-hand lane of a three-lane motorway unless directed to do so, for example, at roadworks or due to a lane closure

• exceed 60 mph.

14.2

Mark one answer

DES s19, HC r98

If a trailer swerves or snakes when you are towing it you should

☐ ease off the accelerator and reduce your speed

☐ let go of the steering wheel and let it correct itself

☐ brake hard and hold the pedal down

☐ increase your speed as quickly as possible

Strong winds or buffeting from large vehicles can cause a trailer or caravan to snake or swerve. If this happens, ease off the accelerator. Don't brake harshly, steer sharply or increase your speed.

14.3

Mark two answers

DES s14

On which TWO occasions might you inflate your tyres to more than the recommended normal pressure?

☐ When the roads are slippery

☐ When driving fast for a long distance

☐ When the tyre tread is worn below 2mm

☐ When carrying a heavy load

☐ When the weather is cold

☐ When the vehicle is fitted with anti-lock brakes

Check the vehicle handbook. This should give you guidance on the correct tyre pressures for your vehicle and when you may need to adjust them. If you are carrying a heavy load you may need to adjust the headlights as well. Most cars have a switch on the dashboard to do this.

14.4 | Mark one answer | DES s2, HC r98

A heavy load on your roof rack will

- ☐ improve the road holding
- ☐ reduce the stopping distance
- ☐ make the steering lighter
- ☐ reduce stability

A heavy load on your roof rack will reduce the stability of the vehicle because it moves the centre of gravity away from that designed by the manufacturer. Be aware of this when you negotiate bends and corners.

If you change direction at speed, your vehicle and/or load could become unstable and you could lose control.

14.5 | Mark two answers | DES s2, HC r98

Overloading your vehicle can seriously affect the

- ☐ gearbox
- ☐ steering
- ☐ handling
- ☐ battery life
- ☐ journey time

Any load will have an effect on the handling of your vehicle and this becomes worse as you increase the load. Any change in the centre of gravity or weight the vehicle is carrying will affect its braking and handling on bends.

You need to be aware of this when carrying passengers, heavy loads, fitting a roof rack or towing a trailer.

14.6 | Mark one answer | DES s2, HC r98

Who is responsible for making sure that a vehicle is not overloaded?

- ☐ The driver of the vehicle
- ☐ The owner of the items being carried
- ☐ The person who loaded the vehicle
- ☐ The licensing authority

Your vehicle must not be overloaded. Carrying heavy loads will affect control and handling characteristics. If your vehicle is overloaded and it causes a crash, you'll be held responsible.

14.7 | Mark one answer | DES s19

You are planning to tow a caravan. Which of these will mostly help to aid the vehicle handling?

- ☐ A jockey wheel fitted to the towbar
- ☐ Power steering fitted to the towing vehicle
- ☐ Anti-lock brakes fitted to the towing vehicle
- ☐ A stabiliser fitted to the towbar

Towing a caravan or trailer affects the way the tow vehicle handles. It is highly recommended that you take a caravan manoeuvring course. These are provided by various organisations for anyone wishing to tow a trailer.

Mark one answer

Are passengers allowed to ride in a caravan that is being towed?

☐ Yes, if they are over fourteen

☐ No, not at any time

☐ Only if all the seats in the towing vehicle are full

☐ Only if a stabiliser is fitted

Riding in a towed caravan is highly dangerous. The safety of the entire unit is dependent on the stability of the trailer. Moving passengers would make the caravan unstable and could cause loss of control.

Mark one answer

A trailer must stay securely hitched up to the towing vehicle. What additional safety device can be fitted to the trailer braking system?

☐ Stabiliser

☐ Jockey wheel

☐ Corner steadies

☐ Breakaway cable

In the event of a towbar failure the cable activates the trailer brakes, then snaps. This allows the towing vehicle to get free of the trailer and out of danger.

Mark one answer

You wish to tow a trailer. Where would you find the maximum noseweight of your vehicle's tow ball?

☐ In the vehicle handbook

☐ In The Highway Code

☐ In your vehicle registration certificate

☐ In your licence documents

You must know how to load your trailer or caravan so that the hitch exerts a downward force onto the tow ball. This information can be found in your vehicle handbook or from your vehicle manufacturer's agent.

Mark one answer

Any load that is carried on a roof rack should be

☐ securely fastened when driving

☐ loaded towards the rear of the vehicle

☐ visible in your exterior mirror

☐ covered with plastic sheeting

The safest way to carry items on the roof is in a specially designed roof box. This will help to keep your luggage secure and dry, and also has less wind resistance than loads carried on a roof rack.

You are carrying a child in your car. They are under three years of age. Which of these is a suitable restraint?

☐ A child seat

☐ An adult holding a child

☐ An adult seat belt

☐ An adult lap belt

It's your responsibility to ensure that all children in your car are secure. Suitable restraints include a child seat, baby seat, booster seat or booster cushion. It's essential that any restraint used should be suitable for the child's size and weight, and fitted to the manufacturer's instructions.

Section fourteen Questions

Case study practice – 14 Vehicle loading

Nathan and his family are going on holiday. Nathan will be driving.

He's loading the newly purchased roof rack on their estate car.

His wife Jane is helping the two young children with their seat belts in the rear seats.

The family dog, Shadow, will be travelling in the rear compartment of the car.

Once ready to go, they call at the service station to buy fuel and make final checks.

14.1 How could the full roof rack affect this vehicle's handling?

Mark **one** answer

☐ Increase road holding
☐ Reduce the stability
☐ Protect the paintwork
☐ Improve journey time

HC r98 DES s2

14.2 How should Shadow be secured for safety?

Mark **one** answer

☐ In a child's seat belt
☐ In a cardboard box
☐ In a special harness
☐ In a plastic dog bed

HC r57 **DES** s2

14.3 Who's responsible for ensuring that the children are wearing the appropriate seat belt or child restraint?

Mark **one** answer

☐ The police
☐ The mother
☐ The driver
☐ The children

HC r99–102 **DES** s2

14.4 Which one of these actions could help reduce the family's fuel consumption?

Mark **one** answer

☐ Removing the roof rack when it isn't being used
☐ Braking and accelerating as quickly as possible
☐ Fitting extra spoilers and larger wing mirrors
☐ Increasing tyre pressures and opening windows

DES s17

14.5 What should Nathan be checking?

Mark **one** answer

☐ For any spilt fuel around the vehicle on the station forecourt
☐ To ensure that none of their luggage has been left behind
☐ That the weather forecast will be good during their journey
☐ That there's appropriate pressure in all four tyres plus the spare

HC p128–130 **DES** s5

Case study
practice

Case study practice

Some of the questions within the test will be presented as a case study.

You'll be presented with a scenario – the case study – which will appear on the left-hand side of the screen. The scenario will be presented in a text format and may be accompanied by a supporting picture or diagram. As you move within the case study, the questions will appear, one by one, on the right-hand side of the screen, and you'll be asked to respond. You can re-read the scenario throughout the case study should you wish to do so.

A case study example is shown below and on the following pages.

In this section, you'll also find five mixed-topic, practice case studies similar to the ones in the actual test. Use these to help you prepare for the real thing.

Answers to all the case studies in this book are in section 16, Answers.

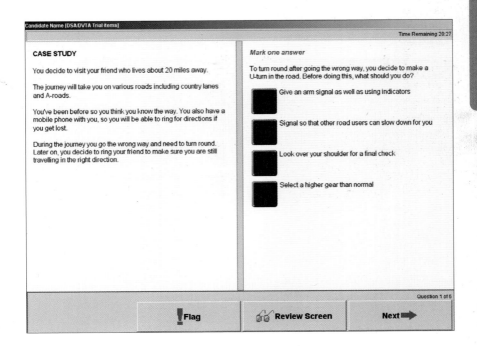

CASE STUDY

You decide to visit your friend who lives about 20 miles away.

The journey will take you on various roads including country lanes and A-roads.

You've been before so you think you know the way. You also have a mobile phone with you, so you will be able to ring for directions if you get lost.

During the journey you go the wrong way and need to turn round. Later on, you decide to ring your friend to make sure you are still travelling in the right direction.

Mark three answers

What should you do as you approach this bridge on your journey?

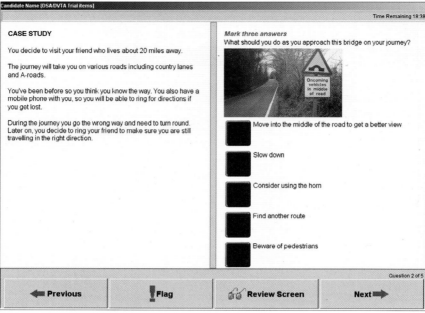

Move into the middle of the road to get a better view

Slow down

Consider using the horn

Find another route

Beware of pedestrians

Question 2 of 5

Previous | Flag | Review Screen | Next

CASE STUDY

You decide to visit your friend who lives about 20 miles away.

The journey will take you on various roads including country lanes and A-roads.

You've been before so you think you know the way. You also have a mobile phone with you, so you will be able to ring for directions if you get lost.

During the journey you go the wrong way and need to turn round. Later on, you decide to ring your friend to make sure you are still travelling in the right direction.

Mark one answer

During your journey, you ring your friend. What is the safest way for you to use your mobile phone?

Use hands-free equipment

Find a suitable place to stop

Travel slowly on a quiet road

Direct your call through the operator

Question 3 of 5

Previous | Flag | Review Screen | Next

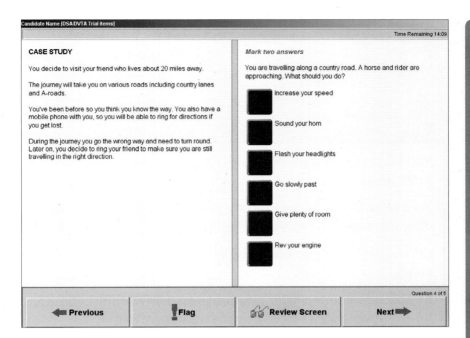

CASE STUDY

You decide to visit your friend who lives about 20 miles away.

The journey will take you on various roads including country lanes and A-roads.

You've been before so you think you know the way. You also have a mobile phone with you, so you will be able to ring for directions if you get lost.

During the journey you go the wrong way and need to turn round. Later on, you decide to ring your friend to make sure you are still travelling in the right direction.

Mark two answers

You are travelling along a country road. A horse and rider are approaching. What should you do?

- Increase your speed
- Sound your horn
- Flash your headlights
- Go slowly past
- Give plenty of room
- Rev your engine

Question 4 of 5

◀ **Previous**   ❗**Flag**   👓 **Review Screen**   **Next** ➡

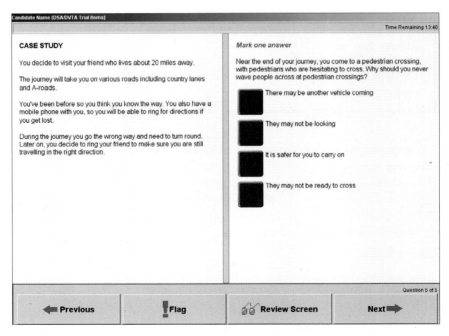

CASE STUDY

You decide to visit your friend who lives about 20 miles away.

The journey will take you on various roads including country lanes and A-roads.

You've been before so you think you know the way. You also have a mobile phone with you, so you will be able to ring for directions if you get lost.

During the journey you go the wrong way and need to turn round. Later on, you decide to ring your friend to make sure you are still travelling in the right direction.

Mark one answer

Near the end of your journey, you come to a pedestrian crossing, with pedestrians who are hesitating to cross. Why should you never wave people across at pedestrian crossings?

- There may be another vehicle coming
- They may not be looking
- It is safer for you to carry on
- They may not be ready to cross

Question 5 of 5

◀ **Previous**   ❗**Flag**   👓 **Review Screen**   **Next** ➡

Case study practice – A

You plan to visit a friend who lives in a town two hours' drive away.

Two weeks before the journey you realise that your tax disc will expire while you're away.

On the morning you leave you're tired after a poor night's sleep.

At the beginning of your journey you reach a roundabout. Another car cuts in front of you causing you to do an emergency stop.

Later you join the motorway where a red X is flashing above the outside lane.

It's just after 11 pm when you park outside your friend's house.

1   What should you do two weeks before you leave?

Mark **one** answer

☐ Transfer the tax disc from another vehicle

☐ Notify DVLA that the vehicle is off the road

☐ Make a note to renew the tax disc on your return

☐ Apply immediately for your new tax disc

HC p122 **DES** s2

2   What should you do on the morning of your journey?

Mark **one** answer

☐ Drink two cups of coffee and rest for 15 minutes

☐ Drink two cups of coffee and leave immediately

☐ Start your journey at 5 am to beat the traffic

☐ Plan your journey so there will be no stops

HC r91 **DES** s1, 11

3   What should you do at the roundabout?

Mark **one** answer

☐ Flash your lights and change lanes

☐ Sound your horn at the other car

☐ Stay calm and continue when it's safe

☐ Continue on your journey immediately

HC r147 **DES** s1

4   What MUST you do on the motorway?

Mark **one** answer

☐ Drive down the outside lane

☐ Overtake in the outside lane

☐ Pull over in the outside lane

☐ Stay out of the outside lane

HC r258 **DES** s11

5   Why MUST you avoid using your horn when parked outside your friend's house?

Mark **one** answer

☐ Because they have children

☐ Because it's before midnight

☐ Because it's after 10.30 pm

☐ Because you're stationary

HC r112 **DES** s13

> Case study practice – B

You're taking your 14-year-old nephew on a day trip.

You drive through town and reach a zebra crossing. A man carrying a white cane with a red band is waiting to cross.

You join a dual carriageway and see a sign which is a white circle with a diagonal black stripe.

As you drive across a roundabout you're involved in a collision with a cyclist. You and your nephew aren't injured. The cyclist is conscious but she's lying at the side of the road and her leg is bleeding heavily.

1   Who's responsible for your nephew wearing a seat belt?

Mark **one** answer

☐ He is

☐ You are

☐ His parents

☐ The police

`HC` r99 `DES` s2

2   What do the markings on the man's cane mean?

Mark **one** answer

☐ He's blind

☐ He's deaf and blind

☐ He's deaf

☐ He has mobility problems

`HC` r207 `DES` s10

3 What does the sign mean?

Mark **one** answer

- ☐ Pedestrian zone ends
- ☐ End of goods vehicle restriction
- ☐ End of minimum speed requirement
- ☐ National speed limit applies

`HC` p106 `DES` s6 `KYTS` p20

4 What should you do at the roundabout?

Mark **one** answer

- ☐ Take your nephew to the hospital
- ☐ Drive to the nearest police station
- ☐ Put on your hazard warning lights
- ☐ Flag down passing drivers for help

`HC` r283 `DES` s16

5 What should you do about the cyclist?

Mark **one** answer

- ☐ Leave her for the emergency services
- ☐ Restrict the blood flow from her leg
- ☐ Help her back onto her bike
- ☐ Give her a drink of water

`HC` r283, p133 `DES` s16

> Case study practice – C

You're driving into the town centre and the weather is cold and very damp.

There are several cars parked down either side of the main road.

It's market day and there are many pedestrians around.

Ahead of you a large van is being unloaded on your side of the road and there's oncoming traffic.

Later you reach a junction with some traffic lights that aren't working. There are several other vehicles in the area.

On your way home your steering begins to feel a little heavy. You stop at a nearby filling station.

---

1   What's the recommended time gap that should be left between vehicles in these weather conditions?

Mark **one** answer

☐ Two seconds

☐ Four seconds

☐ Six seconds

☐ Eight seconds

HC r126, p41 **DES** s7

2   What should you watch out for in this area?

Mark **one** answer

- ☐ Sale posters going up in any of the shop windows
- ☐ The next available free parking space on the road
- ☐ Pedestrians stepping out from between vehicles
- ☐ Traffic wardens who may be working in the area

HC r152 **DES** s7

3   How should you react to the van?

Mark **one** answer

- ☐ Stop and wait until the way ahead is clear
- ☐ Move out and pass as quickly as possible
- ☐ Find another route to your destination
- ☐ Wait until the van is unloaded and moved

HC r163 **DES** s7

4   Who has right of way at the lights?

Mark **one** answer

- ☐ No specific vehicle
- ☐ Any vehicle opposite
- ☐ The largest vehicle
- ☐ The fastest vehicle

HC r146, 176 **DES** s6, 8

5   What might cause the steering to feel this way?

Mark **one** answer

- ☐ Being very low on fuel
- ☐ Battery power is failing
- ☐ Driving at a slow speed
- ☐ Tyre pressure is too low

HC p129 **DES** s7

You're driving to work on a single carriageway road.

It's early morning and there's patchy fog which is very thick in places.

A sports car is travelling too closely behind you.

Later you reach a roundabout where you need to turn right. The approach road is still a single carriageway. There's only one line of traffic.

When you get to work you find that the car park is full. You have to park on the main road facing downhill.

You need to leave some camera equipment in your vehicle until later.

1   What lights would you use under these weather conditions?

Mark **one** answer

☐ Headlights with fog lights as necessary

☐ Full-beam lights at all times on the journey

☐ No lights at all during the whole journey

☐ Sidelights and hazard warning lights

HC r226, 234–236 **DES** s12

2 What should you do about the sports car?

Mark **one** answer

☐ Brake sharply and allow the other vehicle past

☐ Pull over to the side of the road and then stop

☐ Increase speed and pull away from the vehicle

☐ Slowly drop back to allow more room in front

HC r235 **DES** s10, 12

3 How should you position your vehicle when approaching the roundabout?

Mark **one** answer

☐ Move closer to the centre line but give no signal at all

☐ Stay close to the left-hand kerb and signal to go right

☐ Move nearer to the centre line and signal to go right

☐ Stay in the middle of the approach lane but don't signal

HC r184–190 **DES** s8

4 How should you position your front wheels when parking here?

Mark **one** answer

☐ Turned in towards the kerb

☐ Aligned alongside the kerb

☐ Turned away from the kerb

☐ Mounted up onto the kerb

HC r252 **DES** s9

5 What should you do with the equipment?

Mark **one** answer

☐ Leave it on the back seat in a bag

☐ Lock it away securely out of sight

☐ Cover it with a blanket or jacket

☐ Leave it in the passenger footwell

HC p131 **DES** s20

You're taking a friend and their two children to the coast. The children are aged two and six.

With fuel and tyre pressures done, you make other final checks.

After helping the children into the vehicle you set off.

It rained heavily overnight and the roads are still wet in places. However, the sun is now shining and the day is very warm and bright.

Once on the motorway the traffic is very heavy. There's a large goods vehicle travelling in front of you.

Further on you see an overhead gantry with a speed limit of 40 showing above all lanes, including the hard shoulder.

1   What else should you check before your journey?

Mark **one** answer

☐ Oil and water levels

☐ Lights and indicators

☐ Brakes and brake fluid

☐ Interior temperature

DES s14

2 How MUST you seat the younger child?

Mark **one** answer

- [ ] On a cushion with a lap belt
- [ ] In a normal adult seat belt
- [ ] On a booster cushion only
- [ ] In a suitable child restraint

HC r99–102, p32 **DES** s2

3 What hazards might you encounter in these weather conditions?

Mark **one** answer

- [ ] Puddles making the tyres muddy
- [ ] Glare from the sun on wet roads
- [ ] Road surface drying out too fast
- [ ] Dirt splashing on the windscreen

HC r93 **DES** s12

4 What position should you take behind the goods vehicle?

Mark **one** answer

- [ ] Well back so you can see ahead and be seen
- [ ] Close enough to stay out of the sun's glare
- [ ] Just far enough back to stay in its slipstream
- [ ] Well back so other vehicles can pull into the gap

HC r221–222 **DES** s7, 11

5 What does the sign on the overhead gantry mean?

Mark **one** answer

- [ ] There's an obstruction in the hard shoulder 40 yards ahead
- [ ] Only 40 vehicles can use the hard shoulder until further notice
- [ ] This lane can be used as a running lane at a speed of 40 mph
- [ ] Traffic must merge in turn back onto the motorway in 40 minutes

HC r269 **DES** s11, 18

> 1. Alertness

1.1	☐ look over your shoulder for a final check
1.2	☐ slow down ☐ consider using your horn ☐ beware of pedestrians
1.3	☐ Approaching a dip in the road
1.4	☐ overtaking drivers to move back to the left
1.5	☐ pull up in a suitable place
1.6	☐ To make you aware of your speed
1.7	☐ be ready to stop
1.8	☐ Use the mirrors
1.9	☐ allows the driver to see you in the mirrors
1.10	☐ To assess how your actions will affect following traffic
1.11	☐ Stop and then move forward slowly and carefully for a proper view
1.12	☐ restrict your view ☐ distract your attention
1.13	☐ leave the motorway and find a safe place to stop ☐ ensure a supply of fresh air into your vehicle

1.14	☐ even when street lights are not lit ☐ so others can see you
1.15	☐ Using a mobile phone ☐ Talking into a microphone ☐ Tuning your car radio ☐ Looking at a map
1.16	☐ suitably parked
1.17	☐ keep both hands on the wheel
1.18	☐ look round before you move off ☑ use all the mirrors on the vehicle ☐ give a signal if necessary
1.19	☐ slowly, leaving plenty of room
1.20	☐ find a safe place to stop
1.21	☐ Turn into a side road, stop and check a map
1.22	☐ approaching bends and junctions
1.23	☐ Ask someone to guide you
1.24	☐ An area not covered by your mirrors
1.25	☐ divert your attention

477

1.26	☐ Check that the central reservation is wide enough for your vehicle
1.27	☐ Motorcyclists
1.28	☐ Stop in a safe place before using the system

Section 1 – Alertness

1.1	Information about the medicine causing drowsiness
1.2	To maximise his visibility to others
1.3	He becomes drowsy
1.4	Stop in a service area, drink a caffeinated drink and then rest
1.5	Open the window

> 2. Attitude

2.1	☐ give way to pedestrians already on the crossing	**2.14**	☐ To help other road users know what you intend to do
2.2	☐ there may be another vehicle coming	**2.15**	☐ Toucan
2.3	☐ following another vehicle too closely	**2.16**	☐ allow the vehicle to overtake
2.4	☐ your view ahead is reduced	**2.17**	☐ to let them know that you are there
2.5	☐ four seconds	**2.18**	☐ Slow down and look both ways
2.6	☐ Slow down	**2.19**	☐ to keep a safe gap from the vehicle in front
2.7	☐ Bomb disposal ☐ Blood transfusion ☐ Police patrol	**2.20**	☐ Steady amber
2.8	☐ pull over as soon as safely possible to let it pass	**2.21**	☐ Slow down, gradually increasing the gap between you and the vehicle in front
2.9	☐ Doctor's car	**2.22**	☐ slow down and give way if it is safe to do so
2.10	☐ tram drivers	**2.23**	☐ Dipped headlights
2.11	☐ Cycles	**2.24**	☐ slow down and let the vehicle turn
2.12	☐ To alert others to your presence	**2.25**	☐ Drop back to leave the correct separation distance
2.13	☐ in the right-hand lane		

2.26	☐ apply the handbrake only
2.27	☐ keep a steady course and allow the driver behind to overtake
2.28	☐ in operation 24 hours a day
2.29	☐ stop and switch off your engine
2.30	☐ go past slowly and carefully
2.31	☐ slow down and prepare to stop
2.32	☐ Slow down and be ready to stop
2.33	☐ the pedestrians have reached a safe position
2.34	☐

2.35	☐ good
2.36	☐ use dipped beam headlights
2.37	☐ pull in safely when you can, to let following vehicles overtake
2.38	☐ waste fuel and money ☐ make roads slippery for other road users
2.39	☐ your filler cap is securely fastened
2.40	☐ Competitive

CASE STUDY PRACTICE – ANSWERS

Section 2 – Attitude

2.1 Slow down and, if necessary, stop

2.2 Remain calm, slow down and increase the gap

2.3 In the left-hand lane while signalling left

2.4 The vehicle needs more room to turn

2.5 Stop and wait for them to cross

❯ 3. Safety and your vehicle

3.1	☐ Braking ☐ Steering
3.2	☐ between 11.30 pm and 7 am in a built-up area
3.3	☐ reduces noise pollution ☐ uses electricity ☐ reduces town traffic
3.4	☐ help the traffic flow
3.5	☐ traffic calming measures

3.6	☐ toxic exhaust gases
3.7	☐ When tyres are cold
3.8	☐ under-inflated
3.9	☐ Take it to a local authority site ☐ Take it to a garage
3.10	☐ Harsh braking and accelerating
3.11	☐ Distilled water

3.12	☐ Where the speed limit exceeds 30 mph		**3.31**	☐ increase fuel consumption
3.13	☐ air pollution ☐ damage to buildings ☐ using up of natural resources		**3.32**	☐ have a large deep cut in the side wall
			3.33	☐ 1.6 mm
3.14	☐ The braking system ☐ Wheel alignment ☐ The suspension		**3.34**	☐ You, the driver
			3.35	☐ By reducing your speed ☐ By gentle acceleration ☐ By servicing your vehicle properly
3.15	☐ Just above the cell plates			
3.16	☐ Look at a map		**3.36**	☐ having your vehicle properly serviced ☐ making sure your tyres are correctly inflated ☐ not over-revving in the lower gears
3.17	☐ You will have an easier journey			
3.18	☐ it will help to ease congestion			
3.19	☐ Your original route may be blocked		**3.37**	☐ use public transport more often ☐ share a car when possible ☐ walk or cycle on short journeys
3.20	☐ allow plenty of time for your journey			
3.21	☐ increased fuel consumption		**3.38**	☐ Carrying unnecessary weight ☐ Under-inflated tyres ☐ A fitted, empty roof rack
3.22	☐ 20%			
3.23	☐ Brake fluid level		**3.39**	☐ Headlights ☐ Windscreen ☐ Seat belts
3.24	☐ braking system ☐ suspension			
3.25	☐ the brakes overheating		**3.40**	☐ 30%
3.26	☐ have the brakes checked immediately		**3.41**	☐ consult your garage as soon as possible
3.27	☐ a fault in the braking system		**3.42**	☐ the steering to vibrate
3.28	☐ To maintain control of the pedals		**3.43**	☐ steering ☐ tyres
3.29	☐ A properly adjusted head restraint		**3.44**	☐ lock them out of sight
3.30	☐ Worn shock absorbers		**3.45**	☐ Etching the car number on the windows

3.46	☐ The vehicle documents
3.47	☐ remove the key and lock it
3.48	☐ Reducing your road speed ☐ Planning well ahead
3.49	☐ Take it to a local authority site
3.50	☐ To help protect the environment against pollution
3.51	☐ avoid harsh acceleration ☐ brake in good time ☐ anticipate well ahead
3.52	☐ better fuel economy ☐ cleaner exhaust emissions
3.53	☐ Maintain a reduced speed throughout
3.54	☐ Before a long journey
3.55	☐ No, not in any circumstances
3.56	☐ lock it and remove the key
3.57	☐ In a secure car park
3.58	☐ In front of a property entrance ☐ At or near a bus stop ☐ On the approach to a level crossing
3.59	☐ help you to avoid neck injury
3.60	☐ making a lot of short journeys ☐ accelerating as quickly as possible
3.61	☐ walking or cycling
3.62	☐ Take all valuables with you

3.63	☐ Install a security-coded radio
3.64	☐ Leave it in a well-lit area
3.65	☐ vehicle watch scheme
3.66	☐ On the exhaust system
3.67	☐ reduce fuel consumption by about 15%
3.68	☐ missing out some gears
3.69	☐ By reducing exhaust emissions
3.70	☐ Improved road safety
3.71	☐ 1.6 mm
3.72	☐ accelerating
3.73	☐ exempt for medical reasons
3.74	☐ You, the driver
3.75	☐ Oil leaks
3.76	☐ use an adult seat belt
3.77	☐ a suitable child restraint is available
3.78	☐ Switch off the engine
3.79	☐ Deactivate the airbag
3.80	☐ Never if you are away from the vehicle

CASE STUDY PRACTICE – ANSWERS

Section 3 – Safety and your vehicle

3.1 Shorter travel time

3.2 No stopping at any time

3.3 Proceed with care as with an unmarked junction

3.4 Tyres that are under-inflated

3.5 Lock it away securely out of sight

481

> 4. Safety margins

4.1	☐ ten times the normal distance
4.2	☐ ten times
4.3	☐ passing pedal cyclists
4.4	☐ To improve your view of the road
4.5	☐ The grip of the tyres ☐ The braking
4.6	☐ On an open stretch of road
4.7	☐ 96 metres (315 feet)
4.8	☐ 73 metres (240 feet)
4.9	☐ Drop back to regain a safe distance
4.10	☐ 53 metres (175 feet)
4.11	☐ 36 metres (118 feet)
4.12	☐ Pass wide
4.13	☐ 38 metres (125 feet)
4.14	☐ Increase your distance from the vehicle in front
4.15	☐ Reduce your speed and increase the gap in front
4.16	☐ reduce speed in good time ☐ choose an appropriate lane in good time ☐ keep the correct separation distance
4.17	☐ Drive at a slow speed in as high a gear as possible

4.18	☐ the driver
4.19	☐ Slow down before you reach the bend ☐ Avoid sudden steering movements
4.20	☐ steer carefully to the right
4.21	☐ windows ☐ lights ☐ mirrors ☐ number plates
4.22	☐ the highest gear you can
4.23	☐ brake gently in plenty of time
4.24	☐ road holding
4.25	☐ select a low gear and use the brakes carefully
4.26	☐ Turn the steering wheel towards the kerb ☐ Put the handbrake on firmly
4.27	☐ slow your vehicle right down
4.28	☐ braking in an emergency
4.29	☐ loose ☐ wet
4.30	☐ braking excessively
4.31	☐ steer and brake at the same time
4.32	☐ rapidly and firmly
4.33	☐ on surface water ☐ on loose road surfaces

4.34	☐ test your brakes
4.35	☐ The tyres make hardly any noise ☐ The steering becomes lighter
4.36	☐ The steering will feel very light
4.37	☐ in the rain
4.38	☐ a two-second time gap
4.39	☐ By changing to a lower gear
4.40	☐ brake promptly and firmly until you have slowed down
4.41	☐ maximum brake pressure has been applied

4.42	☐ dipped headlights
4.43	☐ reduces the driver's control
4.44	☐ Use dipped headlights ☐ Allow more time for your journey ☐ Slow down

CASE STUDY PRACTICE – ANSWERS

Section 4 – Safety margins

4.1   Allow more distance
      Allow more time

4.2   Gently and slowly

4.3   The road could be icy

4.4   Ease off the accelerator then steer carefully to the right

4.5   Amber

❯ 5. Hazard awareness

5.1	☐ On a large goods vehicle ☐ On a builder's skip placed on the road
5.2	☐ The cyclist crossing the road
5.3	☐ The parked car (arrowed A)
5.4	☐ Slow down and get ready to stop
5.5	☐ Pedestrians stepping out between cars ☐ Doors opening on parked cars ☐ Cars leaving parking spaces

5.6	☐ bend sharply to the left
5.7	☐ slow down and allow the cyclist to turn
5.8	☐ There is reduced visibility
5.9	☐ buses
5.10	☐ Lorry
5.11	☐ behind the line, then edge forward to see clearly
5.12	☐ ignore the error and stay calm
5.13	☐ react very quickly
5.14	☐ A school crossing patrol

5.15	☐ Yes, regular stops help concentration
5.16	☐ Stop before the barrier
5.17	☐ Be prepared to stop for any traffic.
5.18	☐ Wait for the pedestrian in the road to cross
5.19	☐ Stay behind until you are past the junction
5.20	☐ Be prepared to give way to large vehicles in the middle of the road
5.21	☐ They give a wider field of vision
5.22	☐ approach with care and keep to the left of the lorry
5.23	☐ stay behind and not overtake
5.24	☐ The bus may move out into the road
5.25	☐ a school bus
5.26	☐ Car doors opening suddenly ☐ Children running out from between vehicles
5.27	☐ The cyclist may swerve out into the road
5.28	☐ stop and take a break
5.29	☐ travel at a reduced speed
5.30	☐ Because of the bend ☐ Because of the level crossing
5.31	☐ To enable you to change lanes early

5.32	☐ Traffic in both directions can use the middle lane to overtake
5.33	☐ A disabled person's vehicle
5.34	☐ Stop
5.35	☐ It may suddenly move off ☐ People may cross the road in front of it
5.36	☐ If you are turning left shortly afterwards ☐ When you are approaching a junction ☐ When your view ahead is blocked
5.37	☐ Less control ☐ A false sense of confidence ☐ Poor judgement of speed
5.38	☐ Edge of the carriageway
5.39	☐ A steady amber light
5.40	☐ Allow the cyclist time and room
5.41	☐ wait for the cyclist to pull away
5.42	☐ check for bicycles on your left
5.43	☐ there is a staggered junction ahead
5.44	☐ Traffic will move into the left-hand lane
5.45	☐ The two left lanes are open
5.46	☐ Not drink any alcohol at all
5.47	☐ Insurance premiums

5.48	☐ Go home by public transport
5.49	☐ after checking with your doctor
5.50	☐ not drive yourself
5.51	☐ be medically fit to drive ☐ not drive after taking certain medicines
5.52	☐ stop and rest as soon as possible ☐ make sure you have a good supply of fresh air
5.53	☐ stop at the next service area and rest ☐ leave the motorway at the next exit and rest
5.54	☐ wait until you are fit and well before driving
5.55	☐ stopping every so often for a walk ☐ opening a window for some fresh air ☐ ensuring plenty of refreshment breaks
5.56	☐ Check the label to see if the medicine will affect your driving
5.57	☐ continue to the end of the road
5.58	☐ Looking at road maps ☐ Listening to loud music ☐ Using a mobile phone
5.59	☐ sound your horn and be prepared to stop
5.60	☐ calm down before you start to drive

5.61	☐ There are roadworks ahead of you
5.62	☐ keep a safe gap
5.63	☐ find a way of getting home without driving
5.64	☐ Reduced coordination ☐ Increased confidence ☐ Poor judgement
5.65	☐ Some types of medicine can cause your reactions to slow down
5.66	☐ At all times when driving
5.67	☐ Tinted
5.68	☐ Drugs ☐ Tiredness ☐ Loud music
5.69	☐ the licensing authority
5.70	☐ When your vehicle has broken down and is causing an obstruction
5.71	☐ Approach slowly and edge out until you can see more clearly
5.72	☐ Quick acceleration
5.73	☐ allow at least a four-second gap ☐ be aware of spray reducing your vision
5.74	☐ Pedestrians walking towards you
5.75	☐ be wary of cars on your right cutting in ☐ slow down, keeping a safe separation distance

485

5.76	☐ on your own ☐ on the motorway
5.77	☐ When driving on a motorway to warn traffic behind of a hazard ahead
5.78	☐ Reflections of traffic in shop windows
5.79	☐ inform the licensing authority
5.80	☐ To allow vehicles to enter and emerge
5.81	☐ Open a window and stop as soon as it's safe and legal

CASE STUDY PRACTICE – ANSWERS

Section 5 – Hazard awareness

5.1 To check for reflections of any vehicles approaching

5.2 Pedestrians or cyclists could be stepping out

5.3 Stop and wait until the way is clear ahead

5.4 Stop and wait patiently till signalled to go on

5.5 The lane can only be used by buses at all times

> 6. Vulnerable road users

6.1	☐ 
6.2	☐ give way to them
6.3	☐ wait and allow them to cross
6.4	☐ Pedestrians
6.5	☐ overtaking on your right
6.6	☐ cyclists can use it
6.7	☐ By displaying a stop sign
6.8	☐ On the rear of a school bus or coach
6.9	☐ A route for pedestrians and cyclists

6.10	☐ deaf and blind
6.11	☐ Be patient and allow them to cross in their own time
6.12	☐ Give the cyclist plenty of room
6.13	☐ Motorcycles ☐ Bicycles
6.14	☐ They are harder to see
6.15	☐ So that the rider can be seen more easily
6.16	☐ drivers often do not see them
6.17	☐ stay behind
6.18	☐ they need to check for traffic in their blind area

6.19	☐ Cyclists
	☐ Motorcyclists
	☐ Pedestrians
6.20	☐ be prepared to stop
	☐ give them plenty of room
6.21	☐ wait because they will take longer to cross
6.22	☐ Reduce speed until you are clear of the area
6.23	☐ a clear view of the crossing area
6.24	☐ On a school bus
6.25	☐ Any direction
6.26	☐ stay behind until the moped has passed the junction
6.27	☐ stay well back
6.28	☐ Be patient and prepare for them to react more slowly
6.29	☐ Pedestrians
6.30	☐ be aware that the driver's reactions may not be as fast as yours
6.31	☐ hold back until the cyclist has passed the junction
6.32	☐ go in any direction
6.33	☐ They will have a flashing amber light.
6.34	☐ just before you turn left
6.35	☐ slow moving
6.36	☐ With-flow pedal cycle lane
6.37	☐ Slow down and be ready to stop

6.38	☐ children's view of the crossing area
6.39	☐ Watch out for pedestrians walking in the road
6.40	☐ allow extra room in case they swerve to avoid potholes
6.41	☐ Cycle route ahead
6.42	☐ The cyclist is slower and more vulnerable
6.43	☐ prepare to slow down and stop
6.44	☐ deaf
6.45	☐ pedestrians and cyclists may cross
6.46	☐ To allow cyclists to position in front of other traffic
6.47	☐ The cyclist might swerve
6.48	☐ Allow plenty of room
	☐ Go very slowly
	☐ Be ready to stop
6.49	☐ You are approaching an organised walk
6.50	☐ By taking further training
6.51	☐ Get out and check
6.52	☐ give way to the pedestrian
6.53	☐ Children
6.54	☐ Stop, then move slowly forward until you have a clear view
6.55	☐ To check for overtaking vehicles

6.56	☐ Give way to any pedestrians on the crossing
6.57	☐ allow the person to cross ☐ be patient
6.58	☐ Slow down and be prepared to stop for children
6.59	☐ check for traffic overtaking on your right
6.60	☐ look for motorcyclists filtering through the traffic
6.61	☐ Pedestrians may come from behind the bus
6.62	☐ Drive slowly and leave plenty of room
6.63	☐ The rider may be blown across in front of you
6.64	☐ At junctions

6.65	☐ You must not wait or park your vehicle here at all
6.66	☐ Slow down and be prepared to stop for a cyclist
6.67	☐ set your mirror to anti-dazzle
6.68	☐ Be prepared to stop
6.69	☐ You should not wait or park your vehicle here

CASE STUDY PRACTICE – ANSWERS

Section 6 – Vulnerable road users

6.1 Swerve

6.2 Go in any direction

6.3 Children may be crossing the road

6.4 30 mph

6.5 The pedestrian is deaf and blind

❯ 7. Other types of vehicle

7.1	☐
7.2	☐ The large vehicle can easily hide an overtaking vehicle
7.3	☐ stay well back and give it room
7.4	☐ Wait behind the long vehicle

7.5	☐ To get the best view of the road ahead
7.6	☐ Watch carefully for pedestrians ☐ Be ready to give way to the bus
7.7	☐ drop back until you can see better
7.8	☐ drop back further
7.9	☐ allow it to pull away, if it is safe to do so

7.10	☐ keep well back until you can see that it is clear
7.11	☐ Cars
7.12	☐ Slow down and be prepared to wait
7.13	☐ Do not overtake when at or approaching a junction
7.14	☐ 8 mph
7.15	☐ It takes longer to pass one
7.16	☐ Keep well back
7.17	☐ Be prepared to give way if the bus suddenly moves off ☐ Watch carefully for the sudden appearance of pedestrians
7.18	☐ Slow down and give way

7.19	☐ Because they cannot steer to avoid you
7.20	☐ Extended-arm side mirrors
7.21	☐ rear fog lights if visibility is less than 100 metres (328 feet) ☐ dipped headlights
7.22	☐ Allow extra room

CASE STUDY PRACTICE – ANSWERS

Section 7 – Other types of vehicle

7.1   60 mph

7.2   They could be blown off course

7.3   Drop back so you can see more of the road ahead

7.4   Trams are unable to steer round obstructions

7.5   Give way as long as it's safe to do so

⊛ 8. Road conditions and vehicle handling

8.1	☐ When you are in a one-way street ☐ When the vehicle in front is signalling to turn right ☐ In slow-moving traffic queues when traffic in the right-hand lane is moving more slowly
8.2	☐ doubled
8.3	☐ be careful because you can see less ☐ beware of bends in the road ahead

8.4	☐ When oncoming traffic prevents you turning right
8.5	☐ **Humps for ½ mile**
8.6	☐ slow traffic down
8.7	☐ Red
8.8	☐ alert you to a hazard ☐ encourage you to reduce speed
8.9	☐ leave plenty of time for your journey

8.10	☐ you do not dazzle other road users
8.11	☐ slow down and stay behind
8.12	☐ To make you aware of your speed
8.13	☐ white line markings ☐ a different coloured surface ☐ a different surface texture
8.14	☐ stop at a passing place
8.15	☐ To prevent the motorcycle sliding on the metal drain covers
8.16	☐ Your brakes will be soaking wet
8.17	☐ It is more difficult to see events ahead
8.18	☐ You will slow down sooner ☐ The engine will work harder
8.19	☐ be wary of a sudden gust
8.20	☐ steer into it
8.21	☐ In case it stops suddenly
8.22	☐ leave sidelights on
8.23	☐ slow down or stop
8.24	☐ visibility is seriously reduced
8.25	☐ Switch them off as long as visibility remains good
8.26	☐ dazzle other road users ☐ cause brake lights to be less clear ☐ be breaking the law
8.27	☐ when visibility is reduced to 100 metres (328 feet)

8.28	☐ dazzle other drivers
8.29	☐ skidding in deep snow
8.30	☐ By changing to a lower gear
8.31	☐ You will have less steering and braking control
8.32	☐ ten times the normal distance
8.33	☐ always use your headlights
8.34	☐ Dipped headlights
8.35	☐ How fast you are going ☐ The tyres on your vehicle ☐ The weather
8.36	☐ your vehicle is broken down on the hard shoulder
8.37	☐ change to a lower gear
8.38	☐ dipped headlights
8.39	☐ To make them more visible in thick fog
8.40	☐ remember to switch them off as visibility improves
8.41	☐ not drive unless it is essential
8.42	☐ The brakes overheating
8.43	☐ Check that your lights are working ☐ Make sure that the windows are clean
8.44	☐ switch off all your fog lights
8.45	☐ Brake lights are less clear ☐ Following drivers can be dazzled
8.46	☐ reduce your control

8.47	☐ Your vehicle will pick up speed
8.48	☐ The vehicle will get faster
	☐ You have less braking and steering control
8.49	☐ It could be more difficult in winter
	☐ Use a low gear and drive slowly
	☐ Test your brakes afterwards
	☐ There may be a depth gauge

8.50	☐ There is no engine braking
8.51	☐ In poor visibility
8.52	☐ Release the footbrake

CASE STUDY PRACTICE – ANSWERS

Section 8 – Road conditions and vehicle handling

8.1   It could be doubled
8.2   Visibility is below 100 metres
8.3   The other vehicle may stop suddenly
8.4   Wait until the road ahead is clear
8.5   A reminder to make him aware of speed

9. Motorway driving

9.1	☐ give way to traffic already on the motorway
9.2	☐ 70 mph
9.3	☐ any vehicle
9.4	☐ A vehicle towing a trailer
9.5	☐ It allows easy location by the emergency services
9.6	☐ gain speed on the hard shoulder before moving out onto the carriageway
9.7	☐ on a steep gradient
9.8	☐ They are countdown markers to the next exit
9.9	☐ the central reservation and the carriageway
9.10	☐ White
9.11	☐ Green

9.12	☐ in the direction shown on the marker posts
9.13	☐ Face the oncoming traffic
9.14	☐ Red
9.15	☐ Left
9.16	☐ keep a good distance from the vehicle ahead
9.17	☐ In the left-hand lane
9.18	☐ Obey all speed limits
9.19	☐ Learner car drivers
	☐ Farm tractors
	☐ Horse riders
	☐ Cyclists
9.20	☐ Learner car drivers
	☐ Farm tractors
	☐ Learner motorcyclists
	☐ Cyclists

9.21	☐ Overtaking
9.22	☐ Stopping in an emergency
9.23	☐ move to the left and reduce your speed to 50 mph
9.24	☐ are told to do so by flashing red lights
9.25	☐ move to another lane
9.26	☐ keep to the left-hand lane unless overtaking
9.27	☐ there is a queue of slow-moving traffic to your right that is moving more slowly than you are
9.28	☐ the Highways Agency Control Centre
9.29	☐ on a motorway for use in cases of emergency or breakdown
9.30	☐ are able to stop and direct anyone on a motorway
9.31	☐ You should not travel in this lane
9.32	☐ The hard shoulder can be used as a running lane
9.33	☐ reduce congestion
9.34	☐ all speed limit signals are set
9.35	☐ Your overall journey time will normally improve
9.36	☐ When signs direct you to
9.37	☐ Variable speed limits
9.38	☐ If red lights show above every lane ☐ When told to by the police ☐ When signalled by a Highways Agency Traffic Officer
9.39	☐ In an emergency or breakdown
9.40	☐ 70 mph
9.41	☐ stop and wait
9.42	☐ the hard shoulder is for emergency or breakdown use only
9.43	☐ all the lanes including the hard shoulder
9.44	☐ pull in at the nearest service area
9.45	☐ 60 mph
9.46	☐ normal driving
9.47	☐ switch on your hazard lights
9.48	☐ use the emergency telephone and call for assistance
9.49	☐ carry on to the next exit
9.50	☐ Switch on your hazard warning lights
9.51	☐ Continuous high speeds may increase the risk of your vehicle breaking down
9.52	☐ traffic ahead is slowing or stopping suddenly

9.53	☐ in the left-hand lane
9.54	☐ on the motorway
9.55	☐ check your location from the marker posts on the left
9.56	☐ there are lane closures
9.57	☐ Lower speed limits
9.58	☐ in an emergency

CASE STUDY PRACTICE – ANSWERS

Section 9 – Motorway driving

9.1 Vehicles already travelling in the left-hand lane

9.2 Yellow/green

9.3 The left-hand lane

9.4 60 mph

9.5 Continue on until she reaches the next exit

❯ 10. Rules of the road

10.1	☐ National speed limit applies	10.14	☐ indicate left before leaving the roundabout
10.2	☐ 70 mph	10.15	☐ Long vehicle
10.3	☐ By street lighting	10.16	☐ your exit road is clear
10.4	☐ 30 mph	10.17	☐ oncoming traffic is preventing you from turning right
10.5	☐ End of minimum speed		
10.6	☐ not overtake if you are in doubt	10.18	☐ A police officer ☐ A school crossing patrol ☐ A red traffic light
10.7	☐ Horse riders ☐ Long vehicles ☐ Cyclists	10.19	☐ stop, let them cross, wait patiently
10.8	☐ at any time	10.20	☐ Cyclists ☐ Pedestrians
10.9	☐ Waiting restrictions		
10.10	☐ in a one-way street	10.21	☐ You must give way to pedestrians still on the crossing
10.11	☐ overtaking or turning right		
10.12	☐ continue in that lane	10.22	☐ To pick up or set down passengers
10.13	☐ Either on the right or the left		

10.23	☐ keep the other vehicle to your RIGHT and turn behind it (offside to offside)	**10.40**	☐ to get into a property
		10.41	☐ 50 mph
10.24	☐ Vehicles may be pulling out ☐ Drivers' doors may open ☐ Children may run out from between the vehicles	**10.42**	☐ 60 mph
		10.43	☐ park in a bay and pay
		10.44	☐ you must not drive in that lane
10.25	☐ give way to oncoming traffic	**10.45**	☐ keep well to the left of the road
10.26	☐ Turning right ☐ Overtaking slower traffic	**10.46**	☐ Continue to wait
		10.47	☐ Keep going and clear the crossing
10.27	☐ No one has priority		
10.28	☐ 10 metres (32 feet)	**10.48**	☐ Turn round in a side road
10.29	☐ Near the brow of a hill ☐ At or near a bus stop ☐ Within 10 metres (32 feet) of a junction	**10.49**	☐ reversing
		10.50	☐ for longer than necessary
		10.51	☐ get out and check
10.30	☐ carry on waiting	**10.52**	☐ Not at any time
10.31	☐ No waiting zone ends	**10.53**	☐ wait in the box junction if your exit is clear
10.32	☐ not exceed the speed limit		
10.33	☐ be easily seen by others	**10.54**	☐ When the front of your vehicle swings out
10.34	☐ Wait until the road is clear in both directions	**10.55**	☐ In a garage
10.35	☐ 60 mph	**10.56**	☐ set down and pick up passengers
10.36	☐ with parking lights on	**10.57**	☐ not park there unless permitted
10.37	☐ a concealed level crossing		
10.38	☐ A Highways Agency Traffic Officer	**10.58**	☐ Pull into a passing place on your left
10.39	☐ Signal left just after you pass the exit before the one you will take	**10.59**	☐ as soon as the vehicle passes you
		10.60	☐ Outside its hours of operation

10.61	☐ brake lights
10.62	☐ Find a quiet side road to turn round in
10.63	☐ In a well-lit area
10.64	☐ move to the left in good time
10.65	☐ you should not drive in the lane unless it is unavoidable ☐ you should not park in the lane unless it is unavoidable
10.66	☐ A Blue Badge

10.67	☐ When in an incident where damage or injury is caused ☐ At a red traffic light ☐ When signalled to do so by a police or traffic officer

---

CASE STUDY PRACTICE – ANSWERS

Section 10 – Rules of the road

10.1 There are regularly spaced street lights in the area

10.2 Short dashes with long spaces

10.3 Amber

10.4 It's for vehicles that have two or more occupants

10.5 You **MUST NOT** park on pedestrian crossings

❯ 11. Road and traffic signs

11.1	☐ red circles
11.2	☐ 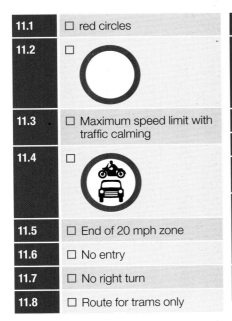
11.3	☐ Maximum speed limit with traffic calming
11.4	☐
11.5	☐ End of 20 mph zone
11.6	☐ No entry
11.7	☐ No right turn
11.8	☐ Route for trams only

11.9	☐ High vehicles
11.10	☐
11.11	☐ No overtaking
11.12	☐ Waiting restrictions apply
11.13	☐ End of restricted parking area
11.14	☐
11.15	☐ Distance to parking place ahead

11.16	☐ Vehicles may park fully on the verge or footway
11.17	☐ Give priority to oncoming traffic
11.18	☐ You have priority over vehicles coming towards you
11.19	☐
11.20	☐ Stop
11.21	☐ Minimum speed 30 mph
11.22	☐ Pass either side to get to the same destination
11.23	☐ Route for trams
11.24	☐ Give an instruction
11.25	☐ On a one-way street
11.26	☐ Contraflow bus lane
11.27	☐ Tourist directions
11.28	☐ tourist attraction
11.29	☐ To give warnings
11.30	☐ T-junction
11.31	☐ Risk of ice
11.32	☐ Crossroads
11.33	☐ Roundabout
11.34	☐ Road narrows ☐ Low bridge ☐ Children crossing ☐ T-junction
11.35	☐ Cycle route ahead

11.36	☐
11.37	☐
11.38	☐ Give way to trams
11.39	☐ Humps in the road
11.40	☐
11.41	☐ End of dual carriageway
11.42	☐ Crosswinds
11.43	☐ Danger ahead
11.44	☐ Level crossing with gate or barrier
11.45	☐ Trams crossing ahead
11.46	☐ Steep hill downwards
11.47	☐ Water across the road
11.48	☐ No through road on the left
11.49	☐ No through road
11.50	☐
11.51	☐ The right-hand lane is closed
11.52	☐ Contraflow system

11.53	☐ Lane for heavy and slow vehicles
11.54	☐ you must stop and wait behind the stop line
11.55	☐ stop at the stop line
11.56	☐ When your exit from the junction is blocked
11.57	☐
11.58	☐ Traffic lights out of order
11.59	☐ Lifting bridges ☐ Level crossings ☐ Fire stations
11.60	☐ No parking at any time
11.61	☐ To pass a road maintenance vehicle travelling at 10 mph or less
11.62	☐ You are approaching a hazard
11.63	☐ On road humps
11.64	☐
11.65	☐ Visibility along the major road is restricted
11.66	☐ Give way to traffic from the right
11.67	☐ Flash the headlights, indicate left and point to the left
11.68	☐ stop at the stop line
11.69	☐ The driver intends to turn left

11.70	☐ On a motorway slip road
11.71	☐ Change to the lane on your left
11.72	☐ Temporary maximum speed 50 mph
11.73	☐ Right-hand lane closed ahead
11.74	☐ The number of the next junction
11.75	☐ an overtaking lane
11.76	☐ On the right-hand edge of the road
11.77	☐ At slip road entrances and exits
11.78	☐ leave the motorway at the next exit
11.79	☐ End of motorway
11.80	☐
11.81	☐ 60 mph
11.82	☐ End of restriction
11.83	☐ follow the route diversion
11.84	☐ To warn of road works ahead
11.85	☐ a compulsory maximum speed limit
11.86	☐ carry on with great care
11.87	☐ Give an arm signal
11.88	☐ No motorcycles
11.89	☐ pass the lorry on the left

497

11.90	☐ Move into another lane in good time
11.91	☐ To warn others of your presence
11.92	☐ unless a moving vehicle may cause you danger
11.93	☐ No parking on the days and times shown
11.94	☐ Quayside or river bank
11.95	☐ hazard warning
11.96	☐ To prevent queuing traffic from blocking the junction on the left
11.97	☐ It is to separate traffic flowing in opposite directions
11.98	☐ To warn you of their presence
11.99	☐ 20 mph
11.100	☐ trams must stop
11.101	☐ At a junction
11.102	☐ Pull up on the left
11.103	☐ Red alone
11.104	☐ Leave the motorway at the next exit
11.105	☐ Stop, even if the road is clear
11.106	☐
11.107	☐ Mini-roundabout
11.108	☐ Two-way traffic crosses a one-way road

11.109	☐ Two-way traffic straight ahead
11.110	☐ Hump bridge
11.111	☐ Direction to park-and-ride car park
11.112	☐ wait for the green light before you cross the stop line
11.113	☐ 'give way' sign
11.114	☐ Wait
11.115	☐ Direction to emergency pedestrian exit
11.116	☐
11.117	☐ With-flow bus and cycle lane
11.118	☐ Zebra crossing ahead
11.119	☐
11.120	☐
11.121	☐ Red and amber
11.122	☐ Tunnel ahead
11.123	☐
11.124	☐ shows the edge of the carriageway

11.125	☐ keep left of the hatched markings
11.126	☐
11.127	☐ Wait until the vehicle starts to turn in
11.128	☐ On a motorway or unrestricted dual carriageway, to warn of a hazard ahead
11.129	☐ under any circumstances
11.130	☐ To avoid misleading other road users

| 11.131 | ☐ As you are passing or just after the junction |

CASE STUDY PRACTICE – ANSWERS

Section 11 – Road and traffic signs

11.1 No motor vehicles

11.2 No overtaking

11.3 60 mph

11.4 Tourist information

11.5 An amber light on its own

> 12. Essential documents

12.1	☐ one year after the date it was issued
12.2	☐ insurance certificate
12.3	☐ Retake your theory and practical tests ☐ Reapply for your provisional licence
12.4	☐ 12 months
12.5	☐ A notification to tell DVLA that a vehicle is not being used on the road
12.6	☐ £5,000
12.7	☐ The registered vehicle keeper
12.8	☐ When a police officer asks you for it

12.9	☐ A valid driving licence ☐ A valid tax disc clearly displayed ☐ Proper insurance cover
12.10	☐ valid insurance
12.11	☐ 7 days
12.12	☐ have a signed, valid provisional licence
12.13	☐ the vehicle is insured for your use
12.14	☐ insurance
12.15	☐ have valid motor insurance
12.16	☐ Injury to another person ☐ Damage to someone's property ☐ Damage to other vehicles

12.17	☐ display it clearly on your vehicle
12.18	☐ Registered keeper ☐ Make of the vehicle ☐ Engine size
12.19	☐ you change your vehicle ☐ you change your name ☐ your permanent address changes
12.20	☐ your health affects your driving ☐ your eyesight does not meet a set standard ☐ you change your vehicle
12.21	☐ take the Pass Plus scheme
12.22	☐ have held a full licence for at least 3 years ☐ be at least 21 years old
12.23	☐ When driving to an appointment at an MOT centre

12.24	☐ three years old
12.25	☐ To improve your basic skills
12.26	☐ damage to other vehicles ☐ injury to others
12.27	☐ Third party only
12.28	☐ You will have to pay the first £100 of the cost of repair to your car
12.29	☐ improve your basic driving skills
12.30	☐ widen their driving experience

CASE STUDY PRACTICE – ANSWERS

Section 12 – Essential documents

12.1 That the vehicle meets the required minimum legal standards

12.2 If she changes her name and address

12.3 Comprehensive

12.4 One month

12.5 Insurance certificate and MOT certificate

❯ 13. Incidents, accidents and emergencies

13.1	☐ a disabled person
13.2	☐ When you slow down quickly on a motorway because of a hazard ahead ☐ When you have broken down

13.3	☐ When stopped and temporarily obstructing traffic
13.4	☐ Keep a safe distance from the vehicle in front
13.5	☐ when an emergency arises

13.6	☐ Apply pressure over the wound and raise the arm
13.7	☐ 10 seconds
13.8	☐ 10 minutes
13.9	☐ 100 per minute
13.10	☐ Pale grey skin
13.11	☐ Check the airway is clear
13.12	☐ seek medical assistance
13.13	☐ go to the next emergency telephone and report the hazard
13.14	☐ Variable message signs
13.15	☐ 4 to 5 centimetres
13.16	☐ Make sure engines are switched off ☐ Call the emergency services promptly
13.17	☐ Switch on your own hazard warning lights ☐ Make sure that someone telephones for an ambulance ☐ Get people who are not injured clear of the scene
13.18	☐ Only when it is essential
13.19	☐ breathing
13.20	☐ Circulation ☐ Airway ☐ Breathing
13.21	☐ check the airway is clear ☐ make sure they are breathing ☐ stop any heavy bleeding

13.22	☐ Keep injured people warm and comfortable ☐ Keep injured people calm by talking to them reassuringly ☐ Make sure that injured people are not left alone
13.23	☐ Reassure them ☐ Not leave them alone
13.24	☐ warn other traffic
13.25	☐ gently
13.26	☐ clear the airway ☐ tilt their head back gently ☐ pinch the nostrils together
13.27	☐ douse the burns with clean cool non-toxic liquid
13.28	☐ Apply firm pressure to the wound ☐ Raise the leg to lessen bleeding
13.29	☐ there is further danger
13.30	☐ keep them in the vehicle
13.31	☐ 2YE 1089
13.32	☐ Driving licence ☐ Insurance certificate ☐ MOT test certificate
13.33	☐ As soon as possible
13.34	☐ It will help to reduce the blood flow

13.35	☐ remove anything that is blocking the mouth ☐ tilt the head back gently to clear the airway
13.36	☐ reassure them constantly ☐ keep them warm ☐ avoid moving them if possible ☐ avoid leaving them alone
13.37	☐ This could result in more serious injury
13.38	☐ 45 metres (147 feet)
13.39	☐ Telephone the signal operator ☐ Leave your vehicle and get everyone clear ☐ Move the vehicle if a signal operator tells you to
13.40	☐ Pull up slowly at the side of the road ☐ Hold the steering wheel firmly to keep control
13.41	☐ Pull up on the hard shoulder. Use the emergency phone to get assistance
13.42	☐ get out and clear of the crossing
13.43	☐ When you slow down quickly because of danger ahead ☐ When you have broken down on the hard shoulder
13.44	☐ for the number on the telephone that you are using ☐ for details of yourself and your vehicle ☐ whether you belong to a motoring organisation
13.45	☐ Remove any sunglasses
13.46	☐ Use dipped headlights
13.47	☐ Carry a fire extinguisher ☐ Check out any strong smell of petrol
13.48	☐ Stop at the next emergency telephone and contact the police
13.49	☐ check out the problem quickly and safely
13.50	☐ Switch on hazard lights then go and call for help immediately
13.51	☐ Drive it out of the tunnel if you can do so
13.52	☐ Switch on hazard warning lights ☐ Try and put out the fire
13.53	☐ make sure your radio is tuned to the frequency shown
13.54	☐ Get everyone out of the vehicle and clear of the crossing
13.55	☐ Fire extinguisher ☐ First aid kit ☐ Warning triangle
13.56	☐ Stop at the scene of the incident

13.57	☐ Whether the driver owns the other vehicle involved
	☐ The other driver's name, address and telephone number
	☐ The make and registration number of the other vehicle
	☐ The details of the other driver's vehicle insurance
13.58	☐ Report the incident to the police within 24 hours

CASE STUDY PRACTICE – ANSWERS

Section 13 – Incidents, accidents and emergencies

13.1 By switching on hazard warning lights

13.2 Location of the incident

13.3 Stay with them and reassure them confidently

13.4 He might be required to supply a witness statement

13.5 Driving licence and insurance certificate

➲ 14. Vehicle loading

14.1	☐ not exceed 60 mph
	☐ use only the left and centre lanes
14.2	☐ ease off the accelerator and reduce your speed
14.3	☐ When driving fast for a long distance
	☐ When carrying a heavy load
14.4	☐ reduce stability
14.5	☐ steering
	☐ handling
14.6	☐ The driver of the vehicle
14.7	☐ A stabiliser fitted to the towbar
14.8	☐ No, not at any time

14.9	☐ Breakaway cable
14.10	☐ In the vehicle handbook
14.11	☐ securely fastened when driving
14.12	☐ A child seat

CASE STUDY PRACTICE – ANSWERS

Section 14 – Vehicle loading

14.1 Reduce the stability

14.2 In a special harness

14.3 The driver

14.4 Removing the roof rack when it isn't being used

14.5 That there's appropriate pressure in all four tyres plus the spare

> 15. Case study practice

Case study on pages 463–465

1 Look over your shoulder for a final check

2 Slow down
   Consider using the horn
   Beware of pedestrians

3 Find a suitable place to stop

4 Go slowly past
   Give plenty of room

5 There may be another vehicle coming

Case study practice A

1 Apply immediately for your new tax disc

2 Drink two cups of coffee and rest for 15 minutes

3 Stay calm and continue when it's safe

4 Stay out of the outside lane

5 Because you're stationary

Case study practice B

1 He is

2 He's deaf and blind

3 National speed limit applies

4 Put on your hazard warning lights

5 Restrict the blood flow from her leg

Case study practice C

1 Four seconds

2 Pedestrians stepping out from between vehicles

3 Stop and wait until the way ahead is clear

4 No specific vehicle

5 Tyre pressure is too low

Case study practice D

1 Headlights with fog lights as necessary

2 Slowly drop back to allow more room in front

3 Move nearer to the centre line and signal to go right

4 Turned in towards the kerb

5 Lock it away securely out of sight

Case study practice E

1 Oil and water levels

2 In a suitable child restraint

3 Glare from the sun on wet roads

4 Well back so you can see ahead and be seen

5 This lane can be used as a running lane at a speed of 40 mph

The official DSA theory test learning materials

The references in this book direct you to these three essential titles (**HC, DES, KYTS**). Every theory test question is taken from the information in these books – make sure you have your copies for complete test preparation.

The Official Highway Code

Keep a copy in your car so you can refer to it at any time.

eBook
Also available as an eBook from your device's eBook store.

Alternative formats:

The Official Highway Code Interactive CD-ROM

Includes a helpful voice over option and quizzes to bring The Highway Code to life.

Learning the Highway Code with British Sign Language – the official DSA DVD and book pack

The full contents signed by professional signers and a book for reference purposes.

The Official DSA Guide to Driving – the essential skills

Packed with advice for all motorists, not just learners.

eBook
Also available as an eBook from your device's eBook store.

Know Your Traffic Signs

Illustrates and explains the vast majority of traffic signs.

Official Highway Code iPhone app

All the rules of the road at your fingertips. Available on the iPhone app store.

Order now at **safedrivingforlife.info/shop** or call **0870 850 6553**.

Also available from all good high street book stores.

We want you!

Learning to drive? Help us make sure the official DSA products are the best they can be.

We'd like to hear your views and feedback so please tell us what you think in one or all of the following ways:

Learner Survey 2013

Complete our short survey.
Simply go to **surveymonkey.com/s/learner2013**

safedrivingforlife.info

Visit our brand new website. With loads of help for learner drivers, new drivers and all road users, we would like your feedback to help make this site as useful as possible for you.

Join the conversation

Talk to us and chat with other learners and driving instructors.

 safedrivinglife   **@safedrivinglife**

Other official DSA publications

From the Driving Standards Agency –
the official route to Safe Driving for Life™

Driving
Standards
Agency

Theory test

Check how much you've
already learnt to see if you're
ready to pass the multiple
choice part, with mock tests
and much more.

The Official DSA Theory Test
for Car Drivers

INTERACTIVE DOWNLOAD
ISBN 9780115532641   £12.99

Alternative format:

The Official DSA Theory Test
for Car Drivers

DVD-ROM
ISBN 9780115532597   £12.99

Hazard perception

Develop your hazard
perception skills and learn
more about this part of the
theory test.

The Official DSA Guide
to Hazard Perception

DVD
ISBN 9780115528651   £15.99

The Official DSA Complete
Theory Test Kit

DVD-ROM AND DVD
ISBN 9780115532603   £19.99

Practical test

For help with practical skills
and advice on what to expect
on the day.

The Official DSA Guide
to Learning to Drive

BOOK
ISBN 9780115530913   £9.99

DOWNLOADABLE PDF*
ISBN 9780115530623   £9.99

Prepare for your Practical
Driving Test – the official DSA
guide

DVD
ISBN 9780115531446
£15.99
*for instant access from
safedrivingforlife.info/shop

For the full range of official DSA titles and to place your
order visit **safedrivingforlife.info/shop** or call **0870 850 6553**.
Also available from all good high street book stores.

f safedrivinglife

🐦 @safedrivinglife

The Official DSA Theory Test Kit for Car Drivers iPhone app

Help for both the multiple choice and hazard perception
parts of your theory test.

Available on the iPhone app store.

TSO (The Stationery Office) is proud to be DSA's official publishing partner.